Urban and Landscape P

CW00683898

Volume 4

Editorial Staff

Isabelle Doucet
Paola Pittaluga
Silvia Serreli

Project Assistants

Monica Johansson
Giovanna Sanna

Translation

Christine Tilley

Aims and Scope

Urban and Landscape Perspectives is a series which aims at nurturing theoretic reflection on the city and the territory and working out and applying methods and techniques for improving our physical and social landscapes.

The main issue in the series is developed around the projectual dimension, with the objective of visualising both the city and the territory from a particular viewpoint, which singles out the territorial dimension as the city's space of communication and negotiation.

The series will face emerging problems that characterise the dynamics of city development, like the new, fresh relations between urban societies and physical space, the right to the city, urban equity, the project for the physical city as a means to reveal *civitas*, signs of new social cohesiveness, the sense of contemporary public space and the sustainability of urban development.

Concerned with advancing theories on the city, the series resolves to welcome articles that feature a pluralism of disciplinary contributions studying formal and informal practices on the project for the city and seeking conceptual and operative categories capable of understanding and facing the problems inherent in the profound transformations of contemporary urban landscapes.

Where Strangers Become Neighbours

Integrating Immigrants in Vancouver, Canada

by
Leonie Sandercock and Giovanni Attili

with
Val Cavers and Paula Carr

 Springer

Authors

Leonie Sandercock
University of British Columbia
School of Community &
Regional Planning
Lasserre Building, 6333
Memorial Road
Vancouver, BC V6T 1Z2
Canada
leonies@interchange.ubc.ca

Giovanni Attili
University of Rome "La Sapienza"
Dip. di Architettura ed
Urbanistica
Via Eudossiana, 18
00184 Rome
Italy
giovanni.attili@gmail.com

ISBN: 978-94-017-7689-9   ISBN: 978-1-4020-9035-6 (eBook)

DOI 10.1007/978-1-4020-9035-6

Photo Credits: All the photos included in this book are courteously taken from the Collingwood
Neighbourhood House Archive except:

- Pages 6, 19, 35, 104, 124, 238, 240, 244–248, 256, 257: photos by Giovanni Attili
- Page 1: "Sculptures by Sara Bonetti", photo by Giovanni Attili
- Pages 110, 235: graphic works by Giovanni Attili
- Chapter 5 and Chapter 10: graphic works by Giovanni Attili taken from the dvd "Where strangers become neighbours"
- Chapter 8: "The Spirit of Haida Gwaii by Bill Reid", photos by Giovanni Attili

Printed on acid-free paper

9 8 7 6 5 4 3 2 1

springer.com

Sculptures by Sara Bonetti

Preface

We have written this book to accompany our film, "Where Strangers become Neighbours". The film tells a very specific story of the integration of immigrants in Collingwood, a neighbourhood of 48,000 people in the eastern part of the City of Vancouver, part of the metropolitan area of Vancouver. The film is even more specific in focusing on the key role of one social institution, the Collingwood Neighbourhood House, in helping strangers to become neighbours. Much of the story is told in and through the voices of immigrants themselves, who have settled in this neighbourhood from many different parts of the world.

Although this is a specific story, it is in many ways a typical one, in telling of the challenges facing immigrants in making the transition from outsiders to fully belonging members of a new society. We live in an "Age of Migration" that began after the second world war and has been accelerating since the mid-1980s (Castles and Miller 1998). A number of factors have contributed to this: growing inequalities in wealth between North and South impel people to move in search of economic opportunities; political, ecological and demographic pressures force some people to seek refuge outside their homeland; and ethnic and religious strife, from Africa to the Middle East to Southeast Asia, lead to mass exodus. In some developing countries, emigration is one aspect of the social crisis that accompanies integration into the world market and modernization.

The result is 21st century cities of extraordinary cultural diversity, cities that are multi-ethnic, multi-racial, multiple. This creates challenges of living together in one society for people from diverse cultures. Migrations change economic, demographic and social structures, and the associated cultural diversity can call into question longstanding notions of citizenship and national identity. Influxes of migrants can lead to the spatial restructuring of cities and regions, in which sometimes the very presence of new ethnic groups leads to the destabilizing of the existing social order. In this new "ethnoscape" (Appadurai 1990), ambivalent new communities are thrust together with nostalgic older ones, and xenophobic fears can quickly turn into territorially based racist politics as the new mix of cultures projects itself onto the urban landscape.

When newcomers with different histories, cultures, and needs appear in existing communities, their presence can be experienced as unsettling to the "oldtimers", who may perceive their whole way of life as being challenged. There is a complicated experiencing of fear of "the Other" alongside fear of losing one's job, fear of a whole way of life being eroded, fear of change itself. This fear is a great threat to the future stability of the multicultural or "mongrel" cities (Sandercock 2003) of the 21st century. Our film explores how one city, and one neighbourhood, have been involved in a positive way in addressing the challenge of integrating immigrants from different cultures, engaging in the active construction of new ways of living together.

The reality of neighbourhoods with increasing numbers of "strangers", or newcomers as we call them in Canada, is becoming a familiar one across Europe. But most of the European cities are at a much earlier stage of accepting the reality of immigration, and of thinking about urban and social policies that can assist integration, reduce tensions, and help to build new, more intercultural communities. It was our intention, in making this film, to provide an example of how one neighbourhood has done this very successfully, albeit not without significant struggles along the way. The film documents the sociological imagination that has made this possible.

But there are of course important differences in political, legal, cultural, and social context, between Canada and European countries. It is the intention of this book, then, to sketch in those differences, to explain what philosophies and policies have made integration successful in Canada, and how these might (or in some cases, might not) translate into the European context. At the very least, we hope our film and book stimulates a more open and less tense and stereotyped conversation in European cities about the presence and contribution of immigrants.

Part I

provides the Canadian context

In **Chapter 1**, we provide some basic information about Canadian immigration and settlement policies, entrance filters and immigrant rights, settlement services, negative elements and difficulties, and the guiding philosophy behind integration, that of multiculturalism. We discuss the Charter of Rights and Freedoms and the Multiculturalism Act as part of a political and legal framework that encourages immigration and establishes and protects immigrants' rights, including their right to their own culture.

In **Chapter 2**, we focus on Vancouver as a multicultural city and recipient of the second largest number of newcomers in Canada each year. We describe the very dramatic demographic changes of the past thirty years and how the city, the province, and grass roots organisations have responded to this new reality. We emphasise the importance of State-civil society collaboration in managing immigrant integration, outline the role of the municipality and of the Planning Department in the City of Vancouver, [within the much larger metropolitan area, population 2.3 million], and discuss some specific interventions and ongoing and evolving policies for coping with the ever-changing influx of newcomers.

Chapter 3 takes an even closer look at how it is possible to "change the mind of a city", establishing a multicultural readiness in the host society, by detailing a case study of an institute that was established by the City in the 1980s to tackle antiracism and diversity training in the public sector.

Part 2
*concentrates on the case study that is the subject of the film,
namely the Collingwood Neighbourhood House*

Chapter 4 introduces the idea and history of Neighbourhood Houses, their origins in the 19th century Settlement House movement in London, and their adaptation in the New World, in recognition of the numbers of immigrants in some urban neighbourhoods, even one hundred years ago. We describe the mission, the governance, the programs and services, and the achievements of contemporary Neighbourhood Houses, as well as some of the challenges they face.

Chapter 5 zeroes in on the subject of the film, the Collingwood Neighbourhood House (CNH) as a local gathering place which is also a unique social institution. We explore how the CNH has become a welcoming place for everyone, bridging cultural differences and building community. We discuss CNH's mission and vision, and core values such as respect, relationship building, collaboration, inclusivity and accessibility, and social justice. We also note the special role of creativity and the arts in community building, and the special place of celebrations in the neighbourhood.

In **Chapter 6**, Paula Carr (the Executive Director of CNH) and Val Cavers (former Coordinator of Settlement Services) reveal some of the stories that were not told in the film, stories of resistance to change, stories of initial fears of and hostility towards newcomers. These stories illustrate just how much has changed during the past twenty two years in this neighbourhood, and how this change came about through the use of extensive consultative processes to deal with people's fears and opposition to particular projects and policies. There are also stories about the ongoing challenges of inclusiveness, which today is manifest in the attempt to offer services and assistance to homeless people in the neighbourhood.

Chapter 7 draws all of this together, asking what CNH's story can teach other cities about building intercultural communities in the mongrel cities of the 21st century, and what is important about the Canadian and Vancouver contexts in enabling such a success story. To go from being a total stranger, to a service recipient, to a full member of a neighbourhood, able to contribute to the lives of fellow residents, is a major life transition for newcomers. Making that transition possible is the extraordinary achievement of the Collingwood Neighbourhood House.

Chapter 8 concludes this section by elaborating the elements of a theory of cosmopolitan urbanism: a sociological imagination of living with difference; a deep political and psychological understanding of difference; and an intercultural political project that addresses the shortcomings of 20th century multiculturalism. We then connect this theory with the actual achievements of the Collingwood Neighbourhood House, as an instantiation of and inspiration for the theory.

Part III
dwells on the relationships between film, social research, and action

Chapter 9 is a sensemaking narrative of the research process which led us to build the documentary about the Collingwood Neighbourhood House. It is an inside view of the different stages, the challenges and the goals which constantly accompanied and shaped our inquiry. Many elements played a significant role in this process: the initial collective work of the students which was carried out during the class "Digital Ethnographies and urban planning", the Cosmopolis Laboratory in the School of Community and Regional Planning, the qualitative research approach, the interviews and the interviewees, the editing phase and the construction of the story, the dissemination process and the educational package.

Chapter 10 offers a more general reflection about the use of film languages in the planning field. It is an inquiry into the new potentialities of digital storytelling and explains the reasons which convinced us to embrace information and communication technologies (ICTs) in telling the story of the CNH. Digital languages can strengthen the expressive possibilities of storytelling, connecting a qualitative study of the city to the potentialities of deeply communicative languages. Digital qualitative inquiries expressively communicate narratives through aesthetic involvements which are crucial in urban interactions. They can give expression to inspiring stories which are potentially able to trigger further planning processes, showing possibilities and sense worlds.

We hope that this book expands on and enhances your understanding of what you see in the film. While the book provides political and legal context, description, and policy analysis, the film provides cascading layers of narrative, much of it through the voices of immigrants themselves, thereby conveying in a more deeply qualitative and experiential way what it feels like to be a stranger in a new land.

Vancouver, Canada   Leonie Sandercock

Rome, Italy   Giovanni Attili

References

Appadurai A (1990) Disjuncture and difference in the global cultural economy. In: Public Culture, 2, 2: pp. 1–32.

Castles S, Miller M (1998) The age of migration, 2nd ed. The Guilford Press, New York

Sandercock L (2003) Cosmopolis 2: Mongrel cities of the 21st century. Continuum, London

Contents

Part I
Context

Chapter 1
Inventing a Multicultural Nation: Canada's Evolving Story

Leonie Sandercock with Samara Brock

1.1 Introduction

We have written this book to accompany and complement our documentary film, "Where Strangers become Neighbours", which tells the remarkable story of the integration of immigrants in one neighbourhood in Vancouver, Canada's third largest metropolis. But that local success story cannot be fully understood without providing some historical and geographical context that locates Canada as a white settler society based on immigration, and some political context that delineates the ways in which the nation has invented and reinvented itself through always evolving and contested policies that both "manage" immigration *and* manage the inevitably associated debates about national identity. These latter debates led to and helped produce Canada's well known philosophy and policies of multiculturalism, as a way of managing the ethno-culturally diverse nation that is the result of Canada's approach to immigration.

The intellectual project of this book is to explore both the political and sociological imaginations that have informed this ambitious attempt at nation building through immigration. Almost a century ago, the Liberal government that was led by Prime Minister Wilfred Laurier decided that immigration was Canada's destiny and proposed an answer to the question of immigration and identity by telling new arrivals, "Let them look to the past, but let them also look to the future: let them look to the land of their ancestors, but let them also look to the land of their children". These words are as relevant today as they were far-sighted then, and they happen to succinctly capture the tightrope that Canadian multicultural policy has teetered along as it has sought to adjust to new waves of immigration since the 1970s from predominantly non-Anglo-European source countries. Canada, then, can be seen as a remarkable social and political experiment in constructing a nation that is not, or rather is no longer based on assumed cultural homogeneity as the foundational citizenship criterion. Precisely *how* national immigration policies propelled by an economic and geo-political

L. Sandercock, G. Attili, *Where Strangers Become Neighbours*, Urban and
Landscape Perspectives 4, DOI 10.1007/978-1-4020-9035-6_1
© Springer Science+Business Media 2009

rationale translate into ways of actually living together in cities and neighbourhoods is the underlying fascination of and curiosity behind our film
and this text.

This chapter provides an account first of Canada as a white settler society pursuing nation building in socially exclusionary ways from the 19th
century until the 1960s and, since then, of the co-evolution of immigration
policy and multiculturalism policy. We trace the changing criteria for and
categories of immigration policy. And we chart the concomitant emergence of legislation and legal changes establishing not only the rights of
immigrants but also the institutions and social policies that would shape
their integration (as opposed to assimilation) into Canadian society. The
final part of the chapter introduces some of the ongoing controversy and
debates that surround both the idea and the actually existing practice of
multiculturalism.

In the next chapter we situate Vancouver within Canada's political and
economic history as a frontier in the westward expansion of Canadian society and therefore as a destination for much of Canada's internal migration; as the entrepot for the opening up of the resource rich province of
British Columbia; as Canada's gateway, since the 1970s, to the Asia-
Pacific region and therefore the recipient of new sources of immigration as
well as capital flows; and as a city that has undergone not only an economic transformation since that time, but also a social, cultural, and political transformation. Vancouver, now widely regarded as a fascinating,
cosmopolitan city, is underpinned by a unique institutional infrastructure
for immigrant integration, and that will be the focus of Chapter 2.

1.2 Canada as a New World Settler Society

Long before Canada's emergence as a modern nation state and industrial-
ized democracy, the lands it now occupies were inhabited by indigenous
peoples.With histories going back in some cases ten thousand years, the
lifeways of these First Nations peoples were initially unsettled by contact
with the first European arrivals, the fur traders, and ultimately dislocated
and dispossessed by successive waves of European settlers who spread
across continental North America claiming land for farming, urban development and resource extraction. These settlers not only brought with them
diseases such as smallpox and measles that were lethal to indigenous peoples but also brought an equally lethal colonial mentality that asserted the
superiority of European civilization. This mentality provided the

ideological justification for the systematic, state-led destruction of indigenous cultures from the nineteenth century to the end of the twentieth
(Harris 2002; Royal Commission on Aboriginal Peoples, vol. 1, 1996).

In this respect, the founding of Canada as a modern nation state followed the same trajectory as other new world societies (Australia, New
Zealand, the United States and South Africa), born in the Age of Empire,
appropriating land, dispossessing original inhabitants, and pursuing nation
building from an immigrant stock peopled entirely from Europe. These
white settler societies were all intrinsically immigrant societies and, in
Canada's case, born from a particular history of bi-cultural and bilingual
compromise, as the two dominant settler groups from the 18th century until the mid-20th were French and English-speaking communities. Thus two
fundamental sets of national policy concerns have developed side by side,
defining and redefining the nation: the first is immigration policy, the second and more recent is the policy of multiculturalism.

Canada's immigration policy has always been driven opportunistically
as well as ideologically: on the one hand by the need to populate and develop a country of vast and challenging geographic scale; on the other, by
the desire to reproduce European civilization. Thus, during the expansion
of the latter part of the 19th century, with the gold rushes of the north west
and the pushing of the railway line across the continent, Chinese male

immigrants were welcomed as labourers but laws were quickly developed to prevent them from bringing families with them or joining them, or owning property except in restricted areas. From the late 19th century onwards, immigration laws were unashamedly racially based. Europeans were welcome, non-Europeans were not. The single most significant change in this approach to immigration policy did not come until the passage of the Immigration Act of 1967 which, in response to the labour shortages of the post-war boom, explicitly ended the racially and culturally based criteria for immigration.

Over the next twenty years or so, the longstanding global pattern of migration to Canada was turned almost completely upside down. The combined proportion of immigrants admitted from Europe (including the UK) and the USA fell from 85% in 1966 to 50% in 1975, 30% in 1985, 22% in 1995, and was just over 21% in 2004 (Hiebert 2006: 7). In this latter year, 47% of immigrants landing in Canada came from the Asia-Pacific region, 22% from Africa and the Middle East, and 9% from Latin America. In other words, almost four fifths of recent immigrants have arrived from "non-traditional" source countries, presenting significant challenges in both economic and social integration to which we will return.

The new Immigration Act of 1967 instituted a "points system" that ranked potential immigrants according to age, education, labour skills, language skills, and financial resources. The underlying economic rationality of Canadian immigration policy is readily apparent from this points system and from the make-up of immigrant categories. There are essentially three categories of immigrant: economic immigrants, family class immigrants, and refugees. Today, the majority of newcomers enter as economic immigrants (58% in 2000), followed by family class immigrants (27%) and refugees (13%).

But the term "economic immigrant" can be misleading, often represented in the media as wealthy businessmen buying their way into the country. In fact, the economic category contains three quite different groups within it.

The first is a very broad category of skilled workers who are identified through the points system and offered entry precisely because of their technical, trade, or professional skills. The second are business immigrants, who come as entrepreneurs, investors, or self-employed business people. The self-employed program is the most restrictive, pertaining mostly to athletes, cultural performers and artists, and farmers. The entrepreneur class was created to facilitate the admission of those individuals intending to establish businesses in Canada. They must have owned and operated a successful business, have a minimum net worth of at least C$300,000, and a credible plan for establishing a business in Canada that will employ at least one person beyond the entrepreneur. These immigrants have three years to fulfill their obligation to establish a business, and must furnish proof of doing so to maintain their status as permanent residents. Investor class applicants are required to have a higher net worth of C$800,000 and to make a minimum investment of $400,000, which is placed with the Receiver General of Canada. And thirdly, there are specifically designated categories of economic immigrants to fill lower-level service positions, the best known of which offers entry to caregivers or domestic workers under the Live-in Caregiver Program (LCP). These workers often work for wages below the statutory minimum in exchange for the opportunity of gaining permanent resident status (leading to citizenship) after 24 months employment. This program has brought significant numbers of Philippina women to Canadian cities in the past decade.

As a generalization, it is fair to say that the business immigrants are the wealthiest, those in domestic employment are among the poorest, and the fortunes of skilled workers are very uneven (Leaf 2005; Hiebert and Ley 2003; Pratt 2003).

This latter issue, of skilled workers unable to find employment appropriate to their skills, is widely seen as the single most striking *failure* of Canada's approach to immigration in the last forty years. (We return to this issue and its probable causes later in the chapter). The single most striking *success* of immigration policy in this same period is the fact that it has enjoyed not only broad bipartisan political support but also that it has widespread public support such that, even at times of specific controversy, the overall approach and actual levels of immigration have not been seriously questioned. And these levels are significant. While the United States continues to be the single largest recipient of international migrants in absolute numbers, Canada takes in approximately twice as many, proportional to total population. Australia is the only country with a higher proportion of foreign born residents, with 21% compared to Canada's 18% and 12% in the USA (Statistics Canada 2003; Hiebert and Ley 2003). What is remarkable is that politicians and policy makers seem to have succeeded in making the case over these past four decades for the economic necessity of immigration. As a highly developed, indeed rich country, with relatively high wages, Canada has essentially completed its own demographic transition: that is, we now have less than replacement rates of natural population growth. The implication of this demographic reality is that the nation is reliant on a continuing intake of immigrants in order to maintain both productivity levels and viable dependency ratios between the working and the aging sectors of the population. So the need for immigrant labour is clear.

What is not so clear, given the Anglo-European origins and ideology of the country's founding as a settler society, is just how the Canadian state has managed the socio-cultural transition from the traditional European source countries to an acceptance of newcomers from Asia and Africa, the so-called "visible minorities" (see Fig. 1.1) whom restrictive immigration policies had previously labeled "non-preferred" (Wallace and Milroy 1999). To comprehend that transition we must turn to the role of multiculturalism policy and its co-evolution with immigration policy since the 1960s.

1.3 Immigration and National Identity: The Evolving Multicultural Response

When a nation state is constructed out of an immigrant population there is always a question of what constitutes membership in the nation, who is a citizen and who is not, and what all this says about national identity. For European nations the answer has always seemed (deceptively) simple. Citizenship is based on long histories of assumed shared cultural and racial identity. This is not so for settler societies, and for Canada it has been doubly complicated by the fact of not one but two "charter groups", the Francophone and Anglophone communities. It was the rivalry between these two groups, often referred to as the (still unresolved) "Quebec question", and the secessionist pressures that arose from desires for cultural recognition among Francophone residents, that seriously unsettled the nation state in the 1960s. Provoked by these pressures and associated terrorist stirrings, a Royal Commission on National Identity was set up and spent five years having conversations with citizens across the country. The favored solution to this problem of the "two solitudes" (Anglophone and Francophone) was to declare Canada an officially bi-cultural nation, and in 1969 the Official Languages Act made Canada officially bilingual. But the result of the five years of conversations through the 1960s was a growing understanding that significant numbers of residents related to neither of these so-called "charter groups". It was for this reason that, in 1971, Liberal Prime Minister Pierre Trudeau's multiculturalism policy was invented, to acknowledge the increasingly diverse demographic profile of the postwar period (Hiebert et al. 2003; Ley 2005; Fleras and Elliot 1999).

Beginning, then, in 1971 when Canada became the first country in the world to introduce an official policy embracing the idea of multiculturalism, this new self-understanding became permanently embedded in political discourse and the Canadian imagination (Canadian Heritage 2006b).

As the idea of multiculturalism evolved, it came to encompass the rights of individuals to retain their cultural practices (as opposed to the idea of assimilation to the dominant culture, or the "melting pot" approach of the USA); the provision of social services to new immigrants; and anti-discriminatory policies (Hiebert et al. 2003).

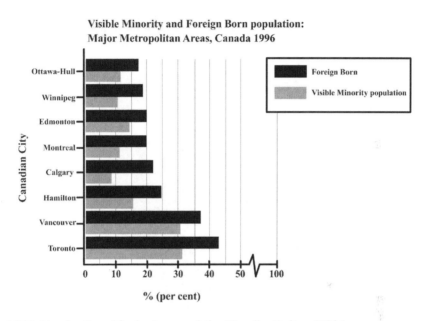

Fig. 1.1 Visible minority and foreign born population (Canadian Heritage 2006a)

Multiculturalism thus became deeply embedded in a broad range of laws, policy statements and international agreements including the Employment Equity Act (1986), the Pay Equity Act (1985), and the Multiculturalism Act (1988). As a central tenet of Canadian society, it was finally enshrined in the 1982 Charter of Rights and Freedoms (Canadian Heritage 2006c). These last two have been particularly important. The legislative and Charter frameworks established since the 1980s now require all federal institutions to formally adopt multicultural policies as part of their working mandates, and the Ministry of Canadian Heritage which implements multiculturalism policy is supported by the position of Minister of State for Multiculturalism. Since the federal government sets policy and establishes funds to implement policies, provincial governments have been forced to follow suit, establishing their own ministries to oversee multicultural affairs. Over the past twenty years, a thick institutional infrastructure supporting the integration of immigrants has evolved, connecting federal,

provincial and municipal governments along with an increasingly important role for non-government organizations, all of which is evidence of
Canada's commitment to actively creating a multicultural society. The
next chapter will illustrate this institutional thickness by describing in
some detail how one city, Vancouver, has adapted to the increasingly diverse immigration flows of the past four decades.

Canadian multiculturalism has encouraged individuals to voluntarily as-
sociate with the culture and tradition of their choice, and there has been
significant spending, through multicultural grants, to support the maintenance of various cultures and languages and to encourage diverse cultural
festivals in public places, as well as the symbolic gesture of public artworks that recognize and celebrate the multiple peoples who make up the
nation. As Mahtani (2002: 70) comments, this is "surely a remarkable
change from conventional strategies of nation-building".

Canada's multicultural policy has been driven by the need for continuing immigration to a country of vast area but relatively small population. From its beginnings as a settler society become modern nation, Canada has always required immigrants as labourers, as a stimulus to its economy, and more recently as tax-paying supporters for an ageing population (Fleras and Elliot 1999; Baxter 1998). The problem for legislators and government officials who saw increasing levels of immigration as necessary for national greatness was how to frame Canada's national identity in ways that would be inclusive of the large number of newcomers who were not part of the traditional streams of immigrants from Europe. Early attempts at resolving this issue had centered on shaping immigration laws to ensure that those who came would be readily incorporated into existing, largely Anglo-European, cultural norms. But this has always been an unattainable ideal. Cultural diversity, beginning with the First Nations, and onwards to early Dukhabors (or "spirit wrestlers" from Russia) as well as large numbers of Chinese immigrants in the late 19th century, had always posed a challenge to Eurocentric notions of what it means to be Canadian. Multicultural policy has thus been about more than managing the coexistence of disparate groups of people in the same country. From the beginning, and at its best, it has been about the story of a nation gradually learning to accept multiple identities, multiple histories, and multiple ways of being at home in the land we call Canada. As Leaf explains: "it is helpful to see the Canadian nation state as fundamentally a modern constitutional polity, rather than a society whose national identity is derived from ethno-nationalist loyalties" (Leaf 2005: 284). But this is, necessarily, an evolving story...

1.4 Multiculturalism: The Ongoing Debates

Canadian multicultural policies are often commended for having promoted the importance of multiculturalism as an ideology not only in Canada but around the world (Fleras and Elliot 1999: 318). The federal government has been relatively successful in making multiculturalism an integral component of governance at the federal level. But an ongoing debate continues about whether Canada has actually succeeded in changing the core story of the nation in which its citizens' lives and identities are embedded. The irony of political discourse centering on multiculturalism in Canada (and elsewhere) is that immigrants, while seen as solutions to economic challenges facing the nation, also seem to challenge the very idea of nationhood as perceived by the host society. To understand the underlying reasons for this, we now turn to a brief history of the idea of difference and diversity in Canadian society.

1.4.1 The Power to Narrate: The Construction of the "Problem" of Canadian Diversity and Multiculturalism

There is a necessarily paradoxical aspect of multiculturalism as government policy. In both Canada and Australia, multiculturalism was introduced by the state as a way of managing increasingly diverse streams of immigration, albeit immigration that was understood as essential for continued economic development of the nation. When a nation state adopts multiculturalism as its guiding philosophy, there is an underlying concern that there is a new problem for the state, a problem that needs managing. If the age of global migrations unsettles the established order of things (notions of belonging, of identity, ways of life taken for granted and thought of as "normal"), then the state responds either by attempting to restore the old order through repressive and exclusionary policies, or by writing new rules for shaping and managing the new order of things. The new rules rewrite some old definitions of belonging and citizenship and create new, different boundaries. Multicultural legislation can be seen as an attempt to define, and perhaps to limit, the extent to which the nation will change as a result of immigration. It reflects and addresses a profound unsettling of norms, and fear of change, on the part of the host society, *at the same time* that it appears to celebrate, and perhaps genuinely desires, this change and seeks to move cautiously towards a new national identity (Sandercock 2006).

So, multiculturalism and the associated legislation is at once very pragmatic in its attempt to manage a new situation and very idealistic in seeking to create new ways of defining the nation. Further, it is likely to be, and should always be contested, at one extreme, by those who wish to see no change to the nation as they understand it, and at the other extreme, by newcomers, as they come to experience exclusion in various ways. In other words, multiculturalism is not an entirely altruistic project, and the language of a virtuous tolerance in which it is often couched needs to be constantly challenged by scrutinizing its actual effects in every policy field. What follows is a brief overview of four significant critiques of multiculturalism. The first is a critique from a First Nations perspective; the second, a critique of the ethno-cultural grounding of the philosophy and policies; the third criticism has been that the apparent tolerance expressed in multiculturalism has actually masked an ongoing and institutionalized racism in Canadian society directed at non-whites (Bannerji 1995, 2000; Hill 2001; Henry et al. 2000); and the final critique concerns the discrepancy between discourses of immigration and multiculturalism on the one hand, and labor market practices on the other.

1.4.2 The Indigenous Critique

Multiculturalism as a guiding political philosophy for the nation presents a significant problem for indigenous communities who argue that their claims, which go beyond calls for "cultural recognition" to demands for land and sovereignty, cannot be accommodated within a multicultural political framework. There is of course a long history behind this impasse, beginning with the ways in which European settlers constructed "the Indian problem" in the nineteenth century.

The first and perhaps most significant problem with multicultural policies is the Eurocentric definition and formulation of these policies (Sandercock 2003; Mahtani 2002; Day 2000; Dei and Sefa 1996; Moodley 1983). Tracing the roots of Canadian multiculturalism back to Western colonial mindsets, Day defines the discourse as one of "Self/Other" differentiation and management (Day 2000: 70). He argues that European discourse on diversity has always been steeped in notions of European cultural superiority. The first instance of a Euro-Canadian ordering of difference came when early explorers encountered aboriginal (First Nations) peoples throughout the continent. They were immediately categorized as "savages" lacking in political organization and thus also lacking any claims to their own land, which, to the European mind, was "terra nullius," or empty land. First Nations were not just a different people, but an altogether different and inferior race, readily identifiable through their divergence from European norms.

This process of differentiation, definition, and denigration of others by Europeans has a long history. Edward Said was one of the first to outline the underpinnings of this colonization mentality with specific reference to "the Orient" of the European imagination in his pivotal postcolonial text, *Orientalism* (Said 1978). "The Orient", and thus also "the Oriental" were European inventions that existed in Western thought as the antithesis of all that was considered "Occidental" and therefore norm-giving. Out of this Western discourse "there emerged a complex Oriental suitable for study in the academy, for display in the museum, for reconstruction in the colonial office, for theoretical illustration in anthropological, biological, linguistic,

racial and historical theses about mankind and the universe" (Said 1978: 460). The imagining of "the Oriental", according to Said, rested on the authority of European texts. These "acquire(d) mass, density, and referential power among themselves and thereafter in the culture at large" (Said 1978: 50). The hegemonic discourse which surrounded these texts thus operated to restrict what could legitimately be asserted about "the Oriental".

A similar totalizing view of cultural Others was applied by Europeans to the peoples whom the early settlers encountered in the New World. The interaction between cultures is always shaped by each culture's understandings of those who are different from themselves. In illustrating how this has shaped European-Indigenous relationships, Brown and Vibert point out that "it is human nature to view and describe other peoples in relation to ourselves: but in doing so, Europeans had the privilege of more power than most. A crucial aspect of that power was the power to narrate" (2003: 14).

According to Dorris, the stereotypes of "the Indian" which Europeans narrated have "become a real and preferred substitute for ethnographic reality" (1994: 99). Europeans have historically defined First Nations cultures in opposition to themselves, incorporating into their narrations a dualistic framework of subject/object, of "us" vs. "them," of standard vs. divergent. The stereotypes about First Nations that were formed in this way have proven to be extraordinarily persistent. Images formed about First Nations by early European visitors and settlers in the "New World" which shaped the European conception of "the Indian" have continued to shape Canadians' understanding, and thus treatment, of First Nations to this day.

This "othering" discourse, as applied to the people whom Europeans encountered in the territory that would become Canada, is relevant to a broader discussion of the ideology of Canadian multiculturalism because both aboriginal and immigrant identities have become similarly colonized by the Canadian state (Day 2000: 116). The way of thinking about one gives insight into the way of thinking about the other. Or, as Bannerji puts, "it is the nationhood of this Canada, with its two solitudes and their survival anxieties and aggressions against "native others", that provides the epic painting in whose dark corners we must look for the later *others*" (Bannerji 1996: 4). This juxtaposition of Canadian norms against those of a cultural Other lays the groundwork for a conceptualization of Canadian identity in terms of who belongs and who doesn't. Day's outline of a postwar conception of Canadian identity is reproduced in Fig. 1.2.

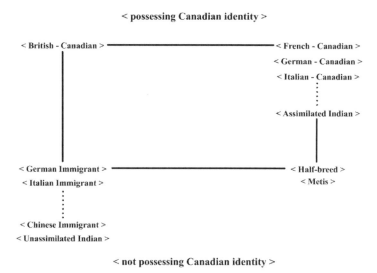

Fig. 1.2 Group identity in Canada, post-WWII (from Day 2000: 174)

This hierarchy of identity has shifted over time. The categorization of different peoples has been shaped around notions of race and more recently ethnicity, both of which are far from static categories. For instance, race was used as an early explanation of difference between French and English settlers. When conflicts emerged between the two groups, their perceived differences became naturalized through the evocation of "fundamental racial differences" (Day 2000: 108). With the Immigration Act of 1869, which was devised to help populate the "empty" western regions (again erasing the prior existence of the First Nations), a new category of Canadian emerged – what Day calls the "Internal Other." An hierarchy of "desirability" thus emerged from Canada's immigration policy. The British, followed by other Northern Europeans, were at the top of this ranking, and debates about undesirables such as Dukhabors and, particularly in British Columbia, Chinese, came to the fore. Discourse ensued about the threat that these "strangers within our gates" posed to our sense of being Canadian – a quality which naturally was understood to be purely Anglo-Saxon (Day 2000: 128; Fleras and Elliot 1999: 300).

There is not room within this overview for an in-depth analysis of the kinds of reasoning and policies that were used to manage immigration from 1869 to 1967. But it is worth underlining the fact that both explicit measures – exclusion Acts and head taxes – and implicit measures – such as continuous journey requirements or restrictions on foreign credentials – have always been used to legislate who did or did not qualify to be a one hundred percent Canadian. As Day puts it, these things were put into place to carefully select those who posed "as little challenge as possible to the existing attempt at order" (Day 2000: 224).

1.4.3 The "Ethnic" Critique: Multiculturalism as an Ethno-Cultural Categorization of a Citizenry

One outcome of this kind of ordering of peoples has been the idea that whereas some possess "ethnicity", others do not. This is the second powerful critique of multiculturalism. Both anglophone and francophone Caucasians in Canada have tended to see themselves as distinct and separate from the so-called ethnic population. In his analysis of multicultural language, Day observes that "*ethnic* is used in everyday language to refer to any person or group other than those whom the speaker considers normal or dominant" (Day 2000: 52). Like race, ethnicity is a cultural construct, with flexible definitions.

One (among many) things that might distinguish a 21st century multicultural project's promise from its 20th century counterpart's limitations, would be to evolve beyond an ethno-cultural approach to the question of belonging and identity. Perhaps *the* defining feature of 20th century multiculturalism was its celebration (but also stereotyping) of ethno-cultural identities. Frozen in the spatialised confines of Chinatowns and Banglatowns and Little Italies and Japantowns (and so forth) of globalising cities is a static understanding of culture that is betrayed by the complexities of identity, and the inevitable mutations and hybridities (mongrelizations) that occur over time as people are exposed to different ways of living and make choices and adaptations. "Culture" cannot be understood as static, eternally given, essentialist. Of necessity, it is always evolving, dynamic, and hybrid. All cultures, even allegedly conservative/traditional cultures, contain multiple differences within themselves that are continually being re-negotiated. Many newcomers have migrated precisely to escape these limiting definitions. It is increasingly offensive to many immigrants to keep having to identify themselves as "ethno", as always a hyphenated member of the nation (Mahtani 2002). In Canada, official language categorises "visible minorities", but in an increasing number of municipalities, these so-called "visible minorities" will soon be majorities, and already are in the City of Vancouver (see Chapter 2).

There are at least four arguments to be made against an ethno-cultural framework, or foundation, for multiculturalism. The *first* is that identities are multiple and cannot be subsumed under an ethnic umbrella. The *second* is that past and current practices of categorizing citizens this way ascribe ethnicities only to non-dominant (or "minority") cultures, while the dominant culture is always assumed to be without ethnicity, in other words, to be the norm against which ethnicity is measured. The third argument is that members of the nation state who are of mixed ethnic ancestry are left out of this categorization: an increasingly significant issue as inter-ethnic and interracial marriages and offspring are on the rise (Bisoondath 2002).

A fourth argument, this one vital to imagining a defensible 21st century multicultural project, revolves around the viability and danger of ethnicity as a marker of identity. Like all other single-issue campaigns, ethnic movements contain within them the power to question the whole politics of the system in the light of a single issue. But they also contain the seeds of their own destruction. Ethnic consciousness is a means of dealing with, and deflecting, issues of discrimination in the same instant. The legitimacy of any ethnic group is tested at the point when it faces a crisis of direction or of internal policy. Ranjit Sondhi, a BBC governor, writes about contemporary Britain:

> in their struggle for equal treatment, for an end to discrimination, blacks may find that they have to align themselves with whites, at times against other blacks. There comes a moment when they choose, either to act as a closed group or, to push the issue where they begin to contradict their own definition and become part of a general campaign for social justice (Sondhi 2002).

But the greatest danger of all is when ethnicity is constitutive of national identity, because it is then that it produces the kind of ethnic chauvinism that leads ultimately to the horrors of ethnic cleansing. Ethnicity entails a sense of belonging and loyalty to a particular set of cultural traditions, a sense of belonging tied to fixed, permanent, unalterable oppositions. The test of any group organized along ethnic lines is the extent to which it is inclusive of other ethnicities, or alternatively, the extent to which it armour-plates itself against them. Can the members of one ethnic group be intimate with those of another, cherishing and celebrating each other's differences as much as their own? Does such a group have an active policy for building staged alliances and allegiances with other groups across the very boundaries that it seeks to preserve? Does it freely grant the freedom to its individual members to move in and out of its ethnic space if they should so choose? To what extent are they prepared to fight for the rights of others to self-determination and equal participation even before their own are fully realized?

Perhaps, in other words, the best type of ethnicity is one that defines a new place for identity by insisting on the fact that its difference is something constructed, not simply found, not "natural". This version of ethnicity is not tied to fixed, unalterable oppositions, and is not wholly defined by exclusions. This means finding a meaning for ethnicity somewhere between fact and fiction. Even as we accept the imagined nature of ethnic identity, we are also required as a necessity to recognize its opposite – the moment of arbitrary closure. There is always a boundary, no matter how partial, temporary, or arbitrary.

Otherwise there is no differentiation, no positioning, no crossing of lines. No change. Accepting the necessarily constructed nature of ethnicity does not stop the ethnic subject from engaging in the politics of difference. But it is an altogether gentler politics, not a brutalizing but a revitalizing force. Perhaps Sondhi (2002) is right: ethnicity is like an act of faith, and like faith, is most attractive when it has lost its recruiting power, and when it freely admits the possibility of multiple identities, of which ethnicity is but a part. Everybody has more than one answer to the question "Who am I?"

When conceived and constructed this way, ethnicity is transformed into something that is not doomed to survive forever, as Englishness, say, has been, by marginalizing, dispossessing, displacing and forgetting other ethnicities. A constructed, "open-ended" ethnicity has lost its recruiting power. As in other forms of identification, there will always be dimensions of power in an open-ended concept of ethnicity. But it won't be quite so framed by the extremes of power and aggression as earlier forms. And by signaling the end of the "age of innocence" of the ethnic subject, the end of an age in which everything ethnic was "right on", it moves us forward into a different politics, a different world of ethnic relations in which a politics of difference can join with a politics of justice.

Federal multicultural policies have not yet succeeded in building an understanding of these issues in the host culture of their own ethnicity (Sandercock 2003; Mahtani 2002). The majority of policies focus on the need for "ethnic" populations to adapt to the dominant society and do not overtly address underlying issues of racism, exclusion or ghettoization nor the need of the predominantly white host society, themselves composed of specific ethnic groups, to co-adapt. This very serious omission limits the policy's effectiveness in bringing about sustainable change in Canada's race relations.

1.4.4 The "Racism" Critique: Multiculturalism as a Product of Racialised Liberal Democracies

Most western liberal democracies are always already racialised democracies. Think of those countries that we call "settler societies", Australia, Canada, South Africa, New Zealand, and the USA. Each was once a colony subordinate to the rule of Great Britain. Each has welcomed, indeed depended on immigration for its growth, while always strictly controlling the kinds of immigrants who were welcome. For most of the 20th century, skin color was a key criterion, thereby reproducing the exclusions and segregations of the former empires of which they were a (subordinate) part.

In discussing this "unresolved postcolonialism" (Sandercock 2003), we need to make an empirical distinction between colonialism and postcolonialism. Empirically speaking, the "colonial" comprises the formal, institutional, racialised governmentalities of the imperial "Age of Europe, 1492-1945" (West 1990). The *empirical* postcolonial refers to the formal disestablishment of colonial institutional arrangements, the official moments of decolonisation and racial desegregation (Hesse 2000: 12). But clearly a colonial mentality, and governmentality, have lingered on in other forms. Thus it makes sense to talk conceptually of an unresolved postcolonial condition in these New World settler societies as well as in the heartlands of former empires (the European capitals). The transition from western imperialisms to the ostensible universalism of western democracies has in fact been a transition to already racialised liberal democracies in which the persistence of institutionalized racism as well as individual prejudices has enormously complicated the politics and management of immigration and the social integration of immigrants. The racism implicit in the 18th century Anglo-European Enlightenment project of "civilizing" the supposedly uncivilized parts of the globe endures, and in that sense we have not arrived at an age of postcolonialism.

What has to be acknowledged, then, is the enduring historical connection between empire, immigration, labor markets, and racism. What has to be remembered in discussing the dilemmas of multiculturalism in the mongrel cities of the 21st century is that these cities are embedded in already racialized western liberal democracies, countries in which there is a history of regarding the cultural/racial/ethnic Other as inferior, less civilized or, in popular parlance, "not like us" and "not one of us".

1.4.5 The Labour Market Critique

A fourth and final criticism of actually existing multiculturalism points to the extraordinary discrepancy between discourses of immigration and multiculturalism on the one hand, and labor market practices on the other. According to this critique, multicultural rhetoric celebrates the pluralist immigrant society, but the labor market valorizes all things Canadian – Canadian education credentials, Canadian work experience, and Canadian English accents – while devaluing all things and people defined as "foreign". For example, the recent report of the Standing Committee on Citizenship and Immigration, "Settlement and Integration: A Sense of Belonging, Feeling at Home" (2003), highlights the common immigrant experience of de-skilling and underemployment and concludes that the stated goals of Canada's immigration policy are being derailed by employment practices (Sandercock 2005).

This critique generally refers to the fortunes of the Skilled Worker class of immigrants within the economic immigrant category discussed previously. There are a substantial number of studies on the economic fortunes of immigrants and visible minorities in Canada and the dominant theme in this research is that immigrants are experiencing more difficulty in finding well-paid work now than was the case in the 1970s. The first studies to identify this issue emerged out of figures reported in the 1986 census which showed that returns to human capital for immigrants had fallen relative to the Canadian population. These concerns deepened after the release of the 1991 and 1996 censuses, although both of those surveys coincided with weak economic conditions. The 2001 census indicated that the circumstances of immigrants had not deteriorated any further, but nor had they improved (Hiebert 2006: 15). The most widely publicized statistic supporting this concern has been the fact that the degree of poverty among recent immigrants increased markedly between the 1981 and 2001 censuses. Immigrants who arrived in the five years preceding the 1981 census had a poverty rate 1.44 times the Canadian-born population. The equivalent figure for the 2001 census was 2.29 times the rate for the Canadian-born (Hiebert 2006: 16).

This narrative of declining fortunes for immigrants has been almost universally accepted in Canadian research, and the media have been quick to report the bad news, accentuating it anecdotally with stories of engineers and other professionals who are driving taxis. There is no consensus among researchers as to the cause of this downturn in fortunes. The explanation most often cited is discrimination in the labour market, which in turn is usually attributed to racism. Other explanations centre on the human capital of immigrants (relative to the Canadian population), usually noting language problems as a barrier; and the broader impacts of economic restructuring, particularly the shift towards a knowledge-based economy.

However, the most rigorous empirical study of the longitudinal fortunes of immigrants in the Skilled Worker program (Hiebert 2006) suggests a much more nuanced picture. Using new data sources, notably the Longitudinal Immigration Database (IMDB), Hiebert shows that the skilled workers who are at the heart of the economic side of immigration policy are achieving earnings parity with average Canadian incomes quite quickly: in about two years for women and five for men (Hiebert 2006: 44). This is not to deny the reality of labour market discrimination, the most worrying form of which is the failure to recognize the credentials of immigrants once they have landed and are applying for jobs. From this critical perspective, the most appropriate policy response would be to ensure a labour market that would be more welcoming to immigrants and minorities. The announcement in 2006 of a national *Action Plan Against Racism* – which anticipates coordinated efforts between the ministries of justice, heritage/multiculturalism, immigration, and human resources – would seem to be a positive step, but it is too soon to comment on the success of this. Two other significant findings of Hiebert's research are, first, that language facility is the single most important form of human capital predicting success in the labour market; and second, and paradoxically, that refugees who arrive without English or French do not suffer long term penalties in the labour market. This latter finding speaks to the great importance of settlement services in shaping economic integration, and we will discuss this in our study of Vancouver in the next chapter.

1.5 Multiculturalism as Ongoing Dialogue: Reconceiving the Role of the Host Society

Clearly, encouraging debate and active renegotiation of multicultural ideals is the only way to ensure their ongoing relevance (Kymlicka 1998; Day 2000; Fleras and Elliot 1999). And there is in fact continuing dialogue about what it means to be Canadian, in the media as well as in academic discourse. In addition to the four critiques outlined above, the question that most requires urgent attention is that of the role and responsibility of the so-called "host society" in co-adaptation to a multicultural reality.

Some authors have turned their attention to this idea. For example, Fleras and Elliot (1999) insist that multiculturalism is not just for "ethnics" but that attention should also be

> directed at the ethnic mainstream – both attitudes and institutions – by modifying public perception of and response to diversity through modification of rules, rewards, structures, mindsets and symbols. In the final analysis, multiculturalism is an exercise in society building by which all citizens are incorporated as legitimate and distinctive contributors to a united and inclusive society (Fleras and Elliot 1999: 317).

But it is not just in the academy that the concept and practice of multiculturalism has been challenged. There has been a distinct shift in symbolic messages at federal level in the past decade with the appointments of the present and previous Governors General, both of whom are members of a so-called visible minority group. And at provincial level, likewise, in both Ontario and British Columbia, members of First Nations have been appointed as Lieutenant Governor. These important symbolic shifts suggest a growing acceptance of and comfort with the multiple narratives and identities that make up the nation. Further significant shifts can be seen on the ground, in actual cities and neighbourhoods. At least in the City of Vancouver, considerable thought has been given to the question of what fully engaging members of the host society would look like. As Chapters 2 and 3 describe in detail, there is real institutional thickness that speaks to the actual engagement of the host society in a variety of programs that do cross-cultural bridge building work. One remarkable initiative in Vancouver in the mid-1980s was the creation by the City of the Hastings Institute, specifically to tackle antiracism and diversity training in the public sector. Notably, the Collingwood Neighbourhood House used Hastings Institute trainers in antiracism workshops for its staff and volunteers, and many of the professional staff, including the Co-Director, Paula Carr, as well as residents who became active on the Board of the CNH, (like Terry Tayler, its first President) had been through Hastings Institute training. That story is the subject of a detailed case study in Chapter 3.

And, as Part II of this book illustrates, as well as the accompanying film, there have been grass roots efforts at the level of cities and neighbourhoods to develop a more inclusive and co-adaptive approach to immigrant integration, one that is increasingly coming to be called "interculturalism". Chapter 8 develops this philosophy explicitly, and links it to the case study of this book, the community building practices of the Collingwood Neighbourhood House.

1.6 In Conclusion: Multiculturalism as a Bold Social Experiment

Multiculturalism is, ultimately, a leap of the imagination. From its beginnings, in Canada at least, it was an idea of what a good country could be. The idea involved welcoming rather than shunning strangers, and not requiring them to abandon their own cultures and lifeways in order to join Canadian society. Most people couldn't describe this idea even now in more than fuzzy terms, or by associating it with food and festivals. There is now and always has been a huge element of expediency and opportunism in the concept. And it's always been a risk. No one has ever known for sure, or indeed knows now, whether a country based on such an idea is really possible, but again and again we leap toward the idea, and hope for the best. And maybe making the leap is the whole point. It's a life-affirming, humanity-affirming project.

As a project, multiculturalism doesn't truly live on the philosopher's page or in the critics' columns. It only lives when it is expressed in actions. And the country doesn't thrive unless we make the leap from our tribe or group or gated community onto the wobbly platform of the idea of a country in which all kinds of people can thrive. The leap requires physical presence and risk: to speak to, smile at, or just even meet the gaze of a stranger, to begin a process of welcoming. The risk, psychologically, is that when we do that, we might all be changed in some way. But the payoff, in terms of mutual understanding, of people connecting instead of colliding, can be so glorious as to make the risks seem small.

The places you'll see this leap of faith are on the sidewalks of the city, on school playgrounds, on subways, at bus stops, in public parks, parking lots, sports clubs, queues in stores, at sports events, in high school gyms, child care centres. In those places, and others like them, the leaps that continue to invent and redefine the multicultural nation continue to be made, day after day. When the leap fails, it looks like the destruction of the Africville community in Halifax, Nova Scotia, in the 1960s (Clairmont and Magill 1974), or the appalling history of the residential schools throughout Canada in their systematic attempt to annihilate indigenous cultures (Haig-Brown 1988; Jaine 1993; Royal Commission on Aboriginal Peoples, vol.1, 1996). When the leap succeeds, it looks like the Collingwood Neighbourhood House, as we explain in Part 2.

There is a magic in the idea of multiculturalism and the actions that embody it, actions such as the creation of the Collingwood Neighbourhood House. There's also a public act of courage in this idea. And those acts are out there each day along with their opposites. This book tells of these acts of courage, in one neighbourhood, as a tangible example of the active construction of a form of intercultural citizenship that addresses some of the current weakness of multiculturalism that this chapter has noted.

References

Alfred T (1999) Peace, power, righteousness. An indigenous manifesto. Oxford University Press, Toronto

Brown J, Vibert E, eds. (2003) Reading beyond words: Contexts for native history. 2nd ed. Ontario: Broadview Press, Peterborough

Bannerji H (1995) Thinking Through Toronto: Women's Press

Bannerji H (1996) On the dark side of the nation: Politics of multiculturalism and the state of Canada. Journal of Canadian Studies 31:103.

Bannerji H (2000) The Dark side of the Nation: Essays on Multicuturalism, Nationalism and Gender, Toronto: Canadian Scholars Press

Baxter D (1998) Just numbers, demographic change and immigration in Canada's future. Vol. 22. The Urban Futures Institute, Vancouver

Bissoondath N (2002) Selling illusions: The cult of multiculturalism in Canada. Penguin, Toronto

Canadian Heritage (2006a) Canadian multiculturalism: An inclusive citizenship. http://www.pch.gc.ca/progs/multi/inclusi (accessed July 30, 2007).

Canadian Heritage (2006b) Diversity in our urban centres: Canada's ethnicities. http://www.pch.gc.ca/progs/multi/reports/ann98-99/ethnicities_e.cfm?nav=2 (accessed July 30, 2007).

Canadian Heritage (2006c) Policy and legislative framework. http://www.pch.gc. ca/progs/multi/policy/framework_e.cfm?nav=2 (accessed July 30, 2007).

Clairmont D, Magill D (1974) Africville: The life and death of a Canadian black community. 3rd ed. McLelland and Stewart, Toronto

Day RJF (2000) Multiculturalism and the history of Canadian diversity. University of Toronto Press, Toronto

Dei G, Sefa J (1996) Anti-racism education: theory and practice. Fernwood Pub, Halifax

Dorris M (1994) Indians on the shelf. In: Paper Trail. HarperCollins, New York, pp122–132

Fleras A, Elliott JHL (1999) Multiculturalism in Canada: The challenge of diversity. Nelson Canada, Scarborough, Ont

Haig-Brown C (1988) Resistance and renewal: Surviving the Indian residential school. Tillacum Library Press, Vancouver

Harris C (2002) Making native space. Colonialism, resistance, and reserves in British Columbia. UBC Press, Vancouver

Henry F et al. (2000) The Color of Democracy: Racism in Canadian Society. Toronto: Harcourt Canada

Hesse B (2000) Introduction: Un/settled multiculturalisms. In: Hesse B (ed) Un/settled Multiculturalisms. Zed Books, London

Hiebert D, Ley D (2003) Characteristics of immigrant transnationalism in Vancouver. RIIM Working Paper Series, n° 03–15.

Hiebert D, Collins J, Spoonley P (2003). Uneven globalization: Neoliberal regimes, immigration, and multiculturalism in Australia, Canada, and New Zealand. RIIM Working Paper Series n° 03–05.

Hiebert, D (2006) Beyond the polemics: The economic outcomes of Canadian immigration. RIIM Working Paper Series n° 06–15

Hill L (2001) Black Berry, Sweet Juice: On Being Black and White in Canada. Toronto: Harper Collins

Jaine L (1993) Residential schools. The stolen years. University of Saskatchewan Extension Press, Saskatoon

Kymlicka W (1998) Finding our way: Rethinking ethnocultural relations in Canada. Oxford University Press, Toronto

Leaf M (2005) Vancouver, Canada. Multicultural collaboration and mainstreaming. In: Marcello Balbo (ed) International migrants and the City, UN Habitat, Nairobi

Ley D (2005) 'Post-Multiculturalism?' Paper presented at Woodrow Wilson International Center for Scholars, Washington DC, Jan 2005

Mahtani M (2002) Interrogating the hyphen-nation: Canadian multicultural policy and 'mixed race' identities. Social Identities 8(1): 67–90

Moodley K (1983) Canadian multiculturalism as ideology. Ethnic and Racial Studies 6(3).

Pratt G (2003) From migrant to immigrant: Domestic workers settle in Vancouver, Canada. RIIM Working Paper Series, n° 03–18.

Royal Commission on Aboriginal Peoples (1996) vol. 1, Looking forward looking Back. Ottawa

Said E (1978) Orientalism. Pantheon, New York

Sandercock L (2003) Cosmopolis 2: Mongrel cities of the 21st century. Continuum, New York

Sandercock L (2005) "A lifelong pregnancy?" Immigrants and the crisis of multiculturalism. Presented February 14, 2005 at the Simon Fraser University Wosk Centre Dialogue "The future of multiculturalism in British Columbia."

Sandercock L (2006) Mongrel cities of the 21st century. Is multiculturalism the solution or the problem? 2006 Laurier Lecture, Vancouver: CBC Radio Audiotape, July 2006

Sondhi R (2002) Equality and diversity issues in Birmingham, unpublished MS for City of Birmingham, March 2002

Statistics Canada (2003) Canada's ethnocultural portrait: The changing mosaic, 2001 Census Analysis Series. Statistics Canada, Ottawa

Wallace M, Milroy BM (1999) Intersecting claims: Possibilities for planning in Canada's multicultural cities. In: Fenster T (ed) Gender, Planning and Human Rights. Routledge, London

West C. (1990) The new cultural politics of difference. In: Ferguson R, Gever M, Minh-ha TT, West C (eds) Out there: Marginalization and contemporary cultures. MIT Press: Cambridge MA

Chapter 2
Integrating an Immigrant Metropolis: Vancouver's Diversity Mission

Leonie Sandercock with Samara Brock

2.1 Introduction: An Age of Migration in an Urban Century

> The closing years of the twentieth century and the beginning of the twenty-first will be the age of migration (Castles and Miller 1998: 3).

International migration is not an invention of the late 20th century, nor even of modernity in its twin guises of capitalism and colonialism. But there has been a growth in the volume and significance of migration since the 1980s, and an equally important qualitative shift since the 1960s and 1970s in those New World countries such as Canada and Australia that changed their racially exclusionary immigration laws at that time. Many authors have also begun to talk about the 21st century being the "urban century" (see Friedmann 2002). Seemingly then, the world is now undergoing its largest human migration in history, and that migration is both international, and from rural to urban, shifting the balance of world population. According to Friedmann (2002:2) it is expected that by 2025 a stunning 60% of humanity will be living in cities, compared with 40% in 2000.

Canadian cities are at the forefront of these global trends. With the second highest proportion of foreign-born residents in the world, Canadian immigration is quintessentially an urban phenomenon. Recent analyses from Statistics Canada show that fully 94% of all recent immigrants are living in Canada's cities, with 73% of them concentrated in the three largest: Toronto, Montreal, and Vancouver. And this is a trend that has accelerated over the past three decades. In the 1970s, 58% of immigrants resided in these three cities, and in the 1980s, that proportion had grown to two thirds (Statistics Canada 2003). With the changes to the Immigration Act in 1967 (described in Chapter 1), the result of this accelerating immigration is that Canada's three largest cities are among the most culturally diverse in the world, what Sandercock (2003) has described as

L. Sandercock, G. Attili, *Where Strangers Become Neighbours*, Urban and Landscape Perspectives 4, DOI 10.1007/978-1-4020-9035-6_2
© Springer Science+Business Media 2009

the "mongrel cities of the twenty first century". The current proportion of foreign-born residents in the CMA (Census Metropolitan Area) of Vancouver is 38%, second only to that of the Toronto CMA at 44% (Statistics Canada 2003). Within the Vancouver metropolitan area there is another interesting breakdown in terms of social geography. The City of Vancouver, with a population approaching 600,000, is by far the largest (although no longer the fastest growing) of the twenty one municipalities in the metropolitan area whose overall population is a shade over two million. And while not the only locus of immigration into the Vancouver CMA, the City of Vancouver has traditionally been at the forefront of both immigrant reception and multicultural policies in the region.

In this chapter, we situate Vancouver within Canada's political and economic history as a frontier in the westward expansion and economic development of the nation and thus as a destination for much of Canada's internal migration during the last century. The city became the entrepot, or funnel, for the wealth created by the opening up of the resource-rich province of British Columbia. Since the 1970s, Vancouver's role has expanded, as it became Canada's gateway to the Asia-Pacific region and thus the recipient of new sources of immigration as well as investment capital. This has brought about a socio-cultural as well as economic transformation, and just how these transformations have been managed, especially within the City of Vancouver, is the focus of this chapter. The next chapter looks in some detail at one local institution established by the City to work proactively on anti-racism and diversity training in the public sector. These two chapters reflect both strengths and weaknesses in the City's approach to multicultural readiness, but neither can be adequately understood without a broader appreciation of Vancouver's geographical, political and economic context, which is where we begin.

2.2 Vancouver's Economic and Socio-Cultural Transformation: An Overview

2.2.1 The First Century

Vancouver is built, literally, on the rich alluvial deposits and fertile soils created after the last major ice age, as the glaciers retreated and rivers flowed out at the base of the Coast Mountains. This physical geography created an environment that was hospitable to Coast Salish First Nation groups long before the city was founded in the late 19th century. The Coast Salish had both seasonal and permanent settlements all around the area, from the Fraser River to the shores of English Bay, for many centuries before the arrival of European settlers and colonists. Situated at the mouth of the Fraser river delta and hemmed in to the north by the steep slopes of the Coast Mountains, whose jagged peninsulas and deep fjords make access almost impossible by land, Vancouver occupies the last available flat land at the edge of the continent and is the most northerly major city on the west coast of North America.

Vancouver was colonized not from the sea, but from the land, unlike superficially similar places such as Cape Town or Sydney. "It is the terminus, not the beginning, of the modern Canadian story" (Berelowitz 2005: 12) and, in fact, its genesis as a city was as the western terminus of the transcontinental Canadian Pacific Railway. It is also the last stop, metaphorically speaking, of a colonization journey that began in the British Isles. The European urbanization of Vancouver has been a double exercise in conquest: first in the displacement of its first inhabitants, the Coast Salish peoples, and their near erasure from the physical and symbolic landscape. And second, a conquest of nature.

Historically, economic development in Canada has been natural resource-based, and this has had a profound impact on the nature of urban development. The resource sector has been instrumental in the formation of urban communities in Montreal, Toronto and Vancouver. Much of the growth of these core regions, until the 1970s, was determined by the demand for transportation, processing and administration generated by the natural resource sector. In the early days of these urban centres, cohorts of resource industry managers, production workers, and capital holders were the backbone of urban society, and they were predominantly of British and Scottish origins (Hutton 1998).

Founded in 1886, some thirty years after the province's capital city of Victoria, Vancouver had only 2,700 residents by 1900, making it very much a 20th century city. By 1931, its population had increased ten-fold, and by the early 1990s, twenty-fold, to pass the half million mark. By 1890, the budding town had established an electric street-railway that developed an interurban system of links and provided a mechanism for suburban growth. The streetcars established the grid of commercial arterial roads whose fine grain of commercial enterprises is one of the city's most endearing qualities and has contributed to its "neighbourhood" feel. These neighbourhoods were further enhanced by enlightened investment in tree planting and landscaping (Punter 2003: 7).

Vancouver's origins as a railway and port city meant that much of its waterfront was initially devoted to shipping and railway yards and then to storage and manufacturing. For its first hundred years, the downtown core was largely blocked from the water by the railways, warehouses, sawmills, and other industries. Reclaiming the waterfront for public use became a major focus of planning policies from the 1960s, as industry moved to cheaper land to the east of the downtown. In the post-second world war era, Vancouver experienced an economic boom driven initially by its traditional resource economy base, but enhanced by port activities, industrial consolidation, and immigration.

Vancouver has always been a city of immigrants. In its first hundred years, it was a predominantly Anglo-Canadian city growing, primarily through immigration of between one and two percent a year. Interestingly, although the Chinese population of the city in the late 19th century (drawn by the gold rush of 1858 and then the building of the railroad) was approximately one in five (Hiebert 1998), the effects of exclusionary racially-based laws since the early 20th century shaped the ethnic composition of the city and province over the first half of that century, determining that the dominant culture of the region would be Anglo-European. This is reflected in the striking proportion of immigrants to

Canada born in Europe (90%), compared with Asia (3%) before 1961 (Leaf 2005: 273). Much has changed, however, over the course of the city's recent metropolitan transformation. These changes, which have both economic and socio-cultural dimensions, are the subject of the next section.

2.2.2 Modernisation and Transformation Since the 1970s: An Asian-Pacific Metropolis

According to the preeminent scholar of Vancouver's economic transformation, Thomas Hutton, Vancouver since 1971 has undergone a major shift of production and employment away from the resources sector and toward the service sector and knowledge economy. There has been particularly strong growth of producer or business services; a dramatic expansion of employment in certain high-level occupational categories (managers and other professionals) which corresponds to the emergence of the information economy and key knowledge industries; a relative decline in traditional manufacturing as a result of firm closures; and a diminishing role for Vancouver's command and control functions for BC's resource-based economy (Hutton 1998: 56–57). There have been massive investments of public and private capital in Vancouver's metropolitan core since the 1980s, greatly accelerated by Expo 86, which have generated new retail, commercial, recreational, educational and institutional infrastructure as well as substantial residential development and redevelopment, and an associated booming construction industry. Major capital projects and an extensive international marketing effort by the provincial government have transformed the city from a relative backwater to a seductive destination for international visitors (both tourists and business travelers) and, above all, as a mecca for immigrants.

Vancouver's most striking transformation since the 1970s is its assumption of the role of Canada's gateway to the Asia-Pacific region, in terms of both human and capital flows (Hutton 1998: Chapter 3). These gateway functions range from trade to finance and investment, travel and tourism to communications, along with a three-dimensional immigration flow: of economic immigrants, family reunification, and refugees. The impacts of this immigration have been vast: from greater ethnic diversity to the introduction of new values and preferences; the emergence of new cultural groups, social institutions and business networks; new ethnic enclaves and neighbourhoods and a new impetus for suburban growth;

new consumption landscapes in the metro core and suburbs; new cultural landmarks and institutions; the reconstruction of residential landscapes; metropolitan densification; and the expansion of a variety of linkages between Vancouver and originating societies, cultures, and communities (Hutton 1998: 91).

What Leaf (2005: 287) describes as "the Asian components of Vancouver's new identity" are an important part of the re-branding of the city from a western Canadian outpost dependent on the provincial resource-based economy to a major urban service centre of the Pacific Rim. Coincident with Canada's opening up of its immigration laws to non-European source countries after 1967, the politics of China (especially the Cultural Revolution) and the position of Hong Kong as a major source of emigrant and refugee movement out of China created a large pool of potential immigrants for Canada. By the early 1970s immigration flows from Hong Kong into Vancouver were already significant, and were enhanced by a bigger wave after the 1984 signing of the Sino-British Agreement for the return of Hong Kong to China in 1997. There have also been significant components of immigration from South and Southeast Asia during the past thirty years, notably from British Commonwealth nations such as India, Pakistan and Sri Lanka.

By the 1990s, 90% of Vancouver's population growth was due to in-migration, with more than two thirds of that growth coming from outside Canada. Asian-origin flows have dominated since the 1980s, and by the 1986 census, the largest component of foreign-born residents were from Hong Kong (13.6%), followed closely by the People's Republic of China (11.5%), the Philippines (5.5%), Taiwan (4.6%) and Vietnam (2.7%). Of a total of 324,815 immigrants in the 1990s, those from East, Southeast and South Asia together comprised 53.4% of the foreign-born residents of the city (Hiebert 1998). One very important consequence of these shifting immigration sources is that Vancouver now has the highest proportion of "visible minorities", (a Canadian legal term defining people who are "non Caucasian in race or non-white in colour"), of any city in Canada, with more than 37% of the total population in 2001 categorised as belonging to a visible minority group. This was a substantial increase from 1991, when only a quarter of the population were so accounted for (Leaf 2005: 274–5).

Vancouver's Chinese population (itself internally diverse, with significant perceived differences between Taiwanese, Hong Kong and mainland groups) is by far the largest of the visible minority groups (at

17% of the CMA population), followed by South Asians (from India, Pakistan, Bangladesh, and Sri Lanka) who comprise 8% of the CMA, and Filippinos at 3% (Leaf 2005: 275). Nevertheless, there is a wide diversity of other ethnic groups who make up the overall mosaic of Vancouver, including folks from the Caribbean, Africa, West Asia and the Middle East. Another very important characteristic of Vancouver's recent immigration pattern is that it is increasingly dominated by economic immigrants, that is, by those admitted to Canada in the business category (as entrepreneurs, self-employed or investors), as skilled workers, or as caregivers. In 2002, economic immigrants comprised almost two thirds of the total (followed by the spouse and family category at 31% and refugees at 7%) (Citizenship and Immigration Canada 2003).

Federal and provincial legislation, programs and policy initiatives have been leading factors in Vancouver's emergence as an Asian-Pacific city. At the federal level, the reforms to immigration policy in 1967 have been critical; but so too has external market development, export trade support programs, and investments in infrastructure such as the City's trade and convention centre. The BC government has also actively supported Vancouver's role as a Pacific gateway city and node of the Pacific urban system. The historic investment focus of BC governments on large infrastructure projects in the province's interior, to open up the resource-rich hinterland, shifted dramatically in the 1980s to such metropolitan initiatives as the funding for Expo 86, the development of a rapid transit system, a 60.000 seat stadium and exhibition centre, and a series of policies undertaken in conjunction with local authorities to encourage the residential redevelopment of the downtown core, most notably by selling a large parcel of provincially owned waterfront land to Hong Kong's wealthiest developer in the late 1980s (Hutton 1998, Punter 2003).

During this period of transformation, the metropolitan regional government (formerly the Greater Vancouver Regional District, recently re-named Metro Vancouver) largely focused on growth management, strategic land use, transportation, environmental enhancement, preservation of agricultural land, and shaping the regional structure. It was the municipalities that found themselves having to deal with the socio-cultural transformation that was underway, and that is the story of the next section.

2.3 Integrating Immigrants in Vancouver: An Intricate Web of Services and Organizations

We turn now from the metropolitan area to the City of Vancouver, which lies at the heart of the region, and the evolution of an institutional infrastructure of urban policies and settlement services to "manage" the massive socio-cultural changes described in the preceding section. Hutton (1998: 96) pinpoints 1980 and the election of mayor Michael Harcourt as the moment when the City started actively exploring opportunities in the Asia Pacific region. A municipal economic strategy was approved by Vancouver City Council in 1983, emphasising the benefits to be derived from developing the city's Pacific gateway functions (port, airport, finance, education and communications). During the early 1980s, the City sponsored a succession of business, trade and investment missions to Asian cities, in cooperation with higher levels of government, the private sector, and the community as a whole.

When Harcourt moved into provincial politics in 1986 the new mayor, Gordon Campbell (now himself Premier of the province) continued to support trade, investment and cultural relationships with Asia, but the real focus of attention of this new regime began to shift to the accommodation of the new immigrant populations from Asia and elsewhere. In particular, the City was increasingly concerned about its capacity to integrate the large inflows of widely diverse cultures (Hutton 1998: 96). For the first

time at the local political level, managing this socio-cultural transition began to be seen as a potential problem, and responses included the reallocation of resources to social planning; adopting regulatory rather than developmental policy approaches; giving less priority to economic policies and programs (Hutton 1998: 98); and creating an institute to conduct anti-racism and diversity training for the public sector (the latter being the subject of a detailed case study in the next chapter). Taken together, these and other policies must be seen as a conscious attempt to build a multicultural society, accept socio-cultural diversity as intrinsic to a changing national identity, at the same time as the metropolitan and regional economy is being transformed.

What is immediately fascinating in teasing out Vancouver's strategies and policies for social integration is what we'll call the institutional thickness of the infrastructure that has been created over the past two decades. This thickness comprises a dense and intricate network of agencies responsible for the wellbeing of immigrants, agencies from all three tiers of government as well as innovative local civil society institutions such as the Immigrant Services Society (ISS), the United Chinese Community Enrichment Services Society (SUCCESS), and the range of Neighbourhood Houses across the City, one of which is the focus of the entire Part II of this book, as well as of our film.

It is actually difficult to separate out the complementary and overlapping programs of national, provincial and municipal agencies, and the civil society organisations, or non-profits, as the latter are largely funded by various government programs and grants. As background, it is important to understand that federal support by way of funding for resettlement and integration programs up until the late 1990s flowed to local community groups and NGOs on a project-by-project basis, with applications being submitted directly to the relevant federal agencies: Citizenship and Immigration Canada (CIC), the Multiculturalism Branch of Heritage Canada, and Human Resources Development Canada (HRDC). New federal legislation enacted in 2001 (Immigration and Refugee Protection Act) has devolved responsibilities from the federal ministries to the provincial level, through BC Multiculturalism, which now resides in the Ministry of the Attorney General. (In 2006, the Settlement and Multiculturalism Branch of provincial policy was shifted from the Ministry of Community, Aboriginal and Women's Services to the Ministry of the Attorney General, indicating a higher profile for the portfolio). That ministry is now responsible for the design, administration and delivery of immigrant services, and in turn BC Multiculturalism funds municipal and NGO projects and programs. And although this devolution has coincided with federal budget cutbacks in this policy domain, it has also coincided with an increased provincial commitment to multiculturalism, as evident in the passage of the Multiculturalism Act in BC in 1996, and the new *Strategic Framework for Action: A Strategy to Stimulate Joint Action on Multiculturalism and the Elimination of Racism* (Province of British Columbia 2005). Such increased provincial commitment, in turn, is likely connected to the efforts mentioned above of both province and municipality to re-orient Vancouver towards the Pacific Rim (Leaf 2005: 289).

The BC Multiculturalism Act outlines policies aimed at reducing racism and violence as well as increasing cross-cultural understanding and encouraging respect for the multicultural heritage of British Columbia (Province of British Columbia 1996). Of course, the existence of legislation is not enough. It must be backed with funds for staff to devise programs, and for the implementation of these programs. In this respect, the policy of multiculturalism is as vulnerable as any other policy domain to fluctuating priorities at both federal and provincial levels of government, as well as to the general scaling back of public spending on social issues under the influence of dominant neo-liberal ("small government") ideology in the past decade. Nevertheless, as Sections 2.3.1 to 2.3.4 demonstrate, there are strong relationships between the provincial government and the many grass roots organizations that have emerged in the past three decades to advocate for immigrants' rights and services, and the mobilization of these organizations exerts continuous pressure on government. From the perspective of these civil society organisations, the financial support of the provincial and federal levels of government is never enough. There is always more that needs to be done, and the closer you are to the problems in communities, on the ground, the harder it is to understand why more support is not forthcoming. But from another (non-insider) perspective, it may well seem that this nested hierarchy of federal and provincial legislation, along with the Charter of Rights and Freedoms, provides a quite remarkable framework for enabling the integration of immigrants and the moving towards genuinely intercultural cities and neighbourhoods.

The new *Strategic Framework for Action*, released in 2005, suggests what the private sector, NGOs, municipalities, and the province can do. These include provincial government sponsorship of multicultural and anti-racism training for community leaders, and protocols for dealing with racist incidents, which would be developed at community level in a collaborative way (Building Safe Communities – the Critical Incident Response Model). Funds are available, on application, for these types of programs (Province of British Columbia 2005). The flaw in this new document is that nobody is mandated to do anything. Communities are merely encouraged to submit proposals for funding, under the guidelines set out in the strategic framework. Inevitably, this means that communities with energetic leaders and existing grass roots organizations will take advantage of what is available, marginalising the most vulnerable and least organized communities.

But what is, in general, remarkable about the immigrant and multicultural policy sector is precisely the strength of grass roots organizations, and their umbrella associations, which have become powerful lobbying forces. The provincial government publishes a Directory of BC Multicultural, Anti-racism, Immigrant and Community Service Organisations which lists more than 50 organisations promoting multiculturalism and immigrant services within the City of Vancouver, and another 200 or so ethno-cultural organizations within the metropolitan area that are involved in the provision of services to recent immigrants (BC Multiculturalism 2006). This Directory is a good indication of the scale and diversity of grass roots organizations addressing immigrant settlement.

Leaf's overview of this diverse array of organizations makes the very important observation that what has been happening for at least two decades in Vancouver is an expanding arena of State-society cooperation in addressing immigrant settlement and integration (Leaf 2005: 290), from the most immediate settlement needs such as language skills and general orientation, to the longer term challenges of cross-cultural community building.

Before we turn to the municipal level and the multicultural readiness of the City of Vancouver, we will briefly summarise the work of four of these grass roots organizations as an illustration of the argument thus far: the Immigrant Services Society of BC (ISS); the Multilingual Orientation Service Association for Immigrant Communities (MOSAIC); the Affiliation of Multicultural Societies and Service Agencies of BC (AMSSA); and the United Chinese Community Enrichment Services Society (SUCCESS).

2.3.1 The Immigrant Services Society of BC (ISS)

Immigrant Services Society of BC (www.issbc.ca) was incorporated in 1972 as the first immigrant-serving agency in the province. Since that time, ISS has grown to be the largest multicultural, immigrant-serving agency in western Canada. The society provides a variety of services to Lower Mainland immigrant and refugee communities, and works with over 23,000 clients each year. ISS has a volunteer Board of Directors, 200 paid staff, and over 600 volunteers. The organisation provides programs and services through two divisions: the *Language College and Career Services*, is a full service training facility that provides a variety of programs and services in Vancouver, as well as in suburban Richmond, Surrey and Coquitlam, for individuals from a wide variety of cultural and ethnic backgrounds; the *Settlement Section,* located in downtown Vancouver, is the focal point for ISS' immigrant and refugee settlement programming throughout the Lower Mainland, providing direct assistance to immigrants and refugees on arrival. A visit to this downtown agency offers a glimpse into the lived experience of a newcomer to Canada who has no prior connections here. ISS staff meet new arrivals at the airport, bring them to the downtown agency, where they are offered accommodation in motel-style rooms above the agency's offices for up to one month. In their first week in Canada, and in the city, multilingual staff help them to open bank accounts, obtain drivers licenses, and eventually, to find longer term accommodation, as well as referring them to language classes and other social services.

ISS coordinates a Host Program (funded by the province) that seeks to ease the challenges faced by newly arrived immigrants and refugees by matching them with trained volunteer Hosts/friends from the community. Volunteers and newcomers engage in a range of activities together, one on one, such as: walks in the neighbourhood, practicing conversational English, visiting the library or community centres, using public transit, and shopping.

ISS also administers the provincially funded English Language Services for Adults (ELSA) from three different metropolitan locations (inner, middle and outer suburbs). The ELSA program is available free of charge for up to two years for newcomers over the age of seventeen. It offers classes in speaking, listening, reading and writing at basic literacy level as well as Labour Market Focused (LMF) English training for higher level students who plan to access employment.

In its thirty-five year existence, ISS has developed an impressive array of programs and services to assist immigrants. In addition to the language classes and the Host Program already mentioned, these include: employment services; foreign credential services; settlement services, family and youth services; and housing assistance. In the past decade, the organisation's activities have deepened to include multi-year community development and capacity building initiatives that target specific ethno-cultural communities, gender and/or age groups within the Vancouver metropolitan region. For example, ISS and a group of Afghan women launched a multi-year process to assist in the creation of an Afghan Women's Sewing and Handicraft Co-op in partnership with various partners and funders. A multi-year Food Security program was established in partnership with Quest and Food Banks targetting primarily Afghan and Kurdish communities in Vancouver, Burnaby and the Tri-Cities (Coquitlam, Port Coquitlam & Port Moody) area. One specific outcome has been a highly successful Kurdish community kitchen in East Vancouver as well as an emerging community kitchen for Afghans in Coquitlam.

Funding for these community development and capacity building activities comes from a mixture of government, NGO and faith-based sources, including the United Way of the Lower Mainland, the Vancouver Foundation, the federal Department of Canadian Heritage, and the Vancity

Credit Union. As is the case with the following three organizations whose work we will discuss, the funding sources in themselves convey a very interesting picture of the enmeshing of grass roots civil society organizations with umbrella support and advocacy groups, all drawing on federal and provincial funds from a range of Ministries, as well as private sector and individual donations through fund-raising, and the ubiquitous financial support role of the United Way.

2.3.2 The Multilingual Orientation Service Association for Immigrant Communities (MOSAIC)

As with the three other organizations discussed in this section of the chapter, MOSAIC (www.mosaicbc.com) came into being in the 1970s, in response to the dramatic socio-cultural transition in immigrant source countries. MOSAIC's origins, like those of SUCCESS (Section 2.3.4), are illustrative of a strong self-help tradition among immigrant communities, in the face of local government inaction in the 1970s.   Over time, organisations that began in response to the specific needs of a small group of new arrivals have expanded both the range of their activities and the number of immigrant communities they serve.

MOSAIC was formed in 1976 as a result of the amalgamation of two separate organizations: Multilingual Social Services, and Language Aid to Ethic Groups. Both had struggled from grant to grant, developing in response to the growing awareness of the daily problems faced by non-English speaking residents of the city. Today, MOSAIC has blossomed into a C$5million organization with more than 120 staff and 250 contractors. Services offered include interpretation, translation, English classes, employment programs, family support programs and family counseling, and community outreach and development programs. MOSAIC is very much a community-based organization, with a bilingual staff who offer services to non-English speaking people in metro Vancouver. Some of their recent initiatives include multicultural parenting groups; violence prevention and counseling programs (including "Men in Change"); the Nu Yu Theatre Project for youth; and the Korean Immigrant Youth Project.

MOSAIC's funding comes from the federal departments of Canadian Heritage and Human Resources Development Canada; provincial ministries such as Community, Aboriginal and Women's Services,

Attorney General, Women's Equality, Children and Family Development, and Human Resouces; as well as the usual staunch supporters, the United Way, the Vancouver Foundation, VanCity Credit Union, and the BC Gaming Commission.

2.3.3 The Affiliation of Multicultural Societies and Service Agencies of BC (AMSSA)

Founded in the late 1970s, AMSSA (www.amssa.org) is an umbrella organization that now brings together more than 85 member organizations in the province that are committed to the goal of promoting social justice and equity in multiculturalism, anti-racism, human rights and immigration. AMSSA's membership contains both ethno-cultural community groups and a wide range of older, local non-profit organizations that have traditionally focused on community building and local social services delivery, thereby building on a long-standing tradition of community volunteerism in the city that pre-dates the more recent socio-cultural changes (Leaf 2005: 297).

AMSSA's work is organized around three major committees, the Collaborative Committee on Multiculturalism (CCM), the Multicultural Health Committee (MHC), and the oldest, the Immigrant Integration Coordinating Committee (IICC). Each of these committees runs projects and programs aimed at building collaboration between member organizations and increasing awareness of immigration and multiculturalism issues more broadly. Combined government funding provides almost two-thirds of AMSSA's C$500,000 annual budget. AMMSA is a remarkably successful networking agency whose main functions are information sharing and advocacy activities and providing a mechanism for collaboration between its many member organizations and the government agencies. Over the years it has also contributed to legislative deliberations on immigration and refugee policies. Above all, in working with this wide range of traditional local non-profit organizations, AMSSA has been spreading the crucial message that immigrant issues and concerns involve not just the immigrant groups themselves, but the whole community.

2.3.4 The United Chinese Community Enrichment Services Society (SUCCESS)

SUCCESS was founded in 1973 at the time of the first new wave of (mostly Hong Kong) Chinese immigrants following the liberalizing of Canada's immigration laws in 1967. Although there was an existing Chinese community which had been in Vancouver since the late 19th century, the new arrivals found themselves excluded from the mutual aid societies of that established community. As the immigration flow increased, so too did the need for bilingual provision of access to social services, legal counseling, and finding housing and schools. Responding to necessity, some of the prominent members of the Hong Kong immigrant community came together to find ways to create a bridging mechanism between these new immigrants and Vancouver's social service agencies (Leaf 2005: 293), and formed SUCCESS.

According to Guo (2004), the organization has gone through three stages of development. The first stage was funded by a three-year grant from the federal department of Health and Welfare for the dual purposes of identifying existing gaps between immigrants' needs and the city's social service programs, and working with social service agencies to develop new programs to assist with immigrant integration. This "Chinese Connection Project" demonstrated a real need for community-based programs serving newcomers. Acting on these findings, then, the organizers of SUCCESS undertook fundraising and new membership development, and succeeded in having their organization incorporated into the United Way, an important umbrella organization of social service and charitable NGOs. This, in turn, gave them access and leverage to more federal funding under the Immigrant Settlement and Adaptation Program.

Interestingly, at this time in the late 1970s and early 1980s, the federal government was facing the settlement challenges associated with accepting refugees from Vietnam, and this provided an opportunity for SUCCESS to extend its activities beyond the Chinese immigrant community. During the 1980s then, in this second developmental stage, SUCCESS developed collaborative relations with existing neighbourhood organizations in those parts of the city where new immigrants were settling; opened three offices in different parts of the city (Chinatown and East Vancouver in the City of Vancouver, and in the adjacent municipality of Richmond); expanded their fundraising strategies; and expanded their range of services, from basic housing and services referral to more English language training, career counselling, and job referral services (Leaf 2005: 294).

The most important aspect of the third stage of SUCCESS's work, in the 1990s, Guo (2004) argues, was the offering of a range of language programs along with outreach to other, non-Chinese immigrant groups. And this pattern is fairly typical of immigrant organisations that start out serving one specific ethno-cultural group but, over time, engage in more bridge building activities with other cultures. SUCCESS now has a staff of over 350 professionals in 11 locations in the metropolitan area, supported by more than 9,000 volunteers, and more than a third of its annual operating budget of C$10million comes from community contributions. The rest of the budget comes from federal (38%) and provincial (26%) grants, with a tiny contribution from the City of Vancouver (about 1%).

There are a number of important messages here in terms of the broader question of the integration of immigrants. The first is the dense network of collaborative relationships in which SUCCESS is enmeshed, from the three tiers of government, to the United Way, to a myriad of neighbourhood and community-based organizations. Through its networking and collaboration, SUCCESS has become an important component of Vancouver's immigrant services landscape. The second is the way in which SUCCESS has morphed from its narrow ethnic roots, serving one ethno-cultural community, to serving many, which negates a popular myth that multicultural policies have encouraged the ghetto-izing of ethno-cultural communities. And the third is the deepening of the work of SUCCESS. As their website reveals (www.success.bc.ca), the range of the organisation's activities has gone far beyond the initial goals of settlement services and immigrant advocacy, to include business development, technology training, healthcare and education, and family and youth counseling. In other words, SUCCESS is now a mainstream, multi-faceted organization that is widely respected throughout the Vancouver region.

This brief portrait of four organizations that have emerged in the past three decades to serve the immigrant community is intended to illustrate the complex ways in which civil society and the State have come together to address the challenges of immigrant integration. Our final task in this chapter is to discuss the ways in which the City of Vancouver, as the preeminent municipality in the metropolitan region, has responded to these same challenges.

2.4 The City of Vancouver's Diversity Mission

City of Vancouver Mission Statement: To create a great city of communities, which cares
about its people, its environment, and the opportunities to live, work and prosper (City of
Vancouver 2006a).

As a municipality, the City of Vancouver enjoys unusual political and
planning autonomy thanks to the Vancouver Charter, granted by the
province of British Columbia in 1953. This Charter gave the City much
greater powers of self-government than those of other Canadian cities,
which remain subservient to provincial municipal Acts. This has allowed
the City Council and the director of planning significant scope for policy
innovation and direct response to local circumstances. The following
account of the City's responses to socio-cultural change also needs to be
understood in the context of local political changes that coincided with the
emergence of a more activist civil society seeking more direct influence
over urban and social development, as well as with the arrival of
newcomers from non-Anglo/European source countries who began to
organize and advocate for themselves, often with the help of existing
community based organisations.

For most of the post-world war two period, until the early 1970s, City of
Vancouver politics was dominated by the pro-business Non-Partisan
Association (NPA) party. By 1972, and coinciding with similar changes in
urban regimes across North America, there was a popular electoral revolt
which resulted in a reform party (TEAM, The Electors Action Movement)
ousting the pro-business and pro-development forces. TEAM had a more
sensitive approach to development (influenced by the writings of Canadian
urban critic and guru, Jane Jacobs), a more inclusive vision for the future
of the City, and a more participatory planning process. The newly elected
Council was very influential in shaping a more socially and
environmentally conscious approach to city building, a vision which has
remained intact for most of the past three decades. The hiring of Ray
Spaxman as the director of planning was intrinsic to the new broom
approach. Ray Spaxman had established a reputation in Toronto as a
planner sensitive to neighbourliness and livability, and his next sixteen
years as Director entrenched a planning culture that was receptive to more
participatory processes and also focused on neighbourhoods as the heart of
the city. His successors, Larry Beasley and Ann McAfee, embodied the
same core values, which in turn reflected a local consensus about the kind
of city that its residents wanted (Sandercock 2005). The urban planning
and social policy culture at City Hall changed accordingly, and it was in

the context of this changing institutional environment that Vancouver's socio-cultural demographic transition unfolded. The more open and transparent ways of operating and relationship between City Hall and the City Planning Department have, arguably, been of considerable assistance in developing flexible responses to the hitherto unanticipated needs of the diverse immigrant cultures that were about to arrive and put down new roots.

In the late 1970s, responding in part to federal and provincial policies and funding, the City of Vancouver sought to develop local multiculturalism-oriented policies, initiatives, programs, and partnerships. In 1977 the City adopted an Equal Employment Opportunity program that outlined the policies and guidelines for hiring a diverse workforce and offered diversity training to City staff. In 1988, possibly in response to pressure from organized civil society advocacy groups (see Sections 2.3.1 to 2.3.4 above), City Council adopted a civic policy on Multiculturalism Relations that addressed the need to recognize diversity as strength, promote freedom from prejudice, and ensure access to civic services for all residents regardless of their diverse backgrounds, including those with language barriers (City of Vancouver 2006b).

In response to this new civic policy, the City developed a variety of multicultural initiatives in the 1980s and 1990s. In 1989 the Hastings Institute was created in response to a growing demand from external organizations for the kind of diversity training the City was offering internally (see Chapter 3). In 1993, the City hosted community forums entitled "From Barriers to Bridges" during which Council reaffirmed its policy of reflecting cultural diversity in all aspects of civic activity. Two years later, Council adopted a Diversity Communications Strategy, developed by staff and community representatives, that included a multilingual information and referral phone service as well as an ethnic media news monitoring service that provides overviews of key messages for staff (City of Vancouver 2006c). The City also keeps an inventory of staff people who speak a second language and who are on-call if language assistance is required.

The CityPlan process, beginning in 1993, was one of the largest public involvement processes undertaken by the City (City of Vancouver 2006d). Between 1993 and 1995, CityPlan staff developed strategies to involve the cultural and immigrant groups in the City in future planning decisions. As Joyce Lee discovered in researching her 2002 Masters thesis, *Visioning Diversity: Planning Vancouver's Multicultural Communities,* which examined CityPlan, the City still has a long way to go in creating innovative processes that effectively engage diverse communities (Lee 2002). However, outreach to these groups does continue to be an important part of the ongoing CityPlan Neighbourhood Visions process, and the City continues to learn and adapt its methods.

A Special Advisory Committee on Diversity Issues was formed in 1994 to advise Council on various policy-related issues concerning better inclusion and involvement of culturally diverse communities. Every year, the committee gives two categories of Cultural Harmony Awards: individual and organizational. In 1999, Council approved $513.600 from its City Grant program for community organizations that service immigrants/refugees or culturally distinct communities (City of Vancouver 2006e). Priority for the funding has been given to services aimed at removing barriers to access for members of ethnic communities and/or facilitating the integration of newcomers. Examples of agencies receiving grants include MOSAIC (discussed in Section 2.3.2 above), the Immigrant Services Society (Section 2.3.1 above), and Metropolis Vancouver (a research centre on immigration). The City also publishes a Newcomer's Guide to the City, which is available in five languages. This variety of approaches

has made Vancouver a leader, at least in municipalities within the Greater Vancouver metro-region, in multicultural readiness, according to a study by Edgington and Hutton (2002).

Within the Social Planning Department, there is one position devoted exclusively to multicultural outreach and inclusion. The responsibilities of that position include outreach to specific ethno-cultural communities and liaising with the many grass roots organizations representing immigrant communities, in order to understand their concerns and bring them into a variety of civic initiatives and policies. A key role of this staff position is to instruct and advise staff in other City departments on engaging diverse communities in civic processes from neighbourhood planning to arts and cultural initiatives. In addition, this position plays a coordinating role on specific City initiatives related to multiculturalism and inclusion, such as the Advisory Committee to Council on Diversity and the Mayor's Working Group on Immigration. The fact that one person has held that position for some time means that many relationships have developed between the Social Planning Department and a wide array of local multicultural organizations and leaders.

There is now a growing literature about the City of Vancouver as a progressive planning agency (Punter 2003; Sandercock 2005). That reputation is the deserved result of the reforms and developments since the early 1970s, and an important part of this has been the role of the Social Planning Department, which has been instrumental in determining municipal responses to changing community needs. Social Planning's specific role within the City of Vancouver is to address community and social issues, particularly as they affect disadvantaged groups and individuals. The department has a variety of long-term engagement initiatives in the community such as *Youth Politik* which involves diverse youth in civic processes and enables them to bring their voices and issues to elected officials. Through its Community Service Grants, the Social Planning department funds a variety of diversity and immigration-related non-profit and social service agencies. Priority for funding is given to programming aimed at removing barriers to services which exist for some members of ethnic communities as well as programming that facilitates the integration of newcomers into community life. Through participation in the City's development and rezoning processes, the department also works to create community gathering spaces for the city's diverse inhabitants. Among the many long-term achievements of the department has been its support of Neighbourhood Houses in the City, including essential assistance with the birth of the Collingwood Neighbourhood House, which is the subject of Part II of this book.

2.5 In Conclusion: Vancouver's Multicultural Readiness

We have now presented evidence that, since the 1980s, Vancouver's civic leaders as well as its urban and social planners have been aware of the challenges to the urban social fabric presented by a rapidly changing socio-cultural landscape and have invented numerous ways of addressing these challenges. What is most striking is the emergence of a dense network of institutions and agencies, as well as policies and programs, to assist with the integration of immigrants, reflecting both acceptance of this new demographic reality and a strong sense of civic responsibility for building new, cross-cultural communities. The path has not been entirely smooth. But when racist and xenophobic incidents were first reported in schools in the mid-1980s, the then Mayor, Gordon Campbell was quick to respond, initiating a series of discussions in the schools and in community fora, in which the City's attitude of welcoming strangers was firmly asserted. The institutional response that followed these incidents was the creation of the Hastings Institute (Chapter 3), which was intended to help "change the mind of the City" (Brock 2006) through anti-racism and diversity training of workers in the public sector, to enable them to deal with such incidents in a positive way.

In the intervening twenty years, many policy adjustments have emerged to accommodate and affirm the multicultural city. In the early days, there was outreach to ethno-cultural communities, and assistance offered to those communities with facilities and culturally sensitive programs.

There are now many examples of increasing sensitivity in urban design, public art, and landscape work, marking the presence of the multiple publics that now constitute the city (including, currently, an Aboriginal-Chinese Storyscape project which aims to reinstate an Aboriginal presence in the urban landscape as well as to tell the story of relationships between First Nations and Chinese immigrants in the nineteenth century). The City, through its Social Planning Department, supports the wide array of immigrant integration work being done by the nine Neighbourhood Houses within the City. City Council meetings are open to the public, and members of the public can address Council and argue policy matters with them in sessions that often continue through the night into the early hours of the morning.

A closing anecdote about just such a Council meeting will serve to illustrate the degree of responsiveness that is possible when a City has become sensitized to cultural diversity. Vancouver residents have a reputation as environmental activists. The city was, for example, the birth place of the Greenpeace movement back in the 1970s and it has an avid cycling and outdoor culture. The health consciousness and awareness of citizens is reflected in the fact that it is illegal to smoke in public buildings and restaurants. This has driven smokers out of doors where, in all seasons, they huddle just outside the doorways of office buildings and public facilities, or in the outdoor patio sections of restaurants and coffee shops. A new bylaw, approved in principle in Fall 2007 and now being drafted by the City Council, will ban smoking on most sidewalks, at bus shelters, and within six metres of any entryway, air intake or window of a public building in the commercial district of downtown. This will effectively ban smoking on most sidewalks in the downtown as well as on restaurant patios. The new bylaw was vigorously but unsuccessfully opposed by smokers at the open Council meeting. But there was one very interesting exemption made to the bylaw. In response to verbal submissions to the discussion from owners of hookah lounges and teahouses in the city, these premises were granted an exemption. Council bowed to the argument that hookah lounges provide an important cultural space for the city's Muslims. Hamid Mohammadian, owner of the Persian Teahouse on Davie Street in downtown Vancouver, spoke on behalf of his clientele. He quoted a 75 year old customer who said, "I will have no other place to go if you close". Mohammadian brought a 600 year old hookah pipe decorated with a ceramic mosaic to show Council members. Another submission, from restaurant owner Emad Yacoub, argued that

> hookah lounges are essential for immigrants from hookah-smoking cultures because it helps them deal with the depression common for newcomers, and gives them places like they have at home' (Bula 2007: A1–2).

Two councilors from opposing political parties crafted the exemption during the Council meeting, in response to these public submissions. Such is the extent to which it is possible for the city's governance to be responsive and flexible.This small anecdote is an example of the much larger issue that we raised in the previous Section 1.5, namely the willingness of the host society to adapt to the lifeways of immigrants, rather than the one way adaptation of immigrants to host society (the assimilationist model). While Vancouver is far from perfect in this respect, the account we have presented does portray a city and society that, for two decades now, has not only been developing institutions and programs to assist with the immediate settlement needs of immigrants, but has also been working at a deeper level on the challenges of social integration, cross-cultural community building, and evolving forms of intercultural co-existence. The next chapter provides more detailed evidence of one such institutional innovation by the City, while Part II focuses on cross-cultural community building in one neighbourhood.

References

BC Multiculturalism (2006) Directory of BC Multicultural, Anti-racism, Immigrant and community Service Organisations. Ministry of the Attorney General, Victoria, BC

Berelowitz L (2005) Dream City. Vancouver and the Global Imagination. Douglas and McIntyre, Vancouver

Brock S (2006) Changing the mind of the city: The role of the Hastings Institute / EEO in building multicultural readiness in Vancouver's Host Society. Unpublished Masters thesis, School of Community & Regional Planning. University of British Columbia, Vancouver, BC

Bula F (2007) Hookah lounges exempt from bylaw. In: The Vancouver Sun, 21st September, A1–2.

Castles S, Miller M (1998) The age of migration, 2nd ed. The Guildford Press, New York

Citizenship and Immigration Canada (2003) Facts and figures 2002: Immigration overview. Citizenship and immigration Canada, Ottawa

City of Vancouver (2006a) Equal Employment Opportunity Program *(EEO)*. http://www.city.vancouver.bc.ca/eeo/index.htm#EEO (accessed August 7, 2006).

City of Vancouver (2006b) City of Vancouver Mission. http://vancouver.ca/ctyclerk/mission.htm (accessed August 7, 2006).

City of Vancouver (2006c) Multiculturalism & diversity: Civic policy on multicultural relations. http://www.city.vancouver.bc.ca/COMMSVCS/SOCIALPLANNING/initiatives/multicult/civicpolicy.htm (accessed 22nd Sept, 2007).

City of Vancouver (2006d) Policy report information: City communications strategy. http://www.city.vancouver.bc.ca/ctyclerk/cclerk/951109/csb1.htm (accessed Sept 7, 2007).

City of Vancouver (2006e) CityPlan: Directions for Vancouver. http://www.city.vancouver.bc.ca/commsvcs/planning/cityplan/dfvf.htm (accessed Sept 7, 2007).

Edgington DW, Hutton T (2002) Multiculturalism and local government in greater Vancouver. RIIM Working Paper Series, n° 02–06

Friedmann J (2002) The prospect of cities. University of Minnesota Press, Minneapolis

Guo S (2004) Responding to the changing needs of the chinese community. In: Vancouver: The contribution of SUCCESS, 1973–1998. RIIM Working Paper Series, n° 04–08

Hiebert D (1998) The changing social geography of immigrant settlement in Vancouver. RIIM Working Paper Series, n° 98–16

Hutton T (1998) The transformation of Canada's Pacific metropolis: A study of Vancouver. Institute for Research on Public Policy, Montreal

Leaf M (2005) Vancouver, Canada. Multicultural collaboration and mainstreaming. In: Balbo M (ed) International migrants and the city. UN Habitat, Nairobi

Lee J (2002) Visioning diversity: Planning Vancouver's multicultural communities. Unpublished Masters Thesis, Master of Arts in Planning. University of Waterloo, Ontario

Province of British Columbia – British Columbia Multicultural Advisory Council (2005) Strategic framework for action: A strategy to stimulate joint action on multiculturalism and the elimination of racism in British Columbia. http://www.ag.gov.bc.ca/sam/framework/pdf/framework.pdf (accessed 22nd Sept 2007).

Province of British Columbia (1996) Multiculturalism Act. http://www.qp.gov.bc.ca/statreg/stat/M/96321_01.htm (accessed 21st Sept 2007).

Punter J (2003) The Vancouver achievement: Urban planning and design. University of British Columbia Press, Vancouver

Sandercock L (2003) Cosmopolis 2: Mongrel cities of the 21st Century. Continuum, New York

Sandercock L (2005) An anatomy of civic ambition in Vancouver. Toward humane density. In: Harvard Design Magazine, n° 22, 36–43

Statistics Canada (2003) Canada's ethno-cultural portrait. The changing mosaic. Statistics Canada, Ottawa

Chapter 3
Changing the Mind of the City: Preparing the Public Sector for a Multicultural Society

Samara Brock

3.1 Introduction

The research outlined in this chapter was undertaken to address the following:

> I would like to plea for more research on the complexities of migrant incorporation into transnational cities. The questions that arise in this context are legion, and we are far from having an adequate theoretical framework for understanding the dynamics of successful incorporation. Before such a framework can evolve, however, many more detailed studies are needed (Friedmann 2002: 66).

The successful incorporation of immigrants is an issue facing not only Canadian but most other polyethnic cities around the world. This chapter takes a closer look at the challenge of preparing cities to effectively receive and integrate immigrants. It examines public policy efforts to engage members of the host society, specifically employees of public institutions, in active multicultural citizenship and to counter institutional racism and discrimination. It focuses on the diversity training and anti-discrimination work carried out by an organization established by the City of Vancouver, namely the Hastings Institute / Equal Employment Opportunity program, in order to illuminate ways in which multiculturalism can be implemented at the city level. With a few notable exceptions, there is not much literature looking at strategies that have been implemented by municipal governments to respond to emerging polyethnic urban landscapes (Edgington and Hutton 2002; Pestieau and Wallace 2003). This chapter provides a unique insight into the outcomes of an innovative and long-term approach carried out by the City of Vancouver, in order to illuminate how this work can be more effectively carried out in emerging polyethnic urban centres around the world.

L. Sandercock, G. Attili, *Where Strangers Become Neighbours*, Urban and Landscape Perspectives 4, DOI 10.1007/978-1-4020-9035-6_3
© Springer Science+Business Media 2009

3.2 The Hastings Institute / Equal Employment Opportunity program (EEO)

Of all of multicultural initiatives undertaken by the City of Vancouver outlined in the previous chapter, the most ambitious has been the Hastings Institute / Equal Employment Opportunity program. The EEO was established in 1977 to achieve the City of Vancouver's goal "to have a workforce that reflects the diversity of our community" (City of Vancouver 2006). The Hastings Institute was founded in 1989 to take some of the internal diversity training and cross-cultural communications strategies developed for the City internally by the EEO, to a broader audience. Both the EEO and the Institute currently deliver training on issues related to employment and service equity, diversity, cross-cultural relations, literacy, and harassment-free workplaces. The EEO does this internally within the City as well as providing informal and formal processes to deal with concerns of discrimination and harassment. The Hastings Institute provides training and consulting services externally for provincial government ministries, municipalities, crown corporations, community agencies and the private sector. In addition, the Hastings Institute / EEO is also responsible for the Workplace Language Program. This is a program that operates both internally within the City of Vancouver and with outside institutions such as the University of British Columbia and the British Columbia Building Corporation. Through the City of Vancouver, employees can receive conversation and literacy training from the program at one half employee time, one half City time.

Currently, there are six permanent staff for both the Hastings Institute and EEO. Four of these are advisors, who carry out tasks such as planning, programming and budgeting. One of these advisors heads up the work of the Hastings Institute, while the rest work primarily for the EEO. In addition to these advisors there are two administrative staff. Finally, there are a number of trainers who work as consultants for the EEO's internal harassment training and Workplace Language Program as well as externally through the Hastings Institute's harassment training. These trainers have an array of academic training and hands-on experience. Though the organizations are closely linked, the Hastings Institute also has it own Board, chaired by the mayor, which governs its operations. This is a direct result of the involvement of then mayor, Gordon Campbell (now Premier of the province of British Columbia) in the creation of the organization in 1989, as well as an attempt in the early 1990s to have the

Hastings Institute and EEO function as separate organizations. Both of these points will be picked up on in the following discussion.

These initiatives offered a prime case study for looking at multicultural initiatives at a local or municipal level as they were set up by a city government, in the context of fast-changing demographics, to prepare its employees and the broader population for these changes. Specifically, these organizations were created to engage members of the host society in a process of co-adaptation. This was a significant and ambitious innovation for a city to carry out and was on the leading edge of multicultural programming in this province and the country. The fact that this programming has been in place continuously for over fifteen years offers a rich case study of the shifting priorities and agendas of local and senior levels of government in terms of multicultural policy as well as the ability to look retrospectively at some of the longer-term impacts that these initiatives had in the city of Vancouver.

3.3 Overview of Methodology

The aim of the research documented in this chapter was to access a diverse array of experiences regarding the cross-cultural training undertaken by the Hastings Institute / EEO. Past and present employees, trainers, and participants in the programs over its twenty-year lifespan were interviewed. They were all given the same set of general questions to answer, but the interviews were left open-ended in order to follow their lead on what they felt was important to pull out from their experience with the Hastings Institute / EEO. Gathering an historical analysis of the work of the Institute and people's perceptions of the work was a key part of the inquiry. This was done in order to give greater context about the work of the Institute and the various forces which have shaped it over time. The ultimate aim of this inquiry was to draw conclusions for what municipalities could be doing in terms of building multicultural readiness for receiving new immigrants.

A number of sources were used. Primarily, the findings are drawn from twelve interviews with administrators, trainers and trainees of the organization. In addition to my own interviews, additional information was gathered from three reports. The first report is an impact assessment report conducted by external consultants on Hastings Institute training in 1990 which was created through interviews, questionnaires and focus groups.

The second is a collection of raw interviews collected for a directed studies project by students at the British Columbia Institute of Technology in 1992. The third is an analysis carried out in 2000 by the City of North Vancouver of different municipalities' degree of engagement with multiculturalism. Finally, I also drew upon the Institute's past and current training material to further inform this discussion.

3.3.1 Setting the Context: Some Background Literature

In order to set the context for this analysis of the Hastings Institute / EEO and the recommendations that emerged from this research, some of the relevant literature in the fields of multiculturalism and cross-cultural training will be discussed. The following section will give brief overviews of the following: transformative learning, anti-racism education, and the role of storytelling, as well as a discussion of a similar initiative carried out in Frankfurt, Germany.

3.3.2 Transformative Learning

> The transformation of our culture and society would have to happen at a number of levels. If it occurred only in the minds of individuals (as to some degree it already has), it would be powerless. If it came only from the initiative of the state, it would be tyrannical. Personal transformation among large numbers is essential, and it must not only be a transformation of consciousness but must also involve individual action. But individuals need the nurture of groups that carry a moral tradition reinforcing their own aspirations (Robert Bellah et al. 1986).

> What we want is a new transformed humanity, not equal opportunity in a dehumanized one (Vincent Harding as quoted in DeRosa 1996).

To be effective, diversity training and cross-cultural communication initiatives must create long lasting changes in people's behaviour. Theorists and practitioners of transformative learning have dedicated themselves to exploring how such changes come about. Transformative learning has its roots in the social learning tradition, used by such groups as the Highlander School which advocated working "with, and from the perspective of the poor rather than from the perspective of state-directed, or expert-centered planning practices" (Sandercock 2003: 81). Thinkers such as Paulo Freire have been central to shaping the field. A key aspect of a transformational approach is the reliance on a continuous cycle of action and reflection. This kind of reflection in practice has its roots in Paulo Freire's notion of praxis or the integration of action and reflection to engage in a critical literacy that entails reading "the word and the world" (Mayo 1999: 74). For Freire, this combination was essential to social change and separation of action and reflection resulted in "either mindless activism or empty theorizing" (Mayo 1999: 63).

More recently, the Ontario Institute for Studies in Education (OISE), one of the premier centres for the study of transformative learning, has developed a definition of transformative learning that is particularly relevant to this discussion:

> Transformative learning involves experiencing a deep, structural shift in the basic premises of thought, feelings and actions. It is a shift of consciousness that dramatically and permanently alters our way of being in the world. Such a shift involves our understanding of ourselves and our self-locations; our relationships with other humans and with the natural world; our understanding of relations of power in interlocking structures of class, race, gender; our body-awarenesses, our visions of alternative approaches to living and our sense of possibilities for social justice and peace and personal joy (Morrell and O'Connor 2002: xvii).

Transformative learning is explicitly aimed at working on both the societal and individual levels (O'Sullivan 2002; Tisdell 2003). It capitalises on times when the society's fundamental beliefs and understandings are being questioned in a way that demonstrates they are no longer functional and so cannot be maintained (O'Sullivan 2002). At the individual level, transformative learning tries to capitalise on an individual's reaction when he or she finds that the assumptions they use to categorise and make meaning consistently give them a misunderstanding or misperception of what is happening (O'Sullivan 2002). Racism and fear of the cultural "Other" are classic examples of times when assumptions are not functional at both the individual and societal level and when transformative learning techniques can be used to shift people's understanding.

Morrell and O'Connor acknowledge that for enduring behaviour change to occur, deeply and often unconsciously held beliefs must be changed. It is important to note that discriminatory thoughts and behaviour need not be the result of what Fleras and Elliot call "red-neck racism" – the explicitly avowed belief that one race is genetically inferior to another. Nor need they involve "polite racism", the kind practiced by people who believe in racial superiority but avoid saying so in public. Rather, such prejudices can be seen as examples of what Elliot and Fleras call "subliminal racism." This sort of racism is found in people who genuinely accept egalitarian values, but who nonetheless, often unconsciously invoke double standards when evaluating or predicting the actions of different racial groups (Fleras and Elliot 1999). This sort of racism is particularly difficult to identify, or to eliminate, since it is found in people who "consciously and sincerely reject all racist doctrines" (Kymlicka 1998: 81). This requires education that moves beyond rational, mind-based techniques to techniques that, while they include the mind, also address a person's emotions, spirit and body (Morrell and O'Connor 2002; Tisdell 2003; Miller 2002). Thus, transformative learning does not rely exclusively on rational methods of education, but expands to create dialogue about other aspects of our lives and acknowledges that multiple ways of knowing are necessary for multicultural understanding (LeBaron 2002; Morrell and O'Connor 2002; Sandercock 1998).

Due to its goal of long-term, fundamental change, transformative learning focuses not only on shifting a mindset but in creating a skill set that enables continual learning to occur. Bell Hooks' *Teaching Community: A Pedagogy of Hope* provides one example of the kinds of skills that are core to transformative learning literature. hooks presents an analysis of teaching in a way that allows "border crossings" or community building across difference to occur. She asserts that "to build community requires vigilant awareness of the work we must continually do to undermine all the socialization that leads us to behave in ways that perpetuate domination" (Hooks 2003: 36). This vigilant awareness is at the root of a key skill needed to actively engage in community, which Hooks calls a "radical openness" to different perspectives and the will and ability to shift one's own mindset (Hooks 2003: 48). Creating abilities such as self reflection, listening, and communication, as well as a long term commitment to using them in active engagement, is at the core of transformative approaches.

3.3.3 Multicultural Versus Anti-racism Education

A focus in diversity education on transformative approaches is outlined in the current literature on multicultural and anti-racist approaches. A key distinction is often made in the literature between these two approaches. This distinction centres on the idea that anti-racist education is a more holistic, challenging and engaging approach to overcoming strongly held beliefs. Effective anti-racism education is seen as a proactive process that "seeks to balance a value on difference with a sharing of power" (Dei 1996). Rather than merely focusing on rights and responsibilities, this pedagogical approach focuses on developing critical insight into issues of power and inequality. It also aims to focus this insight on existing institutional practices, and to pose a challenge to those practices that foster inequity (Fleras and Elliot 1999). This is contrasted to multicultural education, which does not openly challenge racism but is "merely intolerant of racism in its practice (Fleras and Elliot 1999: 353). In their summary of anti-racism training resources, Bina Mehta and Joelle Favreau explain the distinction in this way:

> Generally, anti-racist work addresses issues of power and privilege, while multiculturalism encourages a celebration of one's culture. While anti-racist training acknowledges the need to respect differences, it also tries to address the more complex issues of how people are treated unfairly as a result of their racial background... Ultimately, the goal of anti-racism is the elimination of racial discrimination and prejudice. Anti-racism is more overtly politicized, acknowledges the historical oppression of people of colour and calls for action against racism; by comparison, multicultural training does not often develop beyond celebrations of peoples' different backgrounds, as the primary means for achieving harmonious communities. This is an important distinction (Mehta and Favreau 2000: 4).

A key aspect of the anti-racist approach is a focus on the historical and societal structures that give rise to racism. As Sefa Dei observes, "justice is... not about simply treating everyone the same. Justice is recognizing the different ways individuals and groups have been historically disadvantaged and developing remedial measures that work within the lessons of history" (Dei 1996: 312). Those who advocate for anti-racist over multicultural approaches feel that unless we become critically reflective about the cultural norms in which we are embedded, we will take for granted social norms and cultural codes which determine and distribute power and privilege. It is precisely this lack of critical insight into systems of oppression and domination that has rendered multicultural approaches vulnerable to criticism. Diversity trainer Carl James worries that the very idea of multiculturalism may actually be detrimental to changing racist behaviour. He warns:

> Canadian anti-racism sources are sometimes stifled by the fact that we assume that because, unlike the Americans, we consider ourselves multicultural, then we are accepting of everyone... Obviously that is not the case. Racism is just as prevalent here as elsewhere. So we have to look more carefully at what our rhetoric of multiculturalism covers up in terms of getting at the issues of inequalities and injustice due to racism. Multiculturalism is not anti-racism, there are different tenets that underlie their orientations and actions (James as quoted in Mehta and Favreau 2000: 8).

In her overview of diversity training, Patti DeRosa makes further distinctions between the varied philosophical underpinnings of training approaches. She outlines the "intercultural approach" which sees "ignorance, cultural misunderstanding and value clashes" as the problems and "increased cultural awareness, knowledge and tolerance" as the solutions (DeRosa 1996: 1). She claims that this is the approach used in most international business and student exchanges. The "managing diversity approach" shares many similarities with the intercultural approach, though its focus is more on higher level managers and the need for them to learn to engage with difference in a business context. The "legal compliance approach," on the other hand, focuses on lack of compliance with civil rights regulations and exclusionary procedures within an organization, as the problem. It focuses on education about and compliance with legal frameworks, rather than on personal transformation. The "prejudice reduction approach" focuses instead on activities that promote emotional release. While DeRosa applauds this latter approach for helping to get at the emotional core of prejudice, she argues that often the emphasis is too much on personal hurt and not enough on institutional oppression. The "valuing diversity approach" looks at all aspects of diversity.

> DeRosa argues that in this approach, "since all human differences are up for discussion, the unique histories and experiences of specific groups may be obscured or diluted. Issues of privilege and entitlement of dominant groups' members may not be critically examined" (DeRosa 1996: 3).

For DeRosa, the anti-racism approach is the only one which adequately brings together critical reflection on societal issues of power as well as a focus on individual transformation. She outlines how this approach has moved away from the "in-your-face" style of early civil rights work. For her, new anti-racist approaches effectively combine aspects of other training philosophies:

> New-style AR (anti-racism)... takes a knowledge of cultural dynamics from the Interculturalists and an understanding of the need for legal supports from the Legal Compliance approach. From Managing Diversity, it takes the recognition of the impact of diversity on organizational effectiveness. Like Prejudice Reduction, it is committed to emotional exploration and healing, and like Valuing Differences, it focuses on a wide spectrum of human differences (DeRosa 1996: 5).

In her analysis, new style anti-racism both combines and moves beyond these approaches.

It clearly links the micro-analysis and the macro, the personal and the political. It requires deep self-examination and demands action in our personal and political lives. It is inclusive and transformative, rather than additive, reformist or assimilationist (DeRosa 1996: 5).

Through this discussion, we can see that there is a strong parallel between anti-racism education, as outlined by these authors, and the kind of pedagogical approaches that are extolled in transformative learning literature. Both are looking at using innovative and expansive methods for training and education in order to engage individuals in more fundamental shifts in attitude and understanding. The preceding discussion helps to set the stage for the analysis of the Hastings Institute / EEO's approach to education and training.

3.3.4 The Role of Storytelling

Stories are merely theories.
Theories are dreams.
A dream is a carving knife
and the scar it opens in the world
is history.
(from The Geology of Norway by Jan Zwicky)

The role of storytelling is intrinsic to this case study. Increasingly, in planning discourse and other literature about social change, the transformational role of stories and storytelling is being explored. That discourse is particularly relevant to this inquiry because, as discussed above, it is the stories, both conscious and unconscious, about ourselves and others that create either the cohesiveness or divisiveness of communities and societies. In particular, it is the narration of the cultural "Other" by members of the host society that creates boundaries between those conceived of as "natives" and those conceived of as newcomers (Chapter 1). It is therefore useful to examine how scholars are looking at ways in which stories can be used to reframe our understanding, rather than to entrench long-held biases and prejudices.

Sandercock argues that certain repeated stories serve to create boundaries between urban citizens:

Official urban discourses (those produced by City Council's Departments of Planning, Police Departments, mainstream media) tend to legitimise and privilege the fears of the bourgeoisie, their fears of those Others who might invade or disrupt their homely spaces, their habitus. We rarely hear from those folks whom official discourse classifies as Other, about their fears: the fear for example, of being hungry, homeless, jobless, of having no future in the city, of being unable to provide for one's children, the fear of not being accepted in a strange environment, the fear of police or citizen violence against them (Sandercock 2003: 124).

While this official urban discourse operates to create and maintain boundaries, Sandercock and others have begun to conceptualize how stories can be used in quite a different way. In *Story and Sustainability*, Barbara Eckstein and James Throgmorton (2003) compiled the work of planning scholars who argue for a very different use of stories in increasingly diverse urban centres. These authors show how sharing stories across imagined boundaries can shift the discourse from one of divisiveness to one of shared understanding.

In this collection, Robert Beauregard outlines what urban citizenship entails in his discussion of discursive democracy. He discusses the ideal urban citizen as

an active storyteller who is expressing a view of the world from a personal perspective. She or he is also an active listener to stories told by others. While public spaces might lend themselves to political speeches, harangues, and avant-garde raving, the basic democratic work is only to be done when people interact with each other in ways that allow specific experiences to be set against other specific experiences and to be considered, validated and challenged. Telling and knowing are connected. Stories are told not just to express understanding and intentions to their listeners but also to reshape them. A discursive democracy has to enable private stories to become public… For this to happen, trust and reciprocity must be strong, Deliberations must be non-threatening. In the absence of such conditions, citizens will remain silent or defensive (Eckstein and Throgmorton 2003: 68).

In his discussion, Beauregard is elaborating on Habermasian ideas about discursive democracy, in which mutual dialogue is seen as a key building block for democracy. Central to this idea is the notion that people's opinions are formed through interactions and deliberation. As Beauregard puts it

people's interests are not presocial, but emerge out of social interactions. People reveal their feelings about an issue, listen as others speak, reflect on what they have said and heard, and search for common ground" (Beauregard in Eckstein and Throgmorton 2003: 75).

The challenge these scholars present is that of creating story-telling occurrences and stories that allow people to re-narrate their cities. They argue that we need to create opportunities for citizens to manifest accounts of inclusive rather than exclusive cities and that allow them to expand their notion of community rather than cocoon in the face of difference. Barthel argues in this same collection that

> story at its best creates a sense of commonality; commonality generates a sense of shared history, creates the possibility of community. We need to create spaces and ways to hear, share, draw lessons from, and *act on* these stories (Barthel in Eckstein and Throgmorton 2003: 242).

What these writers are calling for, then, is the creation of spaces for interaction – these spaces include events where different cultures can gather to talk across difference, actual physical spaces which are set up for cultures to gather as well as what Sandercock (following Amin) calls "sites of banal transgressions" where the explicit aim is not formal dialogue, but rather the creation of environments where cultural exchange can occur on a more casual and ongoing basis.

3.3.4.1 Storytelling and Dialogue Creation Through the Arts

One approach to engaging a wide audience in shared storytelling that is gaining a lot of attention in current literature is to create opportunities for dialogue through the arts. In his new book *Better Together: Restoring the American Community*, Robert Putnam, who is well-known for his work on the decline of social capital in modern society, states that "the arts represent perhaps the most significant underutilized forum for rebuilding community in America" (Putnam as quoted in Borrup, 2003: 5). Czech president Vaclav Havel, also a renowned playwright, observed "that arts offer a unique means of connecting us to our common humanity" (Saguaro Seminar 2001: 1). Community arts, undertaken with a community engagement approach, offer unique opportunities to create dialogue around this common humanity. Researchers at Harvard's Saguaro Seminar on Civic Engagement in America have observed that community arts "have a singular advantage in rebuilding social capital: they are enjoyable and fun" (Saguaro Seminar 2001: 4). Other civic activities such as attending meetings or voting, they argue, are akin to "*civic broccoli* because they are good for all but unpleasant to many" (Saguaro Seminar 2001: 4). Community arts are also seen as being especially useful for engaging citizens in cross-cultural dialogue. One example where community arts had a profound impact is outlined in renowned cultural planner Robert Palmer's discussion about the impact that the development of a parade had on cross-cultural understanding in the diverse city of Brussels.

[When] we started to work on the parade… we began to talk to people about… integration. Through our discussions, we began to understand that the real belief was not in integration but in a respect for difference. That was what people actually wanted was a real respect for their own particular cultural positions and identities… They wanted opportunities to develop those traditions and to share them with others… [The parade] offered a visible statement about the importance of cultural differences in Brussels. This parade became a metaphor or icon… [and it] substantially influenced the new way in which the city began to look at cultural diversity (Palmer 2002).

Community arts, from events like parades to murals and mosaics, can give groups a way to express and celebrate difference in an engaging and fun way. As in the example from Brussels, this can help to shift the perspective from one which emphasises the need for new immigrants to integrate, to one where different cultural identities are valued. In this way, communities focus on diversity as an asset rather than a threat. Incorporating these kinds of opportunities for intercultural interaction into the daily lives of citizens is central to building cross-cultural understanding between diverse groups. As Ash Amin points out, "changes in attitude and behaviour spring from lived experience" (Amin 2003: 15).

In using community arts approaches, however, it is important not to revert to the kind of multicultural celebrations that have been criticized by some as supplying nothing more than a veneer of shallow multiculturalism over larger issues of societal racism. In their discussion of successful policy directions for building social cohesion, Waters and Teo emphasize that building connections across group lines best occurs through ongoing strategies. In fact, they point out that "one-time efforts often exacerbate rather than solve tensions" (Waters and Teo 2003: 37). It is important, then, to make community arts and other initiatives into ongoing or part of larger ongoing efforts to create linkages between people. The ultimate aim of this interaction needs to be the creation of what Edward Soja calls intercultural coalitions which "consciously combine formerly separate and often antagonistic racial and ethnic grouping." (Soja 2000: 282). Soja sees these kinds of coalitions as having the ability to open up "spaces of resistance in the Postmetropolis, not jut as figures of speech but also as concrete sites for progressive political action" (Soja 2000: 282). Soja outlines a concrete example of how this occurred in Carson, the most heterogeneous neighbourhood in Los Angeles. He explains that Carson's awareness of its unusual cultural heterogeneity has led to the creation of the country's first Museum of Cultural Diversity, described as a "Forum for Cultural Collaborations through the Arts" (Soja 2000: 296). This substantial arts and cultural initiative worked to create a permanent space to showcase, celebrate and re-narrate ideas of cultural difference. It thus became the kind of ongoing site for interaction and building of understanding across cultural boundaries that these thinkers are advocating.

3.3.5 AMKA: A Complementary Case Study

Having outlined an analytical backdrop for this inquiry in terms of current literature on transformative learning, anti-racist education approaches and the role of storytelling, I now turn to a complementary case study in order to supply further context from which to examine the work of the Hastings Institute / EEO. AMKA (The Municipal Department of Multicultural Affairs) in Frankfurt, Germany provides an instructive comparison with the Hastings Institute / EEO. John Friedmann and Ute Angleika Lehrer analysed AMKA's work in a 1997 article, "Urban Policy Responses to Foreign In-Migration: The Case of Frankfurt-am-Main." The lessons learned from this initiative were then further examined by Leonie Sandercock in her discussion of urban multicultural strategies in *Mongrel Cities* (2003)

The aim of AMKA when it was founded in 1989 was to foster a peaceful multicultural society, through engaging its citizens in a process of "Zusammenwachsen" or "growing together" (Sandercock 2003: 138). Their key objectives included "reducing the German population's fear of the 'Other', encouraging public discussion of migration and social tolerance, engaging newcomers in active participation in public affairs, encouraging the cultural activities of foreign residents, and offering training for members of the municipal bureaucracy in intercultural communication" (Wolf-Almanasreh as quoted in Friedmann and Lehrer 1997). AMKA held three important public hearings and forums: A Hearing on the Situation of Foreigners in Frankfurt, A Hearing on the Situation of Migrant Women, and Suggestions and Demands for an Urban Policy Concerning Frankfurt's Population. All of these were aimed at creating opportunities for diverse groups to listen and be heard as well as creating strategies for how diverse groups could live and prosper together. As well as public dialogues, AMKA focused on additional avenues for newcomers to participate in the political and daily life of the city through such initiatives as a Foreign Residents' Advisory Board, which enable them to attend city council meetings and comment on the municipal budget, as well as through supporting multicultural organizations and events.

Unfortunately, these efforts came to an end when the Red-Green coalition that put them in place was voted out of office in 1995.

From this example, Sandercock outlines a number of key strengths of the organization's work, as well lessons learned that are valuable for setting the stage for the analysis of the work of the Hastings Institute / EEO. First, she summarizes what she sees as particularly significant about AMKA's work:

> It dealt with multicultural citizenship at the level of the city and everyday life
> It was committed to a long-term perspective
> It promoted mutual learning
> It recognized and tried to address fear of foreigners, and the violence that often accompanies this fear
> It addressed the culture of municipal bureaucracy (police, teachers, judges, planners)
> It saw its main role as educational, oriented to learning and communication (Sandercock 2003: 139).

I would add that AMKA wasn't afraid to call a spade a spade. By this I mean that it wasn't afraid to confront the host population with its own racism. While shallow multicultural initiatives tend to dance around the underlying issues of prejudice and racism, AMKA's hearings clearly sought to address these difficult issues. Sandercock also outlines some insightful political conclusions that can be drawn from this example:

> For a project of migrant integration at the level of the city, there needs to be multi-party support... [In addition] support from the national state is essential if conditions of becoming a citizen are to change. A third insight has to do with the micro-politics of integration. The public forums were incredibly important symbolic events, and may also have contributed to the empowerment or confidence-building of those migrant organizations and individuals who took part, but there is also micro-sociological work that needs to be done street by street, neighbourhood by neighbourhood, and across a range of institutions (Sandercock 2003: 139–140).

The work of AMKA gives important insight into the kind of work that needs to be carried out at the city level in order to effectively address co-adaptation of the host society and newcomers. Analyzing its work also offers some insight into the conditions that need to be in place or be created in order for this kind of work to really have long-lasting impact. These observations will now inform the analysis of the work of the Hastings Institute / EEO.

3.4 Analysis of the Work of Hasting Institute / EEO

Many broad themes emerged from the research into the Hastings Institute / EEO. The account that follows is organized thematically to give a picture of the past, present and future of the Hastings Institute / EEO as part of the City of Vancouver's larger multicultural work. It will become apparent, through the interviews drawn on, that there was a focus on "the Kingswood Days" as the heyday of the organization as well as the benchmark against which all future work of the organization would be measured. As stated in a 1995 report to council:

> the "Kingswood years" created a framework of knowledge, awareness and commitment in key areas throughout the province and are the foundation on which the Hastings Institute has built its current programs (City of Vancouver 1995: 4).

More space is, thus, given to a description and analysis of these early years as they provided the foundation upon which all future work of the Hastings Institute / EEO was built.

3.4.1 Origins of the Hastings Institute

In an analysis of how diversity policies originate in municipalities, a report prepared by the City of North Vancouver points out that cities such as Vancouver, Richmond and Burnaby, which were most affected by the wave of Asian immigration that began in the 1980s, were early proponents of policies to do with diversity. Vancouver has since taken its development of diversity and cross-cultural policies and mandates much further than other municipalities. In their analysis, the City of North Vancouver points out that the early and continuing adaptation of these policies by the City of Vancouver was greatly helped by having champions within the bureaucracy (City of North Vancouver 2000: 49). Many interviewees suggested it was the initiative and support of the then mayor (Gordon Campbell) and the City Manager (Ken Dobell) that initially gave rise to the organization. The Hastings Institute was seen as such a high priority that the mayor was installed as the chair of the board, an arrangement that continues to this day. Many felt the early commitment by high level staff was one of the key elements that secured long-term commitment to this kind of endeavour. A past trainer for the Hastings Institute felt that this enabled Vancouver to maintain a commitment to this initiative:

unless the city manager says it is a priority, or the mayor, then it really isn't a priority. You do have people at mid-management and they can do small things, but important things. But really you need people at the senior level to be saying this is significant to us (Interviewee C).

During its initial three years of operation, the Hastings Institute received core funding from the Secretary of State – Multiculturalism and Citizenship Canada, and financial support for program development from provincial ministries and agencies (City of Vancouver 1995: 3). Many of the interviewees felt that this support, financial and otherwise, for the early training carried out by the Hastings Institute arose out of a unique environment. There was commitment to multicultural training during that time from all levels of government. This commitment waned after a few peak years. In describing an offshoot of the Kingswood simulation training aimed at Crown Corporations, (nicknamed "the Crowns"), one ex-Hastings trainer had this to say about how support for the program had tapered off:

the Crowns was a two-day training where a bunch of the Crowns came together – BC Hydro, BCBC, BC Transit, a mix of all of them. It was meant to be mostly supervisors. And we had one of the VPs who would always come and promote the training and that took place in a hotel in Richmond. This was the day when money flowed for training because we would have coffee, tea, muffins and then a fancy lunch… That was the standard. It was expected. That was a costly training. But they were up for it because at that time there definitely was commitment from the Crowns to look at this. They had equity offices and the provincial government was pushing equity… People can't pay for things anymore. The Crowns training we couldn't do anymore. Not with all that money for actors and lunches and people getting away for two days for diversity training in this climate. There has been a shift and that's related to the fiscal climate, the political climate, and the fact that many organizations are so concerned with the bottom line that diversity has fallen off the table (Interviewee H).

Many interviewees talked about how it was the spirit of the times that gave rise to the possibility of the organization and to the City's cross-cultural ambitions (see Chapter 2). It was a time in which there was, in the words of one former Kingswood trainer, "an amazing sense of possibility." A long-term trainer with the Hastings Institute had this to say about the ethos of the time:

in some ways the work that we were doing at Hastings was challenging organizations to reflect on what does it really mean to welcome and value diversity – we say it, but what does it mean to enact it in our organization. It was a very positive and challenging time. It was also a time where people were willing to have that dialogue. That's another reason why I appreciated being involved in that work because people were open to having conversations. Human rights law was in place but human rights jurisprudence was just coming into being. Past practices were being challenged that existed for years – that ethos was being challenged. The language that we used: firemen became fire officers; aldermen became councilors, etc. Not to say that all of these changes came easy. I would argue that it was more than the policy of the City. It was a changing ethos in Canadian society that began to challenge these practices and we just were involved in the education and training of this (Interviewee A).

Some also cited the local political environment as particularly conducive to the emergence of the organization. The Mayor and others wanted to be proactive in addressing the resistance some parts of the community were begin to feel to the increasing number of visible minorities immigrating to the city. A past trainee of the Hastings Institute who now heads up a local non-profit had this to say:

I think at that time Council had enough level of stability that they were able to try some new and innovative kinds of things. It was just after Expo [86] so there was some attention around the city being a world Mecca in some respects. I came from the prairies to Vancouver after Expo – the diversity of the city drew me here. Part of that may have been created through Expo and part of it may have been created by it being a diverse community at that time. My sense is that was when things really began to shift from the city's perspective. And I think after Expo there were still a lot of residual effects. There was lots of development that happened – there was lots of housing development and Hong Kong's time clock was ticking. So there were a number of things that were having huge influences in the community. *I think the City had to react to that. Many people in our community were very resistant to these changes. They didn't want their sleepy little community to become a big city.* They didn't want to have these strangers coming from other parts of the world and changing it. So I think that's kind of what leads to a lot of things. And there were some good innovative things happening at that time. The children's advocate was designated in that period, lots of interesting social housing was being developed. As far as the other levels of government I don't remember the provincial government being very involved at that point. Everything that was really happening around inclusivity and diversity was really coming from the municipality (Interviewee G). (author's emphasis)

3.4.2 Organizational Development

Interviewees focused a lot of their discussion on how the organization had shifted, both positively and negatively, over time. This section will outline the changes they observed and the reasons for them.

3.4.2.1 The Kingswood Years

The first, and, as stated above, to this day the best-known program carried out through the Hastings Institute / EEO was the Kingswood Management Training Program. A quick summary of how it functioned was outlined in a 1995 report to council:

the fictitious City of Kingswood mimicked a civic bureaucracy; participants were drawn largely from government at the municipal and provincial levels and the program was specifically structured around their needs (City of Vancouver 1995: 3).

The foundation of Kingswood was experiential learning principles and training techniques such as role play and simulation. Trainees took on characters for the entire five days of training and were put through various scenarios. This is how one trainee described her experience:

we went away to Qualicum on the island and stayed in a hotel. When we arrived we were each given a character. I think that I was Wilma and I was the volunteer coordinator for some organization and then I had to play that role throughout the whole week and at certain times there were particular tasks that I was called upon to do. And then through the actual scenarios there were some learning and some debriefing afterwards with the whole group and discussions and how somebody would work on issues that we were faced with. I found it very good training in that it had some very hands-on experience but it also looked at policies, city directions and visions and began to not only make you think about what you needed on the ground but also what you needed to create in terms of a vision for yourselves in your community. One scenario I was put through where we had a volunteer and someone had complained because the volunteer was a person from another culture and had some very specific views about that individual and their capacity. And through that discussion and dialogue it was my role to both advocate for that individual but also do some education with that person and also to set some parameters on what we as an organization could do and not do. We could not support his request to remove that person because we did not feel that it was substantiated and had to be diplomatic and not call that person a racist or whatever, but to kind of learn how to bring those issues forward in a way that I think created mutual respect and also modeled that (Interviewee G).

These were well-funded, high-profile training sessions. One past trainer jokingly referred to it as "luxury level training" (Interviewee B). As luxurious as it was, the training was also intended to be challenging and hard-hitting. This past trainer went on to paint the following picture of how Kingswood training looked:

what would happen is that the white well-intentioned and quite comfortable bureaucrat is sitting up in the training room learning about employment equity policy and about the Charter and someone will come up from downstairs and tap them on the shoulder and say we have a situation in your department that we need to deal with. Well, he didn't know he actually had a department so he was shocked to find that out. They would follow you out and you'd take them into a room and sitting in that room is a young black woman who's been passed over for a promotion or has been harassed in the workplace and tells him the story and asks him what are you going to do about it? This is your fault, this is your department, you deal with it, you fix it, and you change it. The whole thing was designed, yes, around role plays but not around you pretend to be this or that. They got thrown into something. They had no idea it was like this whole underworld was there and all of the sudden it really was like a city down there. And she would say and it's that guy and you better talk to him. So he'd send off a memo saying that that person should be disciplined and all of the sudden there would be another person [saying] I'm bringing the union in how dare you say that. So it was very immediate, very hands on. Along with the information and the knowledge and the learning, but the thing was it was in their face all the time about 12 hours a day. It just went straight through (Interviewee B).

Many pointed out that the ultimate purpose of Kingswood went well beyond changing personal opinions, extending to shaping the organizations and communities in which city and other employees worked. One long-term trainer for the Hastings Institute / EEO observed:

this is a very important point. The City provided the resources and we were able to put in place a training program so at the end of the day there would be changed policies and processes that ended up serving a wider population. It was a very creative and effective time (Interviewee A).

One way that Kingswood operated to turn training into concrete action was incorporating plans for how participants would follow up on the training. Participants created a contract which was an action plan for when they returned to their jobs, setting out what they were going to do around specific things such as hiring practices and public outreach.

3.4.2.2 Approach to Training

Those who had been involved in Kingswood as trainers or trainees felt that the program took a unique and innovative approach for its time. A past trainer's analysis of different approaches to training tells us a lot about the philosophical debates and underpinnings of their work at that time:

what we were trying to do was traverse the middle ground on this and we had lots of disagreements between us about what that was about. Kingswood was really going for an experiential piece that if people experienced it, had human to human relationships rather than just information that there was some interaction that really got you to think about what this all meant that this could really change your life. And so Hastings and the Kingswood model was a balance point around how does that best play out. And it was a very powerful piece... One of the things that Hastings was built on was hope and a belief in human beings and in their good. See some training is really based on human beings or parts of them as being of ill-intent or bad or evil. Hastings and the Kingswood model wasn't that way. It was really based on a belief that people could change, on a belief that if people have the right experience and the right information and the right support, the Titanic will turn (Interviewee B).

The impact assessment carried out on the Kingswood training in 1999 also underlines the balance that the training team was trying to create:

members of the training team stressed that the program they deliver is active, experiential, designed to make participants think it is real and to operate at the "gut level." However a substantial amount of effort is put into information and content. Clearly it is not intended to be like an encounter group. The training team's objective is not just to engineer an emotional experience but to include a substantial amount of current information in a learning format that is exciting and challenging. The simulation is designed to take participants out of their real working lives and allow them the freedom to explore other ideas and ways of relating. It is demanding at several different levels: organizational, individual, small group. This is done to enhance the complexity of the training and underline the high expectations of involvement (Berman and Levitan 1990: 4).

3.4.2.3 Changes over Time

Over the years, Hastings Institute training evolved from a five day residential to a two day residential, then to non-residential. It first evolved into a mini-Kingswood program called "Valuing Diversity" which borrowed many techniques from Kingswood and was made more broadly available. Slowly, the focus began to shift from broad diversity or cross-cultural training to more of a focus on harassment prevention. In 1996, Hastings piloted a harassment intervention skills session. In 1999 there was a shift in its primary focus with the creation of a workshop titled "Working Towards a Harassment-free Workplace."

A content analysis of current training documents also shows a shift in training focus away from the deep experiential approach on which early training had been based. Apart from the ongoing training of the Workplace Language Program, there are currently two one-day training sessions: Workplace Harassment Prevention and Harassment Intervention Skills. As indicated by the titles, the focus of these training sessions is on more overt manifestations of discriminatory behaviour rather than focusing on the systemic, underlying causes of discrimination such as societal power structures and colonial history. Part of the focus of the training is, thus, on legal frameworks which guide workplace conduct. For instance, an exercise on the first day of training, "the Harassment Game", focuses on identifying which of a number of scenarios were legally considered harassment. In the first session, there are a couple of video exercises which show people being discriminated against. The aim of these is to elicit reactions as to how one would deal with this situation in the workplace. This is the closest that trainees come to role playing or experiential learning in the first session.

The second session, "Harassment Intervention Skills," is meant as further skill development for supervisors only. This second day began as a follow-up for supervisors after a 4–6 week period. The focus of this day is less on outlining examples and legal definitions of harassment than the first day. For instance, participants talk about injustice and why it is that "we often don't intervene or speak up when we see an injustice occurring" (City of Vancouver 2005). There are also brief role plays in which each participant gets a chance to take on the role of the harasser, the harassed and the intervening supervisor. Participants also take a look at Action Plans that they created after their first day of training and reflect on how they have or have not been able to enact them. Thus, some experiential elements from the original Kingswood training remain in the second training day, though to a much lesser degree than they were in the original training. In addition, rather than being broadly available, these training sessions are for returning supervisors only.

3.4.2.4 Why the Shift in Training Occurred

Interviewees offered many explanations as to why such a dramatic shift in training had occurred, from Kingswood's residential, experiential, multi-day approach, to the current shorter sessions focused largely on harassment prevention and intervention. One ex-trainer who worked for the organization towards the end of the Kingswood programs had this to say about the shift in training:

> Kingswood was a very effective model. Most people would say that it was very valuable and meaningful to them. The downfall of Kingswood was there was no way to build some sustainability when people went back to their organizations. They had this incredible experience at Kingswood and then they went back to their jobs and very little changed because these people were not necessarily empowered to change or given the time to facilitate change. The other element of that is that it is a very costly program. You have a big human resource component to it… They require whatever time release, etc. Plus the staffing model of the trainers was very expensive. While I am very much a supporter of simulation, a five day simulation is not cost-effective especially when you consider the first point I made about having support when they go back to the organization. But the other thing is that Kingswood didn't in a way present solutions or strategies. It presented a real learning in terms of awareness. And you could develop strategies because a lot of things you did in the simulations focused on developing strategies but those weren't necessarily things which you could say, "okay take this strategy you can use it back in your organization." So while you did learn strategies there wasn't necessarily a link as to how to apply that when you got back into your organization. And it might not have been necessarily a strategy going on in the organization. People did learn a lot about exclusion, harassment, all those kinds of things and I think it did change people's behaviour per se but it didn't change organizations so much. It might change the kind of environment that people were in because certain behaviour did change. I think that did assist. But I think also it maybe had run its course. Its time had come and people needed to move on to

something different. And I think some of those differences were to become more organizationally focused in a very specific way. That would be my impression whether that's training people within the organizations to do that kind of facilitation or being change agents within their group or whether it was to begin to work on some specific organizational initiatives like policy and policy implementation and strategic planning and so on. I think overall in the scheme of diversity and multiculturalism there has been that shift generally from more of that kind of generalized training to something that's very specifically focused to help organizations do a specific task or become more inclusive in a particular way. So I think it might have been kind of an evolution process for some of it. And also it wouldn't be funded anymore. It was just not something that people would fund so much anymore (Interviewee C).

A current trainer for the Hastings Institute / EEO explained that training had evolved as a result of a widespread feeling that the original diversity training had been saturated in the organization and that the focus had needed to move from awareness to skills building:

I think there was a sense that diversity training had really been saturated in the organization. That we could realize that from the number of people who were enrolling or not enrolling in the programs... There's only so many ways that you can do awareness training. The thing that is important about the harassment prevention and intervention is that it is very skills-based. And that's what people need. They need skills. When you are looking at diversity issues there is a real challenge in building skills. You can do a lot with awareness with sensitivity, with developing empathy and understanding and giving knowledge and information, challenging biases but it is a challenge to figure out how you build skill around that, and so I agreed with the shift to something that would focus on skills building. Because after all you cannot require people to change their attitudes – you can only educate slowly and people will arrive at their own understandings over some period of time. But you can require certain behaviors in terms of a respectful workplace and you can develop skills for supervisors around how to foster that. And so I really supported that shift (Interviewee F).

There was also a realization that, overall, people's general level of awareness had shifted from the 1980s, when Hastings was established, to the present day. A long term trainer for the organization described how he had seen training change accordingly:

whereas I think about ten years ago doing this kind of training there was more of a requirement to say these are the basics – workplace cultures have changed, we can't do this anymore. Well, people generally know that now. They know that you can't make racist jokes, they know that you can't have pinups. Whereas we can't say ten years ago that that was just generally known and generally accepted. So now we spend a lot more time on the subtler kinds of issues and I think that that is a kind of reflection that people have responded to and taken in an understanding of what the basic requirements are for how we treat each other in the workplace. It's that shift in the nature of the questions to questions that show that people are focusing on areas that may be more subtle or more grey (Interviewee A).

It was these feelings of diversity training "saturation", coupled with lowered budgets and a more widespread diversity awareness, that some interviewees felt gave the impetus to switch to shorter-term training focused on delivering specific information and skills.

However, interviewees had differing perceptions of the change of the organisation from the early years of Kingswood. While some saw it, as outlined above, as a natural evolution given the changing climate, others saw it as a result of poor policy decisions and a shift in priorities. A number of interviewees cited the attempt in the early 1990s to turn the organisation into a revenue generating company as an example of this shift in priorities. In 1992, three years after its creation, the Hastings Institute underwent an expansion which was shaped around the idea that the organisation could generate revenue as a private company, and it became quite separate from the EEO. It moved its offices and grew to more than a dozen staff, mostly trainers. These trainers were paid salaries by the City, but were expected to bring in private training contracts from outside sources such as other levels of government and business (Interviewees C and H). This was a brief experiment, and the Hastings Institute laid off many staff in 1994 and once again became more closely linked with the EEO. According to a 1995 memorandum titled *Proposed 1995 Operating Structure of the Hastings Institute*:

in July, 1994, the Institute informed City Council of the financial difficulties it was experiencing and that a deficit of $136.737 had incurred as of June 21, 1994… Several budget reduction measures were initiated in an attempt to reduce the deficit. Two support staff positions were phased out. A third support staff position was terminated on November 30th. All salary consultant positions have been changed to project based contracts… Anticipating a deficit of $200.000 by the end of this calendar year, the Institute cannot afford to take any additional financial risk next year. The only alternative is to downsize it into a very small organization, merge with the EEO, with no infrastructure or overhead support and maintain minimal activity to slowly repay the deficit loan. (City of Vancouver 1995: 2–4)

The Hastings Institute did downsize dramatically, reducing staff and programming. Financial records showing the changes in funding over time for the Institute are not publicly available. However, there was general agreement among interviewees that funding from the City for the Institute's work had shrunk considerably since its expansion in 1992. It should be noted here that the funding of the EEO, however, has remained stable, and its staffing levels have stayed relatively constant over the past 20 years (Interviewee L).

As mentioned above, some interviewees felt that these shifts in the Hastings Institute were the result of poor planning or a shift in priorities. One ex-trainer had this to say about what she saw as the failed corporatisation of the organisation:

You could have misread the climate. You could have misread that this was something that could develop into kind of a corporate effort separate from the City. But I think it might have been a little bit of wishful thinking. There was a lot of dough, there was a lot of people working there as staff. We were all earning pretty good money and getting a lot of work. But people had to have the money to pay for training and that money did not stay at those levels. It's sustained in the sense that some of that is still going on but on such a smaller scale. A much smaller scale. And I am still making a living at it although there has been a shift; I don't do as much diversity training anymore because few are paying for it. So I am primarily focusing on... you know, still working on systemic change but from a different angle mostly focusing on addressing issues of access for internationally trained professionals. So the shift is because that's where there is energy and money. And I don't know if at the time whether there could have been a broadening of the scope but maybe that just was not possible (Interviewee H).

One ex-trainer suggested that the decision to expand the Hastings Institute and experiment with revenue generation was not philosophically compatible with the staff at the time:

It was really the, then, City Manager and Assistant City Manager [names excluded] who were kind of the managers of that process. And they were the ones who made this decision for revenue generation to take place. And I think there is still probably hard feelings about that. People felt like they had been brought in to do one thing and it turned out to be another. And they weren't necessarily incompatible, but there were some value conflicts that needed to be examined and they weren't examined as such... I think when you are getting into revenue generation...[you have] a particular vision of the way you think the organization is going, that has, in a sense, capitalist values attached to it. And many of us don't (well sure, we are all capitalists to some degree – we make money we try to own houses and cars) but many of us would go on the other side of that to believing that it is about working for social justice and coming for from a socialist agenda and less of a money making agenda (Interviewee C).

One early Kingswood trainer who ceased to work for the organisation as it changed felt the City had chosen to pursue different objectives:

I believe primarily there was a large shift in priorities. If there was a political thing about flavour of the year it was done. On their behalf, it may be that without the funding it wasn't going to be possible to do this kind of stuff. But it looked deeper than that. Because it looked to me – and by this time I was an outsider – it didn't look to me as though there was an attempt to reestablish a set of priorities for the next stage. I mean I'm sure they would say that that is what they have done is work directly with departments and so on. The pull back was so fast except for areas around language training... but the pullback felt so quick that it looked like it was "okay we are done here. Pull the troops back we are out of here." So that people were still there and working in those departments but what they were doing, I haven't seen outcome. I haven't seen huge policy change. I haven't seen them working by going into departments and saying how can we help you with the hiring piece. They may well be doing that but it is certainly not on a large enough scale that it would be visible to someone like me, at least. Cause I am on the outside but not totally on the outside – the world of this kind of training is quite small. So, yes, I would say reprioritizing, just a pull back (Interviewee B).

There were, thus, a complex range of societal, financial and political factors at play which interviewees felt influenced the shift in the Hastings Institute at this time. While interviewees had differing points of view about the main drivers of this shift, they all agreed that dramatic changes took place in the nature of the organisation and the training it carried out. This discussion will be picked up in the following section regarding the current incarnation of the organisation.

3.4.2.5 Current Incarnation and Current Environment

A range of opinions about the current incarnation of the Hastings Institute / EEO emerged from the interviews. Some felt that there is a lack of public profile for the organisation right now. One interviewee, a past trainer, observed that "they are a shadow of their former selves. People think they don't exist anymore" (Interviewee B). A past trainee similarly commented:

It was shocking when I heard the other day that the Hastings Institute was still around. It just has a very low profile. And I also think that the City is in a much different place than it was in 1980. What was interesting in that time was that not only was the training happening but also governments and funders were taking on different ways of getting people to multiculturalize their organizations and they did that primarily by using funding as the tool and so if you were reaching multicultural populations you would be higher priority for receiving funding under certain pools and those kind of encouragements and policies really moved a lot of organizations (Interviewee G).

There were many ways in which interviewees felt that the current work of the organisation did not go far enough. Both the ethos of the time and a shift in funding priorities were seen as the reason for the decline in programming. One ex-Hastings trainer painted this portrait of the current funding climate:

There is a little bit of anti-racism money coming out of the province, but it is a shadow of its former self... Neither Heritage [Canada] nor MCAWS [the Ministry of Community, Aboriginal, and Women's Services] have many resources... So the money's not there.

Heritage has cut what it pays for and they have to be so accountable for every cent that it is like a pain in the neck to go for the money. Sometimes you just get tired. And Heritage said they wouldn't pay for any train-the-trainers anymore because they felt that they had been there, done that. Again people's priorities changed in terms of foundations and federal government what they want to see in place. How they want their money to be spent... It was a big vision and it was brilliant while it lasted but it couldn't have been sustained (Interviewee H).

Another long-term trainer with the Hastings Institute / EEO felt that the current societal climate was at the root of the shift:

To some extent what has happened – we've hit a... not a wall but a plateau – some people say there is kind of a backlash. I don't know if I would use the word backlash. But more of a reflection. An example that I used in some of the training I do – it harkens back to the time that I was going to school in Vancouver. Currently my son is in the same school. During the December period there was a Christmas concert – I am Christian... I look at my son's concert – it's very diverse and multicultural. But people are looking back and asking, "have we lost something?" And I think that is where the plateau happens. I think we are being re-challenged (Interviewee A).

3.4.2.6 Impacts of Hastings Institute / EEO Training

Despite their differing opinions about the current incarnation of the organisation, all of the interviewees spoke highly about the impact that the training carried out by the organisation had had over time. One of the authors of a 1990 impact assessment of early Kingswood training had this to say about her findings:

People who we interviewed talked about transformation as a result of Kingswood. There was a lot of words like that... I think that in the immediate sense Kingswood was incredibly impactful and probably I would say that in a deep emotional way it got people in the gut. We are talking intense. And you create a sense of uncertainty for people who work in a world where they are in control and certain of outcomes. They are the ones running the show. The positive feedback we got (we didn't get all positive because for some of the people it was very negative, they didn't feel safe, particularly the women, and that wasn't good because the Kingswood facilitators did not adequately address that according to them.) But for the deputy chief of police and the fire chief it opened their eyes in a very dramatic way (Interviewee H).

The impact study outlined the specific elements of the training that trainees felt were most effective. These were the simulation experience, the harassment scenarios and the panels from specific communities such as the disabled. Using information gathered from focus groups, questionnaires and interviews, the report explained that:

For a majority of participants the simulation model was the key element in the success of Kingswood as a training program. The simulation models provided a context in which participants could challenge themselves and take risks as a means to enhancing their learning experience (Berman and Levitan 1990: ii).

Of particular interest in this report is the fact that participants felt that the length of the training was appropriate (Berman and Levitan, 1990: 19). In fact

a clear majority thought it was the most cost efficient training program in this area. Although there was agreement that the program is expensive, participants felt the cost of not running the program would be higher (Berman and Levitan 1990: 46).

Despite this, training was shortened in the following years, suggesting that the decision to do so may have been based on budgetary restrictions rather than on the actual needs of effective training. The report further highlights the impact of the training by discussing the way trainees felt upon returning to their workplace:

On returning to work participants reported recognizable changes in their individual perceptions. These ranged from personal changes in attitude and perspective regarding equity issues to a significant emphasis on the urgency of implementing equity in the workplace... All spoke of a clear commitment to take on a more proactive role with regard to equity issues in their departments and/ or organizations. An indicator of greater "equity consciousness" was an increased awareness of incidents of discrimination in their organization. In addition, a majority of interviewees remarked that they became more concerned with organizational policies and practice regarding the physically handicapped, ethnic minorities, and women (Berman and Levitan 1990: 34).

One of the interviewees for my research, who had been a trainer for Kingswood, gave a specific example of how one high-ranking government employee transformed his department after the training he received, expanding the impact from the personal to a policy level:

there was one fellow who I will call John who's quite high up in [the Ministry of] Forestry for the province. He came to the training and he was one of the people who was really a guiding light out of that because he went back into his ministry and I always felt that he stood and looked at it with new eyes. He started creating programs – he created trainings up in the interior. I actually took part in some of them... But it wasn't the training as much as the way he changed policy and the way he put in programming that was different. He started doing pieces with aboriginal firefighter units that hadn't been done like that before. He started hiring things that were different. So what can come out of that piece is a bit of the scales falling off your eyes (Interviewee B).

A series of interviews carried out by British Columbia Institute of Technology students in 1992 with trainees from City of Vancouver departments as diverse as engineering, finance, health, planning , and parks, also highlight many specific impacts of the training they had received from the Hastings Institute / EEO. Many mention the emotional impact that the training had on them and how it has affected their point of view and actions since. One interview summary from an employee from the engineering department states that in the past, the interviewee:

> would have run away and ignored a case of sexual harassment. After going through Kingswood she had learned about her responsibility as an employer to deal with and correct the situation (Mackinnon et al. 1992).

Another interviewee from the Housing and Properties Department felt:

> that the majority of the education of Kingswood has passed through him to the supervisors he manages. Before [interviewee's name]'s attendance at Kingswood in 1987, his department had complaints of human rights abuses and discriminatory practices based on race or disability. Since then, there have been no complaints of discrimination (Mackinnon et al. 1992).

As another example of the impacts documented through this report, an account from an interviewee in the planning department gives a specific story regarding how he has felt more able to take on discriminatory behaviour:

> In past public meetings, there have been comments about monster houses being built. Comments like 'it's the people from Hong Kong that is [sic] causing all this.' It's the Asian immigration. Our immigration should not allow these people in. They are destroying our neighbourhoods.' [interviewee's name] has taken these people to task saying, 'Those people have nothing to do with the issue. Most of the monsters have been built on spec and not for a particular client. You can not blame them for bringing the monster houses into the neighbourhood. It's the spec builder who has done it. And that type of racial comment is unacceptable' (Mackinnon et al. 1992).

In one of my own interviews, a past trainer for the Hastings Institute / EEO outlined specific changes in the library system that occurred in the period after the training began:

> I can remember working with the public library system. I'm not suggesting that the training should take all the credit for this – it was a piece of a larger shift. But if you look at the Vancouver public library system now – you go to any branch there is an elaborate

selection of materials representing a number of backgrounds and in languages other than English. Looking back 10 or 20 years ago that was not the case. So I like to think that the training that was done in the early 90s had some impact into the kinds of services they offer and how they provide those services (Interviewee A).

Interviewees also highlighted other programs of the Hastings Institute / EEO, apart from diversity training, as having a positive impact. For example, a past trainee of the Workplace Language Program who went on to be a trainer for the program felt that that contextual literacy program had really helped her and others:

> going to class at the beginning I didn't really like it because it's something different. Because some people just like me – I am not an open person. I didn't really want to share with a group of strangers. But once you get to know each other you get more open and you have the confidence to share. I think that is very important when you can have a group of people talking together to share experience and it is safe in a way. This is very important it is safe. You don't have to worry that it will spread everywhere. So I think most of the city employees have a similar situation. When they work, they work and they didn't have much time to talk with their co-workers. So once they come to the class they have opportunities... When you go back you be a happier person... And we see promotion after people come to our programs. They get opportunities. For instance a person could be working as a clerical worker because she had no opportunity to take notes because in her job that is not a requirement. So within the class she could just take minutes and then she had the experience so it's a little bit helping her when she gets the promotion later on. I think the city is changing quite a bit now. When I first got into the city almost all those department heads are males. So you can see now there are some women who are getting the higher positions and you can see that it is different groups. You can see the last name and you know that there are from different groups not just Caucasian. I think the city is changing in a good way (Interviewee E).

She also had this story about one employee who experienced quite a shift from participating in the program:

> One of the students who came to our class he was very quiet. He wrote about the sprinkler system at the beginning. After he left our program he became a lot more outgoing. He came several times and after he set up a chi gong class for all city employees where they can go. In his group I think he has over a hundred employees... He's been doing that for years now. Quite interesting because he says if he had never been to the class he never would have done that (Interviewee E).

3.4.2.7 Elements of Good Training and Other Approaches to Creating Change

Throughout the interviews, trainers and trainees alike highlighted many of the elements of effective training and other approaches to creating change. I will now turn to a discussion of some of the key elements that they brought up.

3.4.2.8 Ongoing Impact

The importance of training not being a one-off but, rather, being part of a longer-term initiative was stressed by many interviewees. One past trainer for the Hastings Institute commented:

> You need some kind of ongoing mechanism to keep the issue on the table, to keep it alive for people, to keep reminding themselves about what they have learned and how they can maintain that learning and how they can share that in their organisations... If you look at training alone you are going to see positive impacts after training generally speaking. People come up with new insights about themselves and about the issues and understanding of people's context and their organisation and willingness to do something. Over the long term [with Hastings] I think there are people who sustain that and were helped by the resources that were there. But when those resources don't exist anymore, then I just don't know. I hope that it wasn't a meaningless exercise [and] that that shift can be sustained. But I think you've got to work at it. Particularly in organisations that are in survival mode and not willing to give it the time of day. Because I'm not sure we have moved to a place where people truly understand that issues of diversity are about all that you do in the organisation not just something off the side of your desk or some extra you have to get funding for (Interviewee H).

Many interviewees stressed the importance of follow-up to training. One past Hastings Institute trainer who went on to work for a number of different private and public sector clients summed it up in this way:

> Training has its pitfalls because it is invariably something between a rifle and a shotgun. It's got one load in it. One of the oil and gas companies [I work with] – they instituted hiring teams so that everyone had to be on the hiring team for their co-worker. If you can go in and do ongoing work with that hiring team you can change a lot of stuff... Invariably what we've learned is that training without follow up [is not effective]. And the follow up needs to be over time, over levels of experience, involve different components of practical and emotional and spiritual and actual intellectual shift because humans can't do a one time over and then salvation. For the most part people don't like change, don't want change and fight it (Interviewee B).

A current trainer with the Hastings Institute outlined why the atmosphere in which training occurs was also very important to its impact:

> Training that gets parachuted in a vacuum where there isn't policy support and not consistent messaging from senior management does not, in my experience, have the kind of impact that we would like it to have. Training within the environment of the City [of Vancouver] where there are consistent messages from the council members, the senior management, and the planning department... diversity is just embedded and integrated

and infused in the way the City does business and I think training in that kind of environment is very effective (Interviewee F).

Interviewees generally stressed the importance of longer range rather than one-off approaches to change: for example, continual checking in with the organisation that has received training, including follow-up sessions where they can discuss issues which have arisen. A second suggestion was to facilitate the setting up of committees whose role is to look at all aspects of their organization from a diversity lens. Another idea was that diversity shouldn't just be put on one person's plate in an organisation. A past trainee had this to say about the importance of having ongoing, long-term avenues from which to look at issues of diversity in her organisation:

> There isn't a day goes by that we aren't working on those issues. We just recently started a homeless showering program and we are having the same level of challenges as we did working with our culturally diverse community [which] is just getting people to the place where they get comfortable establishing human relationships with people that they may have seen very differently before. And our communities are constantly transient – we have new people coming and going. For people who may be living in a very diverse community their sensitivity might be very different than someone that comes from something that is a bit more homogeneous. I really do think that having something that is sustainable and ongoing and continues to build on capacity so it doesn't start from a place where people have no knowledge but recognize that knowledge changes and the communities grow and change and the kinds of support will change with that (Interviewee G).

3.4.2.9 The Co-learning Approach

Co-learning was seen by many to be an effective way of getting people to learn with, not at the expense of, others. One trainee of the Hastings Institute looked to the importance of more informal co-learning, where cultures were able to interact through contributing to their community through the arts:

> I think around race relations… some of the things that we have really found to be extremely beneficial is when we can create environments where people are given the opportunity to contribute their skills and their knowledge. There is a focus on the assets rather than the needs so that there is a shift of thinking. Part of this goes along with the shift of community development thinking around not being necessarily needs based but to balance that with the assets in communities. And I know that that was a huge shift in our organisational development that we, for many years, saw our role as being able to provide services – English language services, services around interpretation and translation. Not that we don't continue to see that as our role but we also recognize that we need to do a lot more attitudinally around our changes in attitude in order to create an environment that

is open to other people contributing. One of my greatest examples is when we did the aboriginal carving out here at the neighbourhood house and it was an initiative that came from the aboriginal community that they wanted to do a carving and wanted us to help to get that happening. And we were very excited to do that. In my discussions with them I had talked about how it would be really nice for them to create what they were creating in a more public venue so that people in the community could actually see the creation. So as people got engaged in that process – they carved it out here [in front of the neighbourhood house] – there was lots of traffic. People would stop and see maybe some similarities between the work the aboriginals were doing and their culture. We had people who were Japanese saying this is very similar to how we carve and animistic belief systems got shared. It was just very powerful in that way. From the community perspective that project alone really shifted people's attitudes to see the aboriginal community as not so much a community that really needed child protection, addiction services, all kinds of social housing support but they saw the aboriginal community as just an extremely talented and thoughtful and creative people and the work that they did contributed to our community substantially both in building positive relations but also in beautifying our community with those beautiful carvings. And that's the kind of shifts around policy and activity and how we are approaching things that are much different. So not just seeing ourselves as providing service but that it has to be a whole atmosphere and environment that encourages inclusivity and contribution. So there's both a receiving and giving aspect (Interviewee G).

One current trainer with the Hastings Institute / EEO talked about the importance of creating atmospheres in training sessions which were conducive to co-learning because people were able to learn much more effectively from each other than from abstract examples:

I had another situation where there was an African-Canadian woman in the group... we were looking at issues of what does stereotyping mean and we looked at the diversity wheel and we had said what assumptions do we make about these characteristics. When we see an individual that looks like this, what do we assume about their education, their marital status, their employment opportunities. And it was amazing that we were able to come up with the same kind of immediate assumptions. So as we explored this, a woman in the room said, "you know I have this experience when I go shopping in stores where I am followed and I am stalked and people want to look in my bags. And this doesn't just happen once. It happens over and over." And her co-workers just said, "we can't imagine this. It never occurred to us." And it was much more powerful than some theoretical example that I would give or some statistic that I would give on racial profiling. So I would say that it is the stories that people in the sessions tell that have the impact on others in the room. And that's when I know there's a shift. If I can create the environment where people will share genuinely what their own experiences are. We've had a number of occasions at the City doing this kind of training where someone will say, "Oh yes I had this experience" and then others in the room will say, "Well what did you do? Didn't anyone step up to support you?" And this is great because we are talking about bystanders who don't do anything and now they are horrified that no one stood up to be on this person's side (Interviewee F).

The Workplace Language Program was also highlighted as offering an interesting approach to this kind of co-learning. This is what one trainer for that program had to say about the program:

It's not really ESL… It's really around language and around the idea that most of us when we meet each other we talk about stories. By telling stories we can make connections with people. So in the City of Vancouver there are people from all over and also people who are born here. So when they come to a class they are asked to write. It's a psycho-linguistic methodology. It's based on contextual literacy. Meaning that people write and what they write becomes the exercise. Whatever they put down on the paper that's what we look at. We look at the structure of the grammar and the mechanics, punctuation, spelling. So people are asked to write. Then they are asked to share their writing around the table. So it's quite multicultural because people come from all kinds of backgrounds and what they write is, in many cases, around their family. They write about family, children at school, about job issues and then they share that stuff around the table. It's confidential. In doing so they are exposed to other people's cultures, other people's belief systems and the way other people see the world. I personally think that it's an ideal way to learn of other people's lives and if you can learn around other people's lives I believe that you can make connections… It's pretty simple and we very seldom do it (Interviewee D).

3.4.2.10 Evolution over Time

Another important aspect of good training that many interviewees talked about was the need of training to change as the needs of communities changed and evolved. As one past Hastings Institute trainer pointed out:

I think that the evolution of the training – there's a mirroring of the inside and the outside. The communities change and evolve. The inside has to evolve and then the training has to evolve to meet the needs of how the inside has evolved and how the community has evolved. Because we are into so many more of the visibly different communities we are into second and third generations. So the experience of a second or third generation youth is totally different. We are coming on to forty years from when the act went through – the change in the immigration act. For a long time we acted as though this was something that would pass and Hastings was really about "it ain't going to pass so let's get down to it." At this point in this city nobody in their right mind has any expectation of it passing. It's a reality of everyone's' life. People sometimes still ask for the cookbook – tell us how to deal with them. But that was another thing that Hastings was about – that there is no cookbook so lets get down to what is actually going on here (Interviewee B).

This trainer had a specific example of how she had seen an evolution in a group she did training with over a number of years:

And I know from the police – these guys who are ready to retire who I worked with 10 or 15 years ago. During those years it was a really struggley time but they would have been young sergeants. And it was like, "we have to have our sense of humour, don't mess with our sense of humour"… And then a couple of years later I met a few of them for coffee and they said the weirdest damn thing happened. About three of them had gone down from the Vancouver department to the Canadian police college in Ottawa – so there are police there from all over Canada doing higher level training. And they said that about the second night there they went out to the pub for a drink and as the night went on, I guess the conversation got a little rough around the edges and they said at one point they looked at each other and they had all pulled themselves back from the circle and were sitting there looking back and forth going "holy shit these people are really saying this." And then they said to each other, "what happened to us? That was us." But at this point it was so foreign and offensive and yet that had been where their own brotherhood was. But that shift occurred to the point where people don't talk like that here (Interviewee B).

It was as a result of these kinds of shifts that interviewees felt that training needed to evolve over time.

3.4.2.11 Looking Ahead: Suggestions for Improvement

In addition to detailing the past successes and struggles of the Hastings Institute / EEO, interviewees had a number of suggestions for how the City of Vancouver could become more effective in its training and diversity initiatives in general. As training at the City changed over the years, some felt that it had lost some of its initial transformative learning focus and impact. For instance, some interviewees felt that the City's approach to diversity had to reinstate a more systemic approach. One past Hastings Institute trainer commented:

I personally think that in all organisations (and Hastings I believe has worked towards this philosophy at least initially), that it is everybody's business not just the EEO's, that it is every manager's, every front line worker's... everybody is responsible for creating an inclusive environment. And I think they still hold to that. So that has to be pushed within the organisation and people need to be held more accountable. Like performance evaluations need to be tied in – are managers measuring that as a competency? Is it a skill that people are required to have? I'm not sure how systemic it is. I think that they [Hastings's employees] do good work, they sit on a lot of committees and bring the issue up and with this council... But [do they work] systemically? (Interviewee H)

Interviewees also felt that the City, and other organisations, did not do enough to address the systemic barriers to employment faced by immigrants. One past trainer for the Hastings Institute had this to say on the subject:

I don't believe that mainstream organisations are doing enough. It's like, here I am working with regulatory organisations and it's a surprise to them that they have some responsibility to address this issue... For some of them it's like a wake up call when you tell them that they are liable because of the Charter. I mean, today, you wouldn't expect that I would be saying that about an organization. So we have a long way to go. We still are putting the responsibility on immigrants to get the skills that match Canadian standards as if these ethnocentric standards are superior. We are still stuck. And it's heartbreaking when you see the impact of that. (Interviewee H)

Many interviewees felt that the Hastings Institute / EEO had to look beyond training initiatives to other cross-cultural initiatives. A few looked back to a past initiative undertaken by the City – the Barriers to Bridges community dialogue – as the kind of thing they would like to see the City undertake once again. One past Hastings Institute trainer had this to say:

If the question is, "is the Hastings model an effective way of dealing with this?" I really don't think so. I don't think it does enough. I think what they do is fine. I just don't think it is enough… There was a very successful project a long time ago – probably 10 or 12 years ago called Barriers to Bridges. And it was a community dialogue. They had these dialogues in community centers and people met in various community centers in the city of Vancouver… And it was just getting people to talk about living in diverse communities. And one of the things that they did was to get new immigrants to talk about the immigrant experience. Sharing their stories and trying to use that to facilitate community awareness and understanding of the issues that we face. That kind of community building is very useful in these kinds of diverse communities. And also doing them in places like Dunbar where people don't think it's very diverse but then you have all these ethnic groups and cultural communities come out and you go "oh, it is diverse"… Those kind of things could be partnered in terms of Hasting is working on a part of it and EEO is working an element… And then you got other people in planning or social planning who are working on elements of it. Make it a multi-layered, multi-level City initiative (Interviewee C).

Many interviewees mentioned that they would like to see more diversity at the City as well as at the Hastings Institute / EEO itself. A current trainer for the Hastings Institute / EEO commented:

I would like to see different people involved. I would like to see for Hastings to bring in some of the people who have been through the training doing some more training. Cause sometimes what happens is that is seems like the Caucasian middle class takes over stuff and that's kind of how it is. But it doesn't have to be that way. There can be other trainers and not just based on the fact that they happen to be from one group or another but I mean there are people out there with merit and I think that being true, you also need to waive so called academic and formal learning to bring people in (Interviewee D).

Along with suggestions for how the City could expand its programming and impact, most of the interviewees felt that more funding should be designated from all three levels of government towards these kinds of initiatives. One trainer also stressed that training could not be impactful unless funding was provided to do upfront work to see what kind of training was needed:

> We gotta find some middle ground where we can actually do that upfront work to determine what kind of change practices, behaviors, will be required. It would be nice to get back to that kind of environment where resources were provided for that (Interviewee H).

3.4.3 Summary

In order to bring the myriad of comments and suggestions provided through the interviews and document analysis together, I will spend a few paragraphs outlining the central themes that emerged from this research. It is clear that the Hastings Institute emerged at a special time in terms of commitment to multiculturalism by local government and broader society. Vancouver emerged at this time as a leader in multicultural programming and training (Chapter 2), and the Hastings Institute enjoyed a high profile as a key driver of this innovation. Unlike many other municipalities, the City of Vancouver has shown a long-term commitment to diversity programming and training, despite the apparent lack of public profile of the current incarnation of the Hastings Institute / EEO.

3.4.3.1 Shifts over Time

The organisation's approach to training has shifted through the years due to external factors such as funding, changing government priorities, changes in societal support for diversity issues, and the need to advance to a focus on the development of specific skills rather than on general awareness building. Many highlighted the failed attempt at developing the Hastings Institute using a business model as a pivotal point for the organisation's role and status. Some contradictions developed in interviewees' discussions of the evolution of the organisation. For instance, while many felt that there was a need to evolve the training, others felt that some important elements of the early Kingswood training had been lost. Interviewees outlined many positive impacts that the training had on them and others, especially through the role playing and experiential learning. Most interviewees agreed that training could not be a one-off, that effective follow-up had to be incorporated, that co-learning was crucial and, finally, that self-reflection by trainers was essential.

3.4.3.2 Current Environment and Suggestions for Improvement

Overall, interviewees felt that there was a certain lack of leadership and innovation by the City compared with the past, and they had a number of recommendations for future directions the City could take to improve upon its multicultural work. For example, the City could refocus its diversity training on the more transformative approaches which were a central feature of Kingswood training; it could focus not only on training of individuals but on more systemic transformation of organisations: it could make more efforts to have its own staff reflect the true diversity of Vancouver residents. A related point was that all levels of government had much more to do in terms of reducing barriers to employment currently faced by new immigrants. Other suggestions included the need for community dialogues, such as the City's earlier Barriers to Bridges dialogues, and other community level initiatives, focused on diversity. Finally, it was widely felt that all three levels of government had to make a stronger commitment to multicultural initiatives.

3.5 Recommendations

The Hastings Institute / EEO represents an innovative step taken by a local government to begin to engage its inhabitants, and, specifically, members of the host society, as active participants in multiculturalism. As such, it provides a rich case study from which to make recommendations both to further inform Vancouver's own multicultural work as well as that of other cities with a similarly poly-ethnic citizenry. The following recommendations will look at key strategies that Vancouver could adopt to improve its work, as well as focusing more broadly on what other emerging poly-ethnic cities around the world could do to engage in effective multicultural work. The recommendations have been divided into four general sections: organisational recommendations, training recommendations, recommendations for other municipal multicultural initiatives and, finally, recommendations for senior levels of government.

3.5.1 Organisational Recommendations

3.5.1.1 Reenergise Multicultural Initiatives

One major recommendation that came out of this research was that the City of Vancouver needs to rekindle the energy, innovation, and excitement that set the tone for its early multicultural initiatives such as the Hastings Institute. While it is important to note that the societal mood around diversity and multiculturalism may not be as engaged and receptive as it once was, the City has a role to play in creating and reinvigorating this societal dialogue. Instead of relying on its tried and true approaches, the City needs to be pushing boundaries and engaging its citizenry in an active multicultural dialogue. Recently (in 2005), the City introduced the Mayor's Working Group on Immigration which is linked to the Federation for Canadian Municipalities Big Cities Mayors Caucus Immigration Working Group. This working group represents an exciting opportunity for the City to reinvigorate its multicultural initiatives through critically reflecting on its own work. It also represents an important vehicle through which the City (in partnership with the other organizations and businesses which make up the working group) can take positions and make recommendations on important issues such as barriers to employment faced by immigrants or the need for Canada as a nation to rethink its approach to multiculturalism in order to engage all citizens in mutual co-adaptation (Chapter 1).

The need to keep multicultural work fresh and engaged is an important observation for other cities or municipalities wanting to carry out similar work. Both the example of the Hastings Institute / EEO and the example of

AMKA discussed earlier benefited from the political will and energy committed to the initiatives from high-ranking officials. While the Hastings Institute did not suffer the same fate as AMKA, which ceased to exist when the party that initiated it was voted out, the Hastings Institute / EEO has still had problems maintaining the initial drive and enthusiasm behind its work. An understanding that the building of a truly multicultural city and society is a long term, multi-generational task, should be built into organisational planning for these initiatives to ensure that steps are in place to move the work forward and to keep its approaches relevant and engaging. Some more specific ideas for the kinds of approaches the City of Vancouver, and other cities wishing to undertake this kind of work, might take in order to keep their multicultural initiatives fresh will be looked at in the recommendations for training and recommendations for other municipal multicultural initiatives sections.

3.5.1.2 Diversify City Staff

Another key organisational recommendation that came out of this research was the idea that the City of Vancouver, and the Hastings Institute / EEO itself, needs to further focus on the diversification of staff. While it was acknowledged that the City had gone some way towards diversification in the last 20 years, a number of interviewees felt the City still has a ways to go in terms of modeling the kind of approach its citizens could be taking to welcoming diversity. The Equal Employment Opportunity program is valuable in its work towards ensuring that applicants for positions at, and employees of, the City of Vancouver are not discriminated against and have a vehicle through which to launch a complaint if they are. However, there is still much to be done in terms of explicit policies which aim to incorporate those with barriers to employment into the organisation, from people with physical disabilities to new immigrants whose foreign professional accreditation is not being accepted. A vital step for Vancouver, and any city government with a poly-ethnic citizenry, in creating a culture of inclusion is to have staff reflect the diversity of the inhabitants they serve.

3.5.2 Training Recommendations

3.5.2.1 Focus on Transformative and Anti-racism Approaches

The main recommendation concerning training that comes out of this research is the need to focus on transformative training approaches such as those used in the early Kingswood programs. Currently, the harassment intervention approach of Hastings Institute / EEO training focuses only on the most in-your-face aspects of discriminatory behaviour. It doesn't get into underlying societal racism nor the assumptions and biases that are part of our day-to-day lives. These sessions tend to focus on case law, legal definitions and policies which address extreme cases rather than systemic racism and discrimination. In order to address this discrimination, training needs to focus on broader historical and societal issues. It also needs to incorporate self-reflection which enables trainees to critically examine their own behaviour and understanding and to work towards cultivating what Bell Hooks has termed a "radical openness" to difference . According to interviewees, the best way to get trainees to do this is through co-learning, meaning putting people together (for example having training groups which are composed of members of the host society as well as new immigrants) to learn from each other's experience. This mutual learning approach was also one of the key strengths that Sandercock outlined in similar work undertaken by AMKA.

3.5.2.2 Follow up and Ongoing Evaluation

This research also found that training should be seen as part of an ongoing process rather than a one-off event. Follow up to training, for example, taking the next step after awareness-building to look critically at the policies of an organisation, is the most effective way to ensure that real organisational transformation occurs. The City of Vancouver, and other organisations undertaking training, should develop long-term plans for how training will be followed up in different departments and areas. Evaluation of training programs is also an important ongoing aspect of training. In order to gauge the effectiveness of their training initiatives, it is crucial to develop strategies for follow-up evaluation with participants. An important precursor to training, therefore, should be to develop clear goals and objectives of training programs and strategies for evaluating these. Data gathered from evaluations can help to inform future training initiatives. One approach is to have programs evaluated by an outside body which can more objectively gauge their effectiveness. A similar recommendation to this was made in the 1990 impact study of Kingswood training discussed above, which suggested that an external consultant be hired to collect qualitative and quantitative data 6, 12 and 18 months after completion of the training (Berman and Levitan 1990).

3.5.3 Recommendations for Other Municipal Multicultural Initiatives

3.5.3.1 Civic Re-narration Through Dialogue

Creating community dialogue around issues of diversity, immigration and multiculturalism is another recommendation that emerges from this research. Many of the interviewees talked about a past initiative carried out by the City of Vancouver, the Barriers to Bridges dialogues, as something that should be attempted once again by the City. Both formal and informal occasions for dialogue could help to engage residents in active multiculturalism. If changes in attitude and behaviour come out of lived experience, then creating public dialogue events, such as the public forums undertaken by AMKA, as well as less-formalized opportunities for groups to mix and share their stories and experiences, is an important catalyst for getting groups to communicate and collaborate across difference. Cities need to focus on opportunities for dialogue to re-narrate the idea of a city as a place where diverse cultures enrich each others lives, rather than create incompatible enclaves.

Opportunities for members of the host society to renegotiate their own cultural narratives in order to see their shifting role in a poly-ethnic society is an important part of this. As one interviewee commented, community cultural development is one powerful means by which this can be accomplished. In addition, as community based non-profits such as Neighbourhood Houses are often the loci of such community-based multicultural initiatives, it is vital for cities to work actively with the non-profit sector to create opportunities for dialogue, to support transformative programming, to train their employees and to provide long-term support to successful cross-cultural projects at the neighbourhood level. Ultimately, this would strengthen the city's initiatives through dispersing them more effectively throughout the city in order to carry out what Sandercock terms "the micro-sociological work that needs to be done street by street, neighbourhood by neighbourhood and across a range of institutions" (Sandercock 2003: 139, and Chapters 7 and 8 in this book).

3.5.4 Recommendations for Senior Levels of Government

3.5.4.1 Provide Ongoing Direction and Funding for Cross-Cultural Policies and Programs

In order to create a climate of acceptance for multicultural policy innovations as well as to have the resources to make them happen, it is vital that there is a multi-tiered approach in which all levels of government play a role. Senior levels of government must offer cities, which are the loci of immigration, both direction and the long-term funding needed to create effective programs. This finding is consistent with the analysis of AMKA's work in Frankfurt. In the absence of multi-party support as well as funding from the national state, that city's multicultural initiative ceased to exist. In the case of the Hastings Institute, the attempt to turn from government funding to private funding to carry out their cross-cultural training work was less than successful and led to the downsizing of the organisation's role and status in the city.

Governments, therefore, need to look at strategies for the creation of long term engagement in cross-cultural dialogue between members of the host society and immigrant populations. Senior levels of government, particularly federal governments, are usually the drivers behind immigration policy and the creation of opportunities for new immigrants to come to Canada and other polyethnic nations. As part of their responsibility for implementing this strategy, senior levels of government need to focus energy and resources on effectively co-integrating new immigrants and current residents. In order to accomplish this, they need to explicitly support programming in cities which attract the most immigration. This would be a vital step towards creating an environment conducive to immigration.

3.6 Concluding Thoughts: Canada and Beyond

Arguably, it is new immigrants to Canada, experiencing systemic barriers to employment and overall acceptance in Canadian society, who have the most to lose in the current climate where the onus is on immigrants alone to adapt to their new home. They are faced with the expectation that they should integrate into a society that hasn't yet come to terms with their existence and participation within that society.

However, Canada's host society loses out as well in this environment. Firstly, a national schism exists. There is a tension between who we think we are as Canadians, as reflected in our core story of being a welcoming, tolerant nation, and evidence that points to this being far from the truth. Without ever having been exposed to the idea that multiculturalism is about two-way co-adaptation, it is easy for the host culture to blame any friction on newcomers. This can become a self-fulfilling prophecy: if certain people are seen as a challenge to the existing order, then they likely will be.

This schism applies equally to nations throughout the world whose ideas of themselves as tolerant and welcoming are currently being challenged by new waves of immigration. These are becoming urgent issues. The social policies of increasingly poly-ethnic nations need to operate in tandem with their immigration policies. Approaches such as those developed by the Hastings Institute / EEO, that have had some successes in helping the host society to co-adapt, can be built upon. There is a lot of work to be done to change fear to curiosity, to see difference as a strength rather than a weakness, and to see the hybridities that emerge from cultures mixing as the foundation for new, exciting, truly cosmopolitan societies.

These ideas will be further developed in the five chapters of Part II, where they are exemplified in the approach of one local institution in one neighbourhood in the City of Vancouver, which is also the subject of the accompanying DVD. This study of the Hastings Institute did not undertake the kind of quantitative research that would enable us to make definitive statements about the impact, over time, of the Institute's work across the institutional landscape of Vancouver's multicultural policy sector. But, interestingly for the case study that follows in Part II, of the Collingwood Neighbourhood House, there is a very clear connection. Both the Executive Director of CNH, Paula Carr, and the first President of the Board, Terry Tayler, had undergone training at the Hastings Institute, and CNH has regularly used trainers from Hastings to run anti-racism and diversity training sessions for staff and volunteers. And the transformative learning approach permeates everything that CNH does, as we shall see in the chapters that follow.

References

Amin A (2003) Unruly strangers? The 2001 Riots in Britain. In: International Journal of Urban and Regional Research 27(2), p. 460

Beauregard RA (2003) Voices of decline: The postwar fate of U.S. cities. Routledge, New York

Bellah RN (1986) Habits of the heart: Individualism and commitment in American life. Harper & Row, New York

Berman S, Levitan A (1990) Impact study of the Kingswood management training program: Equity principles in personal and organizational change. Unpublished

Borrup T (2003) Toward Asset-Based Community Cultural Development: A Journey through the Disparate Worlds of Community Building. Community Arts Network. http://creativecommunities.org.uk/pdf/1.2BorrupTowardABCCD.pdf

City of North Vancouver (2000) Multicultural policies and practices in selected BC municipalities: Eight case studies. Prepared by Parul R. Penner. Available through the Hastings Institute / EEO Archives

City of Vancouver (1995) Proposed 1995 operating structure of the Hastings Institute. Available through the Hastings Institute / EEO Archives

City of Vancouver (2005) Harassment intervention skills day 2. Prepared by the Hastings Institute. Available through the Hastings Institute / EEO Archives

City of Vancouver (2006) City of Vancouver Mission. http://vancouver.ca/cityclerk/mission.htm

DeRosa P (1996) Diversity training: In search of anti-racism. The system for adult basic education support. SABES, Boston

Dei SGJ (1996) Anti-racism education: Theory and practice. Fernwood Pub, Halifax

Eckstein BJ, Throgmorton JA (2003) Story and sustainability: Planning, practice, and possibility for American cities. MIT Press, Cambridge, Mass

Edgington D, Hutton T (2002) Multiculturalism and local government in greater Vancouver. RIIM Working Paper Series n° 02–06

Fleras A, Elliott JHL (1999) Multiculturalism in Canada: The challenge of diversity. Nelson Canada, Scarborough, Ont

Friedmann J, Lehrer U (1997) Urban policy responses to foreign in-Migration: The case of Frankfurt-am-Main, Germany. In: Journal of the American Planning Association 63(1), pp. 61–78

Friedmann J (2002) The prospect of cities. University of Minnesota Press, Minneapolis

Hooks B (2003) Teaching community: A pedagogy of hope. Routledge, New York

Kymlicka W (1998) Finding our way: Rethinking ethnocultural relations in Canada. Oxford University Press, Toronto

LeBaron M (2002) Bridging troubled waters: Conflict resolution from the heart. Jossey-Bass, San Francisco, Calif

Mackinnon A, Saucier K, Woodland T (1992) BCIT directed studies project. Interviews collected for the equal employment opportunity program.

Mayo P (1999) Gramsci, Freire, and adult education: Possibilities for transformative action. Zed Books, New York

Mehta B, Favreau J (2000) Educating against racism: an annotated bibliographic tool of anti-racist resources for activists and educators. http://www.crr.ca/Load.do?section=26&subSection=38&id=475&type=2 (accessed August 7, 2006)

Miller JP (2002) Learning from a spiritual perspective. In: O'Sullivan E, Morrell A, O'Connor MA (eds) Expanding the boundaries of transformative learning: Essays on theory and praxis. Palgrave, New York, N.Y.

Morrell A, O'Connor MA (2002) Introduction. In: O'Sullivan E, Morrell A, O'Connor MA (eds) Expanding the boundaries of transformative learning: Essays on theory and praxis. Palgrave, New York, N.Y.

O'Sullivan E (2002) The project and vision of transformative education: integral transformative learning. In: O'Sullivan E, Morrell A, O'Connor MA (eds) Expanding the boundaries of transformative learning: Essays on theory and praxis. Palgrave, New York, N.Y.

Palmer R (2002) Cultural Planning 101. http://www.creativecity.ca/members/conference/2002/CCN-2002-Cultural-Planning-101.pdf (accessed August 7, 2006).

Pestieau K, Wallace M (2003) Challenges and opportunities for planning in the ethno-culturally diverse city: A collection of papers – introduction. Planning Theory & Practice 4(3), pp. 253–258.

Saguaro Seminar On Civic Engagement in America (2001) The arts and social capital. http://www.bettertogether.org/pdfs/Arts.pdf (accessed August 7, 2006).

Sandercock L (1998) Towards cosmopolis: Planning for multicultural cities. John Wiley & Sons Ltd, Toronto

Sandercock L (2003) Cosmopolis 2: Mongrel cities of the 21st century, century. continuum, New York

Soja E (2000) Postmetropolis: Critical studies of cities and regions. Basil Blackwell, Oxford

Tisdell EJ (2003) Exploring spirituality and culture in adult and higher education. Jossey-Bass, San Francisco

Waters JL, Teo SY (2003) Social and cultural impacts of immigration: An examination of the concept of 'social cohesion' with implications for British Columbia. http://www.riim.metropolis.net/Virtual%20Library/2003/wp03-03.pdf (accessed August 7, 2006).

Part II
The Neighbourhood House: Concept and Reality

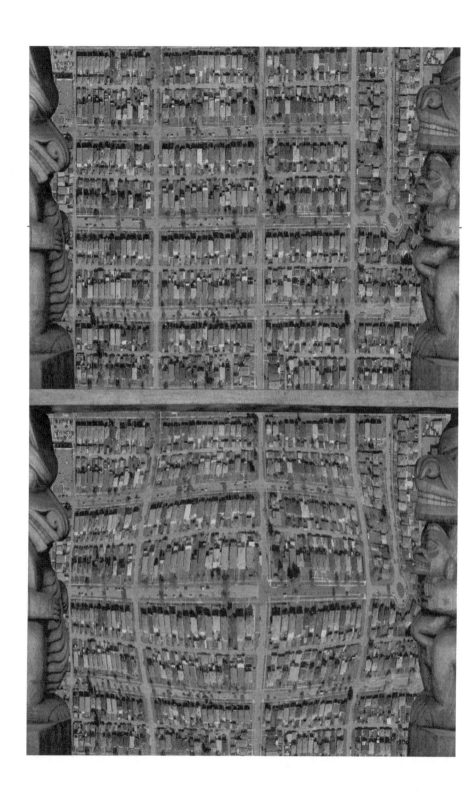

Chapter 4
What Is a Neighbourhood House?

Leonie Sandercock

Our hope of social achievement …
lies in a complete mobilisation of the human spirit,
using all our unrealised and unevoked capacity
(Jane Addams *The Second Twenty Years at Hull House*)

Today's Neighbourhood Houses are the descendants of 19th century Settlement Houses. The Settlement House concept was developed in mid-19th-century England by Samuel Barnett and his wife Henrietta Rowland. Barnett was a Church of England curate and after his marriage to Henrietta, they were sent off to what was described as the worst parish in London. St. Jude's in east London became the birthplace of the settlement movement. From 1874 to 1881 the Barnetts oversaw the development of adult education, parks and playgrounds, arts and especially music performances. They started a book lending library, oratory clubs, public lectures, and social housing.

Samuel Barnett later met Arnold Toynbee at Oxford University. Toynbee was an economic historian who had studied the effects of the Industrial Revolution and who understood the moral, cultural and economic effects of the great urban changes that were taking place in London. Toynbee spoke to his students about the gifts of the poor and how they had been undervalued in society by the wealthy classes. Following Arnold Toynbee's death, the Barnetts opened Toynbee Hall in tribute to him. Toynbee Hall was a commons in the middle of a poor east London neighbourhood. It became a place where university men lived among workingmen and learned about their plight through discussion; in return they would provide teaching, research and public service. The chief beneficiaries of this education were to be the wealthy students who would pay for the privilege of living among the working classes. Toynbee Hall caught on as a model and other settlement houses were established offering adult education, organising job clubs, offering youth and adult recreation, sports, art and music programmes, public health services, and advocating for improved living and working conditions for the poor and working classes (Cavers et al. 2007).

L. Sandercock, G. Attili, *Where Strangers Become Neighbours*, Urban and
Landscape Perspectives 4, DOI 10.1007/978-1-4020-9035-6_4
© Springer Science+Business Media 2009

When the idea crossed over to the New World, settlement houses served similar functions but with one major difference; immigration was a much larger concern and the inclusion, indeed assimilation, of newcomers became the guiding principle for most settlement houses. The spread of settlement houses in North America began in 1889 with Jane Addams' establishing Hull House on the south side of Chicago, and quickly spread to New York and throughout the eastern United States and Canada. Neighbourhood Houses, as some came to be known, also offered English language classes and schooling for immigrant children.

The first neighbourhood house established in Vancouver was Alexandra House, which began as an orphanage in 1894 and later became British Columbia's first Neighbourhood House (now known as Frog Hollow NH). Today there are nine Neighbourhood Houses in the City of Vancouver; seven of them are members of the Association of Neighbourhood Houses, an umbrella organization, the other two, including Collingwood, which is the subject of the next four chapters, are independent of the Association. Although only a few of them receive settlement program funding from the government, all of them, in one way or another, provide services and programs that directly or indirectly help newcomers settle into and integrate with the local community.

Modern Neighbourhood Houses share some of the original philosophy of Toynbee Hall, especially in recognising and nurturing the gifts of all classes and races, although not the paternalism that was typical of 19th century English reformers. One of the keys to the success of the idea is that Neighbourhood Houses are working to forge a new society through learning and sharing cultures and predicaments. They are not simply trying to make others fit into what may be already established. They see change as an opportunity. In a de facto way, Neighbourhood Houses serve as the neighbourhood reception centres for immigrants. Although most NHs receive no funding for newcomer settlement services, their programs and their staff provide the first contact and first line of resources for newcomers needing to access and navigate the complex formal social service system. Federal government settlement service funding is administered through the Provincial governments in Canada, and only a few Neighbourhood Houses receive any of that funding. Other than federal funding, there are very few financial resources available to support newcomers' settlement services, particularly for those immigrants who have been in Canada for more than three years (which officially marks the end of the "settlement" period) and have become citizens.

Although each Neighbourhood House is different, most provide multiple services in response to local needs, covering a wide range of target groups: preschool childcare, after-school programs for children and youth, seniors' social clubs, social and educational groups for parents, community kitchens and gardens, employment counselling programs, volunteer opportunities and so on. They also provide a variety of intergenerational programs, particularly festivals and cultural celebrations. These programs and events provide opportunities for families not only to have fun and relax and get to know their neighbourhood, but also as a means for people from different cultural and racial backgrounds to meet each other and connect by sharing in activities together.

The flexible and multi-service nature of Neighbourhood Houses is a reflection of their mission, which most describe in terms of building and strengthening community by addressing community needs through a highly accessible and inclusive service approach (Yan and Lauer 2006: 13). The most striking thing about Neighbourhood Houses, distinguishing them from both community centres and settlement service organisations, is their focus on building community. And since newcomers are a significant percentage of most neighbourhoods in cities like Vancouver (see Chapter 2), immigrant issues are likely to be the most significant community issues, requiring the attention and support of the whole community.

Neighbourhood Houses are directed by voluntary Boards of Directors, recruited from residents of the neighbourhood. Many are former users of the services of the Neighbourhood House. The Boards are responsible for the setting of policies and deciding the organisation's service direction. Volunteers are the backbone of most Neighbourhood Houses, supporting and usually far outnumbering the paid staff. The volunteers help to organise events, staff programs and services, provide translation assistance, work on committees, and above all, help with the task of making newcomers feel comfortable and welcome.

Historically, federal government funding for settlement services in British Columbia has been allocated, through the Provincial government, to organisations that have a specific mandate to assist newcomers to adjust and settle in the first few years after arrival. But the needs of newcomers are numerous, and there are many advantages in Neighbourhood Houses addressing these needs. For one thing, they are local, and people can get to them easily, often by walking. They are also flexible, designed to respond to local needs. And they are a multi-service facility, offering something for all generations and cultures. While Neighbourhood Houses are therefore playing a vital de facto role in not only the settlement but perhaps more importantly the ongoing integration of newcomers into local communities, their visibility in public discourse is quite low.

Neighbourhood Houses face two main challenges. One is raising public awareness of the vital role they perform, in order to attract more funding for what they do, thus reducing the amount of time spent by staff in writing grant applications, and enabling them to spend more time providing the actual services and programs. The second challenge is raising the awareness of newcomers about the existence of these Houses. Some newcomers come from countries without this kind of social institution, or from cultures that do not encourage seeking public help in resolving personal (family) problems. Other newcomers simply do not hear about the existence of Neighbourhood Houses and what they have to offer. We hope, through our film, to raise this awareness.

To go from being a total stranger, to a service recipient, to being a full member of a neighbourhood, able to contribute to the lives of fellow residents, is a major life transition for newcomers. Helping significantly with that transition is the extraordinary achievement of Neighbourhood Houses.

References

Cavers V et al. (2007) How Strangers Become Neighbours: Constructing Citizenship through Neighbourhood Community Development. Vancouver Center of Excellence for Research on Immigration and Integration in the Metropolis, UBC, Vancouver

Yan MC and S Lauer (2006) Bridging Newcomers in the Neighbourhood Scale: A Study on Settlement/Integration Roles and Functions of Neighbourhood Houses in Vancouver. Vancouver Center of Excellence for Research on immigration and integration in the Metropolis, UBC, Vancouver

Chapter 5
The Story of the Collingwood Neighbourhood House: A Unique Gathering Place

Leonie Sandercock and Val Cavers

5.1 Birth

In the early 1980s, Vancouver was preparing to host the 1986 World's Fair, Expo '86. One of the promised "legacies" of the event was a state-of-the-art public transit system, the first of its kind in Vancouver. The proposed Skytrain would travel along a historic transportation route once used by the famed Interurban Railway that brought people from New Westminster into the heart of Vancouver. In its day, the Interurban travelled directly through the centre of Collingwood, a working class neighbourhood and high immigrant settlement area at the eastern boundary of the City of Vancouver. Today, thirty feet above the derelict tracks, the Skytrain runs through and has several stops in the Collingwood neighbourhood.

L. Sandercock, G. Attili, *Where Strangers Become Neighbours*, Urban and Landscape Perspectives 4, DOI 10.1007/978-1-4020-9035-6_5
© Springer Science+Business Media 2009

The building of the Skytrain presented problems and opportunities to the residential areas that it traversed. In Collingwood, it galvanized the residents and sparked a movement towards local social change. The dream of the Collingwood Neighbourhood House (CNH) evolved through a lengthy series of meetings between planners from the City of Vancouver and local residents, as well as a "more objective" study of local needs by the planners. The most obvious needs that surfaced were for services for families and children. But what also became clear through these discussions was the need for a gathering place, somewhere for people to come and get together and meet others and develop what was clearly missing: some sense of community. The opening of CNH in 1985 was the first bold step towards real community development. Starting in a rented storefront with a skeletal budget of $30,000, the House quickly established programs for children and adults and developed services that previously did not exist in this area. But the notion of a "gathering place" was equally significant in the birth of this local institution. Gathering places and good public spaces are all too rare in modern urban neighbourhoods and cities, places that allow you to meet your neighbours, share ideas, and collaborate on projects. Places where people can come together. Vancouver, like many other New World cities of Anglo-Saxon and Anglo Celtic origins, was not designed around public squares or gardens.

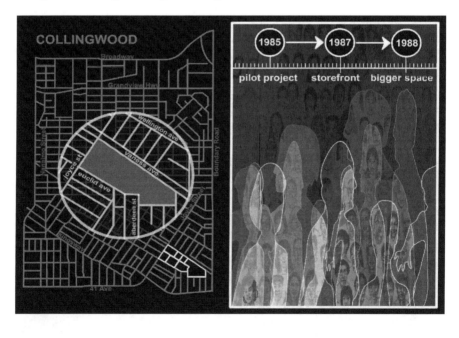

So, unlike many other cultures in which people traditionally have gathered in public squares or boulevards or gardens or around temples, that arena for public life has been missing. While shopping malls may seem to be the new public space, they are not open to everyone, they're not a connecting force. Their purpose is to lure visitors into spending money. Neighbourhood Houses fill this void. They welcome everyone equally, they are non-judgemental, they are non-commercial, they are democratic. And most importantly, they invite people to get involved. They help those in need to define and achieve their goals. They are a hub of information and resources. They foster leadership. They provide a framework, a focus, and resources for neighbourhood residents with aspirations to improve their community. They build relationships. They bring people together through their children, as well as through a set of shared values that emerge as people come together.

When people from many different cultures find themselves living in the same neighbourhood, they need a neutral place to meet, a place where they can participate as equals and relate to one another on a common topic or interest, not even necessarily in the same language. People come to CNH to play badminton, for example, and they may only have badminton in common, initially. But that leads to an interaction that would not have happened otherwise. Gardening is the same. People who were interested in helping start a community garden came together through a love of gardening. The Neighbourhood House, as a place, is the perfect catalyst for these types of interactions, which then create the opportunity for other connections. And in the Collingwood neighbourhood, where 73% of residents speak English as their second language, intercultural interaction has become the norm.

Classes in English as a second language, and childcare programs are the obvious places where this interaction begins. But the Neighbourhood House provides so many more possibilities for people to engage on multiple levels. Neighbourhood Houses are different from community centres in Vancouver. The latter are run by the municipality. The Neighbourhood House, on the other hand, is a grass roots organization, run by and for residents and funded by a wide variety of sources. While community centres tend to focus on provision of recreation, the mandate of the Neighbourhood House is community development. The resident Board that directs the CNH establishes the guiding values and desires for improvement and sets the goals. They can take risks and react quickly to local needs. CNH has never been about protecting the status quo.

As a rapidly changing community, demographically and socio-culturally, its mission has always been to create a welcoming place for everyone, newcomers as well as oldtimers, the comfortable and the poor, seniors and children. They have attempted to establish a set of common values, human values, that look beyond culture and religion and all the other differences that tend to divide people. This chapter focuses on those core values, the soul of the place, and illustrates these through some human stories. But first, some vital statistics of growth and development.

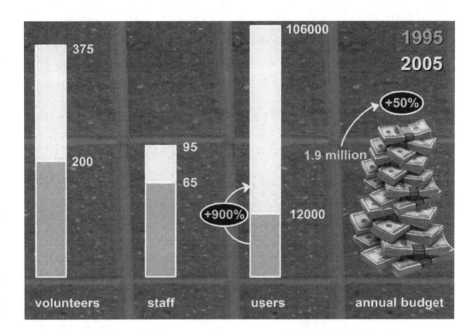

5.2 Vital Statistics

In recent years the catchment area of CNH has expanded to include the neighbouring community of Renfrew. The combined areas have a population of 45,000, only 27% of whom speak English as a first language. Of the 40 or more different countries of origin of residents, the biggest of the newcomer groups are Chinese (50%) and Punjabi (10%), with smaller percentages of Vietnamese, Korean, Philippino, Chilean, as well as African and Middle Eastern groups. There are older immigrant groups such as Italian and Portugese and German, and a mere 20% (compared with more than 50% twenty years ago) of the first settler stock of Anglo-Celtic and Anglo-Saxon residents. There are also almost one thousand Aboriginal residents who are Canada's very first settlers, or First Nations people as they prefer to be called.

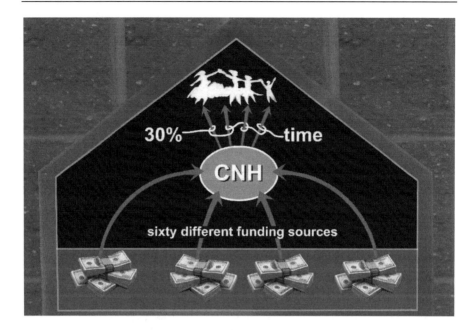

The operating budget has grown from $30,000 in 1985, to $3.5 million in 2006. This money comes from more than 60 different funding sources, the most important of which are the City of Vancouver, the Government of Canada, and the Province of British Columbia. Combined, these three government sources represent 36 individual program streams. At least twenty other funders provide annual grants of between $500 and $55.000, and there is an important revenue stream that comes from fees charged for programs and services, including daycare and recreation programs.There are 100 people on the payroll, representing 39 full-time positions, 32 part-time, 48 casuals and two temporary positions. The current staff represents 30 different cultural and language groups, and CNH maintains a local hiring practice that favours residents of Collingwood when all other factors are equal. CNH is a unionised workplace and there has been a collective agreement with the Canadian Union of Public Employees since 1999. An astonishing 300–400 people volunteer each year at the Neighbourhood House, doing jobs that include being Directors on the governing Board, committee members, child minders, translators, kitchen helpers and cooks, teaching English, office assistance, recreation aids, and information and referral workers. The Volunteer Coordinator interviews all potential volunteers, and together they choose the most suitable tasks. Some volunteers work in special arrangements under certain conditions and are mentored by staff. This includes members of the homeless program and "at risk" youth, whom staff determine as being ready to participate as volunteers. CNH is governed by a Board of 14 residents. In addition, the Executive Director and a representative from the Collingwood Community Policing Centre also attend Board meetings. The current Board of Directors is drawn from seven different cultural and language groups, and at least one position is reserved for a youth member. The selection of Board members is very deliberate in its diversity, following a template developed in the 1980s. The Board leaves the day-to-day management of CNH to the staff and Executive Director and focuses its energies on emerging issues and broader community and regional responses and advocacy. In 2006 a staggering 165,000 people used CNH. Since its programs and facilities are only available to residents of the neighbourhood, what this means statistically is that every member of the neighbourhood is using the NH at least three times a year. What it actually means, according to CNH's own research, is that their programs and services are reaching approximately 75–80% of local residents. In addition to the roughly one hundred programs offered each year, there are short term workshops, clinics, and classes, as well as a number of single day celebrations and parades and festivals and the week-long Multiweek celebration of the many diverse cultures living in Collingwood. Programs cover children (from birth to 12 years), Youth (10–18 years), Seniors (55+), and Adults, Family and Community Programs.

Community development initiatives are wide ranging, including: Aboriginal Canoe Club, Amlat'si Family Place, Families Branching Out, Renfrew Collingwood News, Slocan Park Art and Development, Inventories of Cultural Skills, Public Art and Heritage Sites, Visual Artist Gatherings, Presentations and Art Shows, Renfrew Collingwood Leadership Institute, Renfrew Ravine Annual Clean up, Collingwood Days, Homelessness Committee, Renfrew Collingwood Drug and Alcohol Committee, Neighbourhood Small Grants Project, Norquay Business Development, Renfrew Collingwood Food Security Institute, Renfrew Collingwood Youth Project, Safe Community Initiatives with the Collingwood Community Policing Centre, Skytrain Community Improvements, and Windows of Opportunity – focusing on early childhood development.

While these vital statistics indicate a thriving organization, they do not convey the essence of CNH, the soul of the place, which starts with its core values.

THE COLLINGWOOD NEWS

VOL.1   NO.1   FEBRUARY 2000

Collingwood
Neighbourhood House

5.3 The Soul of Collingwood Neighbourhood House

CNH is a values-based organization. The particular constellation of values that now define this local institution has evolved over time, a result of countless conversations between Board members and residents.

While the central mission, informed by a sense of social justice, has always been to create a place for everyone, the twin values that underpin this are family and community. Ways of embodying these values include relationship building, reciprocity, leadership and capacity building, creativity, and anti-racism education.

These values are also manifested through fostering civic engagement, collaboration and cooperation with other agencies, advocacy work and, last but by no means least, through celebrations.

There are many stories that illustrate these values in motion, embodied in individuals whose lives have been changed by and through their involvement with CNH. But the values are also embedded in the building itself. The 25,000 square foot current home of CNH on Joyce Street was built in 1994 after the organization had rapidly outgrown its earlier premises.

More than a thousand people were involved in the consultation process around the design and construction of the building. From staff to users of the House, people were encouraged to view the drafts, comment, and bring their personal experience to the design. People with first hand experience in childcare and special needs were consulted to ensure safety and accessibility. Details, down to the color scheme and textures, were decided by the people who would be seeing them in their day-to-day lives. Local artists painted a colorful mural in the entrance hallway, depicting the many faces of the neighbourhood. The large reception area is designed to be welcoming and is the first place that newcomers can find assistance and referral information. The height of the reception desk is designed for the accessibility of children and people in wheel chairs.

People arriving at CNH pass through a totem gateway outside the front entrance that was carved by a local Aboriginal artist, Gary Sheena, and his two youth apprentices. The gateway shows a mother bear on one side holding a cub, symbolizing family, and on the other side a wolf, symbolizing community. Across the top of this unusual totem structure (which purposely departs from the typical vertical totem pole form) is a line of creatures representing all of the various cultures who now call Collingwood home. The carvers deliberately chose to create a gateway with the world's creatures on the same plane, rather than competing for the top of a vertical totem pole. The two symbols dominating the totem gateway reflect the twin core values of family and community. Many immigrants who arrive in the neighbourhood have lost their family in the process of leaving or fleeing their homeland. Through CNH, they find a larger family that welcomes them. Many of the people who work there now, but who first came to CNH as users of its programs, talk about the House as a "blessed" or even "sacred" place. It is certainly more than just a physical space. Comfort Adesuwa Ero came to Canada from Nigeria. She is a playwright, stage director, and magnificent storyteller. Comfort organizes an African Storytelling Festival at CNH called Hut Tales, which combines storytelling and drama with a unique African mix of drumming and dancing.

The event reminds Comfort of her home in rural Nigeria, where storytellers would gather the villagers together in the commons and perform their stories and the audience would participate by calling back responses. Through these rituals people interact with each other, learn through old stories, and create new ones. Comfort had grown up surrounded by stories, in a place that valued them. When she moved to Collingwood she searched for that commons where she and others could

tell stories, and she found it in CNH. She has now performed for thousands of children during Multiweek (an annual, week-long celebration of multiculturalism). She has performed in classrooms, on a church stage, in a teepee. The space is not as important as the coming together of people to share stories.

The development and design of the CNH premises is one example of how to increase community interaction. Resident involvement ensured that the place is relevant to the community, reflecting both current and future needs, building on existing assets (like local artists), creating ownership of and care for the building and all that it embodies. Subsequent CNH projects, such as the reclaiming of Slocan Park and Renfrew Ravine (Chapter 6), the Renfrew Library, and various community garden sites, have built on this initial experience of community-based design.

The values embodied in CNH practices have been and remain its core strength.

5.4 Family

Terry Tayler, a founding member and first President of the Board, searched for people within her neighbourhood that shared her valuing of family and who would help to form the Neighbourhood House in 1985 to ensure that there would be local services for her small children. Over the years, service development for families included childcare, family places, youth leadership, parenting classes, community events, advocacy for family housing and child- and youth-friendly planning. Terry now takes her grandchildren to activities at CNH and is mentoring her daughter in civic engagement.

Newcomers to Canada also consider family among the most important values. Generations of newcomers will tell you that they came to Canada for a better future for their children, and they will rank access to appropriate programs for their children and good schools among their top personal values. The Neighbourhood House exemplifies family values in all that it does, including the treatment of staff. CNH is an extremely family oriented employer, allowing staff to put the needs of their families first, being flexible in terms of schedules, and providing unconditional support. The Neighbourhood House is supportive of staff who have family members in various parts of the world and tries to understand what their special needs may be.

Canadian-born parents have found CNH to be a place where they can work to provide their children with a sense of cultural community. Emmanuela Sheena, for example, is married to Native carver Gerry Sheena, and although she herself is not Native, she feels a deep responsibility for her children to be connected to their father's Interior Salish culture. Emmanuela first got involved with CNH through the Slocan Park revitalization project and then found a niche for herself at the Neighbourhood House. Gerry was initially commissioned to carve a totem pole for the Synala Housing Co-operative. He then got involved in three other carving projects, one of them in Slocan Park. Emmanuela has brought her own talents in First Nations' crafts, her knowledge of the community and her amazing organizational skills to the Neighbourhood House. She now co-ordinates the Canoe Club that mentors Native youth in traditional cultural practices. Emmanuela and Gerry's children are learning about their traditional culture right in their own community, while educating the non-Native community and sharing with them the extraordinary arts, crafts, and practices of their culture.

5.5 Community

Building a sense of community where none previously existed has been the other core task of CNH. Central to that task is an emphasis on inclusivity and on intercultural connection rather than on offering programs to ethno-specific groups. From its very beginning, CNH has emphasized an intercultural mission, of working to bridge the differences that divide people, whether of culture, religion, age, ability, or any other difference.

One excellent example of intercultural programming is found in one of CNH's oldest running programs. Family Place is a casual meeting place for small children and their caregivers. Participants must register for all but two of the sessions (these two are drop-in). The registration process ensures that the children, and the adult who accompanies them, build a strong connection to a group. Children from the Family Place program are prepared for other preschool or day care programs and eventually for school. For the adults, this may be the only way that they have of connecting with other parents, sharing experiences and finding out about other resources from each other, the group leader, and from special guests that regularly visit the program.

it's a blessed place

The children are also exposed to English, which is the only time during the week that this happens for many of them. They learn songs and stories in English that benefit them in later learning. From Family Place, adults have gone on to join such things as parenting programs, the Leadership Institute, recreation programs, and volunteering. Every session is supported by several volunteers, often newcomers, many of whom would like to enter the early childhood education field. Approximately 25 volunteers have gone on to become teachers, and children who came to Family Place have returned as youth and adults to volunteer. Many newcomer families are linked up to the Family Place through involvement in an English as an Additional Language class.

Over the years, Satinder Singh, the first and current Co-ordinator of this program, has provided a model for other women arriving from all over the world and wanting to participate in a meaningful way in Canadian society. Satinder arrived in Canada in the early 1990s from India. She had no formal training as an early childhood educator, but she had small children of her own, and she recognized her natural and magical connection with preschoolers. Eighteen years later, Satinder now has her Early Childhood Education Certificate, and she is able to counsel women who are interested in following that path. The Family Place program thrives in part due to Satinder's magic and in part due to the fact that it is inclusive and intercultural. People are brought together rather than kept apart from one another, and in the process they learn that, for all that is different, what they do have in common is parenting.

Another interesting example of the way in which CNH values all types of diversity is seen in its intergenerational programming. A recent initiative is bringing youth leaders together with seniors in the community. Team 16 is a project of the Drug and Alcohol Committee in which youths work on projects throughout the year with elementary school kids, focussing on topics like drug and alcohol abuse prevention, anti-bullying and anti-racism. The youths hold a huge prevention fair every year, attracting more than 600 participants from local schools. When asked who they like to talk to in their families, they told the committee they felt most comfortable with their grandparents. This led to the idea of pairing seniors with the Team 16 youth. Seniors, who often express fear of young people, also needed to bridge that gap. During a water crisis that hit Vancouver, Team 16 members were able to carry bottled water to help isolated seniors, and shovel their walkways after a snow-storm.

The most basic aspect of building community involves relationship building: one person reaching out to another, as well as one organization reaching out to another in a spirit of collaboration and cooperation. CNH regards it as critical that staff have the time and flexibility to devote to this very valued work. Nancy Sweedler is the Co-ordinator of the Families Branching Out program. While she does run several regular programs, her job is to build leadership within those programs so that the participants will run them on their own. Nancy is very adept at this, helping them to recognize and further develop their strengths, passions and ideas. She can spend a lot of her time working individually with people, building strong and trusting relationships with some of the most marginalized members of the community.

One example of how newcomers are quickly drawn into services and connected to the community comes from Satinder Singh, the Family Life Education Co-ordinator. Recently, Satinder was called to the reception area to speak in Hindi to two newcomer families. The families had just moved to Canada and to Collingwood, and someone had suggested that they come to the Neighbourhood House for help in answering the many questions that they had. Satinder was able to immediately assess the families' needs and to provide referral information for them. She also took the opportunity to sign them up for Family Place, and to connect them with the Hindi speaking nurse at the neighbouring health unit. One of the mums was pregnant and the nurse works in the Healthiest Babies Possible program, a program that Satinder had been associated with for many years. Both women later attended Family Place, and it was there that the other mums took over from Satinder. They also quickly assessed the needs of the two women, and took it upon themselves to help with information, support, and friendship. As Satinder has pointed out on many occasions, Family Place is a neutral ground, where people come as parents; they may be from India and mix with people from Pakistan, but those political issues are swept aside to deal with issues affecting people in a similar predicament.

Many people come to the Neighbourhood House for very basic needs, and end up forming life-altering relationships that even replace tattered or distant family relationships. Noel Allan-Hughes is one such person. Noel came to the Neighbourhood House when past events in his personal story were bleak, and had left him penniless, distraught, and lonely. His own family had turned on him, and robbed him of his grandparents' inheritance. He was left with very little strength, and even less self-esteem. He happened upon the Collingwood Neighbourhood House one day, and his luck began to change. Being a helpful and caring soul, Noel immediately saw an opportunity for himself to help out in the Seniors' lunch program.

He washed dishes in exchange for a cup of coffee. From that first encounter with the Neighbourhood House, Noel soon became indispensable in several programs. His warm character and sense of humour endeared him to staff and participants alike. The small meals that he took home improved his health, and regular outings to the Neighbourhood House improved his sense of himself. Nancy Sweedler, the Families Branching Out Co-ordinator, developed a relationship with Noel and helped him to find a niche at CNH. He worked in most of the kitchen programs, including the Monday night family dinner, where he eventually met his soul mate, Sandra. Noel and Sandra are now married and raising two children in the Neighbourhood House community.

Three years on, Noel still helps out in the kitchen, but he is also sharing his computer skills by volunteering to run the computer lab as well as a computer class for youth. CNH has become Noel's adoptive home and family, with the love, guidance, and support his life had been lacking. The appreciation and encouragement Noel received provided the motivation and the energy he desperately needed to involve himself in the community.

5.6 Reciprocity

An important extension of the relationship building work involves the valuing of and emphasis on reciprocity. This ensures that people are treated not just as having needs, but also as possessing the capacity to help themselves. But this model only works if people and organizations see their role as both meeting needs and giving back, thereby establishing a system of reciprocity.

Many of the stories that are told in the film show the level of reciprocity that exists at CNH. One untold story stands out as an example of someone who is reaching for his full potential with some help from the Neighbourhood House and, in return, has contributed a great deal back to the community. Jude Chun wanted desperately to find a place for himself at CNH.

He felt comfortable there because it was one of the few places where he felt that he could fit in, where he was not perceived as different in a negative way. In fact, CNH actively welcomed Jude. His uniqueness was appreciated and people took the time to talk to him, to laugh with him and to coach him into finding a place to share his skills. Michael McLenaghen, Director of Community Services at Collingwood, recognized Jude's uniqueness and together they found a fit. Jude became the indispensable aid in the Parents and Tots gym program, tirelessly hauling out the equipment twice a week, setting it up and putting it away again.

Jude was doing that job for three years when he expressed an interest in working in the Homeless Breakfast program. He is now a regular volunteer, helping in the kitchen, serving food and connecting with participants. In many ways, Collingwood has been the beneficiary of Jude's dedication, and Jude himself has grown and developed social skills that had previously been a challenge for him. These are people who bring all that they have to contribute and share it willingly, and, as in any volunteer organization, these are the people that make the difference. CNH values the right and responsibility of individuals to civic engagement and is hugely indebted to its volunteers.

Reciprocity is also created with local service providers. Within a neighbourhood, each service provider has special gifts and different perspectives to offer as well as challenges with leadership and resources from time to time. The neighbourhood agencies, working together, play an essential role in capacity building. One example is the Family of Schools, where CNH offered space, grantsmanship, lobbying to develop a school board position in the community dedicated to youth leadership, and in response the schools opened up their facilities for family and settlement services and supported CNH´s proposals for development.

The Collingwood Community Policing Centre is another example. It offered safety audits, members to sit on committees and Boards, access to prevention and emergency police services, and police checks for volunteers. In return, CNH provided fundraising and grantsmanship support, advocacy to sustain the policing centre, and learning about community development as a way to build safe communities.

In another case, the Renfrew Park Community Association offered education to residents on Parks resources and systems and supported resident-led projects initially supported by CNH. In return, CNH offered knowledge and education about broad policy changes affecting the neighbourhood, connection to resident leaders for their Board, fundraising support, assistance in building their capacity for political advocacy and community development.

Operating programs in off-site locations adds to the network of community connections. For example, Collingwood Neighbourhood House operates its government-funded adult English as an Additional Language classes, with child minding, at the First Lutheran Church. This relationship has led to a greater understanding between the traditional congregation and immigrant newcomers. One positive spin-off has seen congregation members volunteering in the classrooms. The church also benefits financially from the rent paid for the space, which has contributed to the stability of the church in the community.

5.7 Leadership and Capacity Building

For some residents, seeing themselves as having assets as well as needs requires a considerable shift in self-perception and development of self-esteem. There is one space in CNH that tends, more than others, to attract people, and to involve them immediately. Not surprisingly, that space is the kitchen. The large, commercial kitchen at CNH is located on the ground floor, right next to the reception desk. The door is usually open and there is some activity there at almost any time of any day. One fateful day, Teresa Dalby passed by. Her curiosity and her inclination to help out drew her into the warm and friendly Families Branching Out family dinner program. Teresa is a single mother who is raising her son, Dale, while tackling her own physical disability. She had recently found a space for Dale in the CNH day care program, and was preparing to get her life in order. Her first stop was the kitchen. Teresa was quickly recognized as someone who had a lot to give and the willingness to help out. She and Dale became fixtures in the family dinner program. Teresa's involvement in this program led to her being asked to attend the Renfrew Collingwood Leadership Institute, and after she finished the Institute course, she was chosen to join other parent leaders in a provincial Parents and Leadership program.

Teresa gained self-confidence and parenting guidance while enriching the programs that she was involved in with her special insight and experiences. Dale, too, proved to be a natural leader and became a big brother figure to many of the other children, while still a preschooler

himself. Living with a disabled single parent has given him a mature sensibility, and his mother's involvement at CNH has provided a place for him to flourish.

Nurturing community leaders is a natural consequence of the work that CNH does. Nina came to Canada in the early 1980s, fleeing the Chilean dictatorship of Augusto Pinochet. The violence and injustice that enveloped her country left her little choice but to seek refugee status in Canada. When Nina came to Canada, she had lost a lot of her life, everything that she had built for herself, her self-esteem, and connection to her family. Nina had been living in the Chilean Housing Co-op in the Collingwood community for several years before she was introduced to CNH. A friend had offered to take her son to Family Place, and one thing then led to another. Nina felt an immediate kinship to the House. She recognized that she shared the values of what was then a small community organization with a family focus. Her love of children led to an opportunity to work as a substitute child care worker in the Nobody's Perfect parenting program.

Seventeen years later, Nina is now the Child Care Co-ordinator for the adult English as an Additional Language program. Working with newcomers comes naturally for Nina. As a non-native speaker of English, she often feels unable to fully express herself, leaving her feeling as though she cannot reach her full potential. A fully participating, confident leader in her native Chile, Nina recognizes what it feels like as a newcomer to be spun backwards in your life and to have to prove yourself once again in a new culture. This personal experience has made Nina a leader at CNH. Not only does she mentor volunteers, many of whom have arrived under similar circumstances and are now getting their new start in Canada, but she also takes the concerns of parents in her programs seriously and personally helps as many families as she can, including inviting them to special celebrations at her co-op. Nina's story points to the enormous benefit of hiring staff who have been recent immigrants themselves and can identify strongly with the needs of newcomers.

Mr. Hoo is a senior in the Collingwood community who immigrated to Canada from Hong Kong. Mr. Hoo became connected to CNH through language classes and quickly joined the senior wellness program for companionship and to learn more about Canadian culture. Mr. Hoo loves to cook and share his culture. He often hosts Chinese lunches for the seniors, decorates the facility for Chinese New Year, volunteers at many of

the childcare programs where the children have language challenges, and also sits on an advisory committee to further develop senior services and increase elders' involvement in the neighbourhood. Mr. Hoo is one of many examples where Senior citizens contribute their skills and ideas and are committed to life-long learning. In doing so, they increase their personal health and happiness and the capacity of the community as a whole.

The Youth Centre and Youth Buddy Program offer healthy alternative activities for kids aged 10–18. The Youth Centre is a twice-a-week meeting place for all youth. In addition to games, cooking and recreational activities, the Centre provides homework help and actively promotes interculturalism by involving youths in specific celebrations and art projects. The Youth Buddy Program runs out of five local schools and matches younger newcomer youths with older youths who have been in Canada longer or were born in Canada. The "host" and "buddy" take part in group activities that strengthen awareness of personal safety, and that help the "buddies" to become more comfortable in their new environment. These Buddy Hosts learn leadership skills, and bring them to other areas of the house. Youth Board members are now a fixture on the CNH Board of Directors, providing legitimate and meaningful leadership roles for other young people.

CNH, along with other neighbourhood houses, offers a neighbourhood grants program supported through funds from the Vancouver Foundation. Residents can apply for a grant of up to $500 to improve their community. A committee of residents promotes the program and reviews applications, establishes links and supports and hosts a celebration where recipients are able to share their stories. This community development approach has enabled new leadership to emerge in the community and it has helped people who were isolated, because of culture, to feel more a part of their neighbourhood.

Volunteers at Collingwood are encouraged to take on the roles and responsibilities associated with both organizational and community leadership. That's why, in early 2000, CNH explored the idea of a Leadership Institute where community members would have the opportunity to learn more about leadership relevant to their community and based on their individual learning needs. The Renfrew Collingwood Community Leadership Institute ran as a pilot project in 2002 and continues to evolve, offering hands-on learning experiences designed to recruit new leaders and strengthen the capacities of existing volunteer leaders in the community. The curriculum is based on a set of core competencies for community leaders and changes annually to reflect emerging needs. In the past, workshop offerings have included: Leading Community Processes, Chairing Effective Meetings, Promoting Your Community, Creative Community Fundraising, Community Mapping, and Writing Effective Grant Proposals. Seasoned CNH staff and local residents facilitate the workshops. Over a three-year period, 456 Renfrew/Collingwood residents attended the 35 skill development workshops. The Leadership Institute has proven to be an outstanding way of developing leadership skills, connecting with others in the community, facilitating the exchange of information, and generally contributing to the empowerment of residents to shape their own community.

What all of the above stories demonstrate is the value of an integrated approach to community development, in which staff in any one program are always making connections for participants across programs, suggesting new possibilities for engagement, encouraging participants to become volunteers, and so on, in a kind of cross-pollenising practice. Sanjeev Karwal is one of the many success stories attributed to integrated approaches, through which an apparently single purpose program like Family Place can concurrently be building community and building community leaders. Sanjeev is the current Youth Co-ordinator for Collingwood Neighbourhood House, and is a great role model for youth leadership. Sanjeev was taken to Family Place as a baby, a toddler and a preschooler by his grandmother. He went on to volunteer at school as a youth Buddy Host, and he now runs the Youth Centre and the youth Buddy program.

5.8 Creativity

In the mid-1990s, after being absorbed in the provision of much-needed programs and services such as childcare, recreation, and immigrant settlement services, CNH underwent a fundamental shift back to its community development roots. One of the first community development projects that the Neighbourhood House undertook was the creation of a Cultural Skills Inventory, which was accomplished with provincial funding for a Multiculturalism Week project. The idea was to create a database that would store all of the cultural assets in the community. This could then be tapped by any community group or individual. The project uncovered a treasure of artists, musicians, visual artists, weavers, carvers, dancers, and traditional healers. Fourteen of these people were showcased during Multiweek celebrations and many of them were invited to perform at other neighbourhood events. Some of the artists and performers who were "discovered" through this project later became permanently involved in community development initiatives. The project left CNH with a reputation for initiating community art projects. At the same time, the visual arts programming was expanding in the recreation department, and the two groups quickly got together, leading to a strong visual arts presence in the community and a succession of public art projects that continues today.

Artists and musicians, dancers and organizers seemed to be drawn to the Neighbourhood House and, in the wake of MultiWeek, set to work on beautifying Slocan Park and the Renfrew Ravine (see Chapter 6). This was the beginning of big celebrations such as the Moon Festival and Collingwood Days. Artists were needed to improve the wall beside the new community gardens, and banners had to be painted to replace aging city-issue banners. There has never been a shortage of projects, or ideas, or dreams. January Wolodarsky, who initiated the Slocan Park revitalization, is now the Director of Community Development at CNH, overseeing and supporting a range of cultural, educational, social and environmental initiatives envisioned and led by local residents.

Yoko Tomita was an artist working as a Japanese tour guide when she arrived in Canada in 1989. She had no previous experience working in community art but, following a few key connections, she became immersed in the beautification of Collingwood and the use of art for community development. In 2002, Yoko met Cecilia Boisier, the Visual Arts Instructor at CNH and also a member of the Arts Pow Wow, and it was Cecilia who introduced Yoko to community art. She began helping out at classes and then running workshops, coming to grips with processes that involved many people and incorporating their ideas into artwork. It was a struggle for her initially. There were times when no one would show up at a workshop, and the threat of cancellation was always there. She had to make art that fit criteria that someone else had come up with. She had to learn about motivating, networking and marketing herself. Yoko enrolled in the Renfrew Collingwood Leadership Institute, to which she credits learning many of the skills necessary to be a community development artist. She learned to co-ordinate children and non-artists, and to work with multicultural community members expressing many ideas on a single canvas, murals or street banners. It was a challenging experience but, ultimately, Yoko recognized the value in this process and began to thrive on the energy and ideas.

Since 2002, Yoko has worked on more than twenty projects in the Renfrew-Collingwood neighbourhood, including running the summer art camp for children and lantern workshops for the annual Moon Festival. Last year, she hand-painted twenty new street banners, involving participants from different programs, including the homeless program. A few homeless participants were transformed by painting and creating. One man who had been coming to the program for months but had never spoken to anyone, suddenly opened up and shared his vast knowledge of art while helping to paint a dragon on a banner. The banners were hung on the lamp posts outside the Neighbourhood House on what is now called the Cultural Harmony Walk. Yoko is now the Visual Arts Instructor at CNH and is living her dream of supporting herself through art.

5.9 Anti-racism

Early in the film about CNH we hear two oldtimers, Terry Tayler and Chris Taulu, talking about what kind of a neighbourhood Collingwood used to be. In the early 1980s, they tell us, before the building of CNH, there was a lot of fear of and hostility towards immigrants. People were locking their doors, they were hiding, and they were saying things like "What are they doing here?" And "why don't they go back where they came from?" Oldtimers of Anglo-European ethnicity didn't understand large extended families, or so many people living in a house, not to mention unfamiliar religions, foods, and so on. And some of these oldtimers, the ones that couldn't handle these kinds of changes happening in their neighbourhood, "just up and moved out to Surrey". That was twenty years ago, and when Vancouver audiences watch the film they laugh at this line, because Surrey (the second largest, and fastest growing municipality, on the south eastern fringe of the metropolitan area), is now every bit as multi-ethnic as Collingwood was becoming back then. In other words, there is no "hiding place" from this changing complexion of our neighbourhoods as a result of immigration.

So the film tells us that there was initial resistance to the arrival of newcomers from non-Anglo-European countries, and that "it wasn't always a respectful community", in the words of Paula Carr, the Executive Director of CNH. What the film does not convey so well is just how much of a struggle it was to overcome that resistance, that level of societal racism and prejudice that Canada shares with European countries as well as with other New World settler societies. The reason we (as filmmakers) could not convey this was that no-one wanted to re-live those times, or talk about it at length, on camera, feeling that they had moved on to better attitudes and that there was no point in digging this up. Nevertheless, as Comfort Ero, the Nigerian storyteller says in the film: "There are so many instances when people are racist to you, but you can't hold them to ransom. So many instances I cannot pinpoint here, not only from the mainstream Canadians but also from people from other cultures". So what is fascinating is how this has changed over the years, and why. It's indicative of the courageousness of the Board of the Neighbourhood House that they decided to tackle racism head-on, through extensive education and training programs. They put their own staff and volunteers through anti-racism and diversity training (see Chapter 3). And they mounted anti-racism programs in the community at large, and among youth groups.

For six years, CNH ran an Anti-racism Community Committee that consisted of one staff person and five community members representing the various cultural communities in Collingwood. The Committee's work was wide-ranging. They organised a discussion forum after the arrival of the Chinese "boat people". After 9/11, they organized several evening forums for the Muslim community within Collingwood to share information about Islam and answer questions. One offspring of this was the formation of a Peace and Humanity Committee, which organized an evening of storytelling called "Stories of Peace and War". Six residents told their personal stories of persecution, fleeing war, surviving peril, and escaping to Canada. These powerful stories, told in poetry and prose and through visual art, helped other community members recognize the struggles that their neighbours have faced. CNH has always recognized the need for education in order to build empathy and respect.

The Anti-racism Committee also sponsored several anti-racism sessions during Multiweek, including sessions for parents who want to raise children who do not inherit society's prejudices, and for immigrant youth who find themselves straddling two cultures, that of their family and that of their new country and school. The Committee organized training for staff, giving them tools to support victims of racism. The Committee's largest project was the creation of a video that gave Native youth an opportunity to tell their personal stories of experiencing racism, along with the development of a teaching guide to accompany the video.

And each year, the youths who participate in the Youth Centre at CNH organize their own anti-bullying and anti-racism workshops with and for their peers, dramatizing through scenarios various examples of racist, sexist, and other discriminatory behaviours. The longer term result of these efforts is a spreading understanding of what constitutes these behaviours and why they are not acceptable in Canada, which has an Anti-Discrimination Act and a Charter of Rights and Freedoms precisely to protect people from such experiences.

5.10 Conclusions

What this and the next chapter tells us is that the extraordinary accomplishments of CNH in the past twenty two years have not come easily. Building community where none existed, enabling strangers to become neighbours on an ongoing basis, overcoming deep-seated societal prejudices such as racism, and coaxing civic engagement has taken hard work, focus, and commitment.

As a relatively young organization, CNH has never been afraid of change. But the values that give the place its soul have remained its core strength. Conceived by people committed to social justice and inclusion, these fundamental beliefs are passed on through staff and Boards and volunteers in a virtuous cycle. There are issues yet to be resolved, and emerging needs that have to be addressed, and we discuss these in Chapter 6.

But hearing the story of CNH may make it a little easier for other communities to imagine a different, more connected way of being and relating. All it takes, in the words of the founding President, Terry Tayler, is "dreaming big, and opening your heart".

THE COLLINGWOOD NEWS

VOL.1 NO.1 FEBRUARY 2000

Visual Arts Workshop
"Fruits", Teresa Ha, Winter 1999

City Council Phases Out Endowment for Child Care

On January 13, 2000, Vancouver's newly elected City Council voted to wind down an endowment fund that supports Infant/Toddler programs throughout the city. The decision will affect the funding for three seperate agencies operating under-3 child care, including Collingwood Neighbourhood House. Recently, the YWCA closed Granny Y's, a long standing Infant/Toddler centre on the grounds that it could no longer afford to operate the program.

The City's Infant/Toddler endowment fund was established in 1994 as part of the City's Child Care Strategy to address the extremely high cost of providing licensed under-3 child care in the City. The endowment was created from contributions by developers on City projects. Collingwood Neighbourhood House has been operating Infant/Toddler care since opening its new facility in 1995.

continued on page 13

Chapter 6
CNH: The Ongoing Challenges of Change

Val Cavers and Paula Carr

In its 21 year history, the Collingwood Neighbourhood House transformed from a small storefront office to a 25,000 square foot facility with over 100 regular programmes, 90 regular staff, over 300 volunteers, and serving over 160,000 residents each year, making it the largest neighbourhood house in British Columbia. In those years, the operating budget grew from $30,000 to $3.5 million. Along with growth and development came pitfalls and struggles of all shapes and sizes, among them the ongoing struggle for financial sustainability, and the recognition through sustained funding from government, of the value of the work done at the community level.

Recently, the provincial government of British Columbia recognized the important role that neighbourhood houses play in the integration of immigrants by granting multi-year funding for settlement services like English as an Additional Language Classes and immigrant first-language information services, but that recognition came after 12 years of struggle and year-to-year funding, and at the expense of other service providers who were part of an extensive and critical network. Neighbourhood Houses in Vancouver continue to lobby for sustainable funding. They believe there is substantial evidence that a block funding approach from all three levels of government may serve the community and government in a better manner and still provide the level of accountability needed. Neighbourhood Houses are one of the few types of organizations that receive ongoing support from all three levels of government as well as raise significant dollars through fee based and entrepreneurial approaches. This is a model that governments promote in their rhetoric, yet multi-funded organizations often lose out when one level of government chooses to change funding programs.

The four stories that follow are examples of other struggles that the Neighbourhood House has faced and continues to face. All of them came with learnings that helped the organization grow. The building of the Duke Street Child Care Centre was early on in CNH history and was the House's first encounter with public disapproval. The move towards integrated programming was a lesson learned through the English language classes and has since permeated the philosophy of the Neighbourhood House and

L. Sandercock, G. Attili, *Where Strangers Become Neighbours*, Urban and
Landscape Perspectives 4, DOI 10.1007/978-1-4020-9035-6_6
© Springer Science+Business Media 2009

its current programmes. Slocan Park marked CNH's move back into community development work and became an 11-year symbol of resident-powered achievement. The most recent struggle, involving outreach to homeless people, presents perhaps the most intense challenge yet to the ethics and values of the Neighbourhood House. The initiation of a homeless shower and breakfast programme has brought out the best and the worst in the community and forced the Board of Directors to confront the community in what could become the next catalyst to change the direction of the Neighbourhood House.

6.1 The Challenge of Neighbourhood Opposition: Building a Childcare Centre

In 1993, Collingwood Neighbourhood House was preparing to move from a small storefront space to a 25,000 square foot building on Joyce Street. The building of the new facility mobilized the Board, staff and community, and launched a huge capital campaign. The plans for the new House included the building of an infant toddler centre, a day care for 3–5 year olds, a preschool and day care. At the same time, the Neighbourhood House was working with the First Lutheran Church to open a day care in the church's social housing project, Sarah House. Collingwood, already a local force in the provision of day care, was expanding its childcare operations from relatively small preschool and after school care to become one of the City of Vancouver's major providers.

Around that same time, the City introduced the Portable Purchase Programme, the purpose of which was to install pre-fabricated and inexpensive structures in communities to alleviate the cost of building stand-alone centres and to quickly address the need for more childcare spaces. CNH was seen as an organization with a track record in childcare in a high need community and was chosen to participate in this new initiative. All that was needed was an appropriate site. With the help of the City of Vancouver, the neighbourhood house chose a quiet corner of a local park. No one anticipated that this would become the first major challenge that Collingwood Neighbourhood House would have to face.

The park site was chosen for its convenient location on a major bus route, access to an existing playground, and because it was a park. The Parks Board approved the location in principle, but because it was a park, a lengthy consultative process came into play. CNH recognized that a park

could be a contentious place, so they carefully researched the site, watching to see who if anyone used that corner of the park. When they felt confident, the Parks Board began the consultation process, which included the door-to-door distribution of leaflets. Since they were talking about childcare, and the community need was clearly identified, CNH, the City and the Parks Board didn't anticipate a lot of reaction. Of the 1000 leaflets that they distributed, only a handful came back with negative comments. The Parks Board called a public meeting, and the House and City spoke to the need for childcare, and the desire to use the park for this facility. It was at this meeting that the opposition grew. People objected to the use of park space for anything other than a park. They were concerned that there would be an increase in traffic congestion, with the dropping off and picking up of children. Some folks even objected to children in the park. Most people didn't go that far, but shared concerns about obstructed views, noise and dirt.

The phone calls flooded in to the Neighbourhood House as the discontent spread around the community. The tension escalated and the Neighbourhood House found itself embroiled in a struggle in which it had more to lose, in terms of community support, than to gain. There were several meetings to try to resolve the situation. CNH was afraid that without this location, the money would be lost for the construction of the facility. With no imminent solution, and not wanting to make enemies in the community, the Neighbourhood House pulled out of the project.

At that point, some of the most vocal opponents came forward and offered to help find another location. Working with the City Realtor and CNH, these "opponents" found a piece of land on quiet, residential Duke Street. The property had an easement for a sewer, making it undesirable for most projects, and not very marketable. The opponents of the park location now became the greatest allies in appealing to the neighbours at this new location. Duke Street neighbours were canvassed door-to-door and although there were some who were concerned, most saw the benefits and in the end there was overwhelming support for the project.

The second part of this story is that the Portable Purchase Programme was a new project for the City. The portables were custom-designed day care centres and were unique. The centre ended up being delayed by nearly one year as both the development and building processes and the construction processes for this new type of centre took much longer than anticipated. Being behind schedule on Duke Street meant that in 1995 there were 8 new programmes all opening at the same time. Four of the programs were in the brand new Joyce Street building, another on Wales Street, and three at Duke Street. The logistics of hiring and training new staff, and ordering, furnishing, and setting up brand new spaces are mind-boggling. It was a chaotic time in CNH history, but one that helped to develop relationships with the community on an entirely new level.

6.2 The Challenge of Transcending Cultural Specificity: Introducing Language Programs

Collingwood Neighbourhood House describes most of its programming as "intercultural", which means that programs are not provided to or for culturally specific groups, such as Chinese or Vietnamese people. Rather, they are open to all groups, and participants communicate in English or receive help from multilingual staff, volunteers or other participants. CNH *has* run culturally specific programming, and the results have been less successful.

In the late 1980s, CNH was just beginning to develop its capacity to work with and engage new immigrants. The Board, volunteers and staff had been through sensitivity training, which was a new area of training being developed by consultants and the Hasting Institute in Vancouver (see Chapter 3). At this time, the challenge of welcoming new immigrants to services and citizenship was being felt by a number of organizations and public institutions. CNH started providing English as an Additional Language (EAL) classes for newcomers in a segregated fashion. The demographics at that time, the early 1990s, showed three prominent language groups represented in the community: Cantonese, Punjabi and Spanish. These three groups were targeted by the Neighbourhood House for EAL classes. A space at the First Lutheran Church was secured and teachers were hired, as were three bicultural/ bilingual assistants to provide additional support to the students.

These students all shared the same plight in that they all needed to learn English to fully adapt to their new country. But by separating them into culturally specific groups, they were unable to experience this plight together. Instead, tensions flared around cultural stereotypes: one group was described as poor and lazy, another as snobbish, and so on. Eventually, putting all these people into the same classroom stripped away the superficial stereotyping. Having them all together in the same predicament encouraged them to see each other's struggles as fellow human beings and enabled them to dispel the stereotypes. It wasn't an easy struggle to get to a place of understanding. The three groups and the staff were entrenched in their fears and sometimes loathing. In order to make the change to an integrated classroom philosophy, CNH brought in a cross-cultural facilitator to work with the students and staff. You wouldn't know, now, that there had been an issue among the various communities. Today's EAL students are absorbed by the real issues that face them all, learning English and learning how to live successfully in Canadian society. This is not to say that there are never tensions between cultural groups, or that no-one experiences the subtle racism that ignorance breeds. These issues still occur from time to time, but the teachers and support staff are now in a much better position to deal with such issues when they arise within a mixed group and they can be seen for what they are.

6.3 The Challenge of Participation in a Multi-Ethnic Neighbourhood: Revitalizing Slocan Park

The story of Slocan Park is perhaps typical of many other community struggles in the sense that it involved a lot of committed residents, some opposing residents, some misunderstandings and a lot of bureaucratic red tape. Slocan Park is located in the centre of the Collingwood community and is traversed at ground level by the Skytrain. It was a fairly nondescript place, with a children's play ground and wading pool, two tennis courts, a playing field and a field house inhabited by a City-employed caretaker. Due in part to the Skytrain access, and the public washrooms in the field house, the park became a hang-out for drug dealers and drug users. The caretaker reported picking up dozens of discarded syringes, neighbours complained of dealers hanging around and stashing their drugs in the bushes, commuters would walk all the way around the park for fear of crossing it in the dark. It became a neglected and unsafe place.

In the mid 1990s, Collingwood Neighbourhood House underwent a fundamental shift back to its community development roots (Chapter 5). The organization had become absorbed by the provision of programmes and services, by the huge expansion into the areas of childcare, recreation and settlement services, and by the capital campaign and move into the new facility on Joyce Street. By 1996 the time was right to begin working again with the aspirations of residents.

January Wolodarsky was a mum attending Family Place with her new baby girl at this time. She had just returned to Canada after spending 11 years in Japan working as an environmental artist in Tokyo; designing and installing large-scale urban beautification projects using gardens,

SLOCAN PARK
Landscape Concept

A   Duchess Walk

TOPOGRAPHICS
December 6, 2000

SLOCAN PARK
Landscape Concept

B   Open Air Theatre

TOPOGRAPHICS
December 6, 2000

sculptures and water. She now found herself in Collingwood with a small child and a new set of priorities. Her idea was to do something about the neglected park near her house, which happened to be Slocan Park. While attending the Family Place program, she became familiar with the Neighbourhood House and was connected by the Co-ordinator of Family Place to the Executive Director, Paula Carr. Paula was beginning to conceive of the return to community development, and January arrived at exactly the right moment. Together with two other residents, Julie Cheng (a community developer and Slocan Park neighbour) and Cecilia Boisier (an artist and art educator), they conceived of and began work on the community Arts Pow Wow and the Slocan Park revitalization project.

These three women residents understood that ordinary things like lamp posts and benches could become beautiful objects that enrich experience of the park and create ownership over it through community public art making, and that it could eventually be returned to the commons. The group advertised meetings and held neighbour gatherings in the park to elicit input from neighbours and park users. The initial meetings were disheartening, as few people showed up. Through reflection and debriefing, they recognized that a different strategy to reach people needed to be developed based on neighbourhood meeting places and connections.

Julie and Cecelia and January went door-to-door, to schools, and to seniors' centres. On a few occasions they met people who had photos and memories of how the park used to be. They heard those stories and were further inspired. Sadly, at that same time there was a home burgled in the area, and as a result people stopped opening their doors. But the three organizers weren't deterred. They went on to invite people to the park for free hot dog days to give input into the plan. They had a multilingual student from the local highschool go to the park and talk to people there, take pictures and collect people's ideas. They went to school fairs and had children draw pictures of the park, and anything else they could think of to get people to express what they wanted their park to be.

As a young mother, Emanuela Sheena recalls being told by neighbours not to take her kids to play in Slocan Park. Instead, she regularly drove her kids to other parks to play. Living close to the park, it didn't seem fair that she should have to avoid one of the only green spaces in her community, and so she joined the growing number of people calling for changes. Her initial view was that increased police presence was the way to improve the growing drug problem. But Emanuela quickly became a convert to the proposal being put forward by January, Julie and Cecilia. She helped to organize meetings and attended park gatherings, talking to neighbours and using the park herself.

There was another group of residents who were initially opposed to any changes to the park. Their houses backed on to the park and they seemed to see it as an extension of their back yards. When they found out that plans were being developed to make changes, they became concerned. Some were even enraged. They circulated a petition and shouted their opposition at meetings. They spread a rumour that there were plans to build a skateboard park and gathered supporters who were opposed to that.

The Neighbourhood House and the residents' group came together at a meeting with the Parks Board's landscape architect to talk about the proposed plans, and these residents came to voice their opposition. What became evident was that these residents had for many years been taking an interest in this neglected park. Their calls to the City for changes had long gone unheeded; so their frustration had led them to become sceptical of this new plan. Eventually, when they saw the plan and felt that they had been heard, they backed off and the plan went ahead, leaving development around their houses for a later date.

One of the largest groups of people using the park, then and still today, is the Chinese T'ai Chi group. Every morning there are between 50 and 80 seniors gathered together for their daily exercise. They are there early, before many of them go home to spend the day looking after their grandchildren. It was especially important and challenging to have them involved in whatever plan was being made for the park, but language and culture acted as barriers.

On one occasion, January Wolodarsky was treated with mistrust and misunderstanding when she tried to approach them. Julie Cheng realised that she had a connection, through her father, who had studied T'ai Chi with a friend of one of the leaders of this group.

Through this channel, January, Julie and Cecilia were able to gain the seniors' support. In fact, the T'ai Chi seniors became great allies and enthusiastic participants in the planning process. They have just recently seen their dream of a covered area fulfilled. On the rainiest days in Vancouver, they can now practice their art under a beautiful cedar and metal structure. The seniors recognised that the most pressing issue facing the park was safety, and they graciously put their covered area plans on hold until the safety initiatives could be addressed.

One of the first things that the residents wanted to do in the park was to paint the field house, a seemingly innocuous activity. In fact, this became a huge issue for the City, which was loath to see it painted, especially by children. Cecilia then approached the neighbouring school and asked if she could work with children on some mural painting in the basement of the school. Cecelia painted four murals there, using the park and community as a theme and inviting children, parents and grandparents to attend. It was a fun time; many parents and grandparents did not speak English and were not artists, but were brought together for this project. One mother used the time as an opportunity to learn English with her child, bringing pictures of things and practicing the English descriptions with us. Once Cecilia had proved her skills and shown the City what she and a team of children could do, they gave their approval for the field house to be painted. It took two whole years to get that approval. And they were only ever allowed to paint one side of the building. Interestingly, one of the mural projects at the school showed how children perceived the world around them, and how powerful outside influences are. When asked to paint a scene showing their community and the people around them, these students, who were predominantly Chinese, Indian and Vietnamese and lived in a community where only 27% of people speak English as a first language, painted blond, white, blue-eyed children on the mural. This experience gave Cecilia the opportunity to talk to the kids about representing themselves in art work, and taking pride in who they are.

Another project in Slocan Park was to have kids build a model of an ideal city using huge cardboard boxes. A load of fridge and stove boxes were brought from the local appliance store and the kids set about organizing a cardboard community. They painted the boxes, and played in them until they fell apart. This helped to draw parents and kids to the park, and to give them the opportunity to have input into the planning for the new park. Other new things began to happen.

On Sundays, the park was now a venue for a drumming circle, and a local artist donated her time to paint portraits and give art classes. An environmental group became interested in the plans and started to work with the growing committee of people committed to the restoration of the park. At this point, other stakeholders were brought in. The City had already begun to meet with January and Julie and Cecilia, but it was Translink, the regional transit authority, that was really needed as an ally. Translink runs the Skytrain, a mass public transit system that runs through the entire community, stopping at one point in the middle of Slocan Park. On the park side of the station there are two exits and entrances. One of the complaints that the group heard repeatedly was that there was insufficient lighting for commuters when they entered or exited the station on this side. Commuters felt unsafe. The Skytrain was seen as being culpable in the number of drug dealers and users that used the park, so it was critical to have Translink involved in the project. They were initially slow to become involved, saying that it wasn't their jurisdiction, but eventually they put some money towards lighting. Over time, the resident group was able to soften their "tough on crime" approach, and Translink also became a reasonable partner.

At the same time, the whole Arts Pow Wow project was receiving support from the Saidye and Samuel Bronfman Foundation (Urban Issues), several Federal Provincial, and municipal funding programs, and the Vancouver Foundation, which allowed the park project to gather momentum. The City, Translink and the Parks Board agreed to build the Duchess Walkway, a path that intersects the park and leads from Duchess Street to the Skytrain entrance. The finished walkway has four lantern motif lamp standards. The metal cut-outs on the lanterns represent the four elements and the four seasons and were designed in community workshops, as were the pebble mosaics that travel along the path. At the top of the walkway is an eagle, The Guardian of the Park, an enormous totem. The eagle is held up by four men facing in four directions. At the south end of the park, under the huge cottonwood tree, a garden was

planted to display dozens of indigenous plants. (Unfortunately, the plants were later dug up and stolen.) Another native plant garden was installed closer to the station with the help of a local youth leadership group and Evergreen (the environmental organization), which, despite having some plants go missing, is still being pruned and tended by a local gentlemen who immigrated to the community.

This stage of the project began with a parade from Collingwood Neighbourhood House to the park, a distance of two kilometres, and a party to celebrate the revitalization, complete with an African Storyteller who worked with a local puppeteer on a special tale that celebrated the enormous cottonwood tree at the end of the path that eventually became the Duchess Walkway. The following year, a "Mosaic Madness" event brought people out to work on the huge pebble mosaic that was installed along the Duchess Walkway. Later, community artist Yoko Tomita held banner-painting workshops for the lantern banners.

The project grew incrementally from there. When there was money for murals, a site close to the park was chosen. When funding came available to improve City playgrounds, the committee made sure Slocan Park was on the priority list. By this time, commuters were walking through the park, cyclists were using the bikeway that winds through the park, the City cut back dense foliage that hid drug stashes, and planted a circle of fruit trees with the agreement that residents would care for them and harvest the fruit. Now, 10 years into the project, there are new ideas, new users, and a totally revitalized green space in Collingwood.

6.4 The Challenge of Difference and Fear of "the Other": Initiating a Homeless Shower and Breakfast Program

Perhaps one of the greatest learnings for Collingwood Neighbourhood House has been the acceptance of the economic underclass, including the homeless, in the community. The homeless program has been a true test of the values of Collingwood Neighbourhood House. Gaining community respect for the homeless, for drug addicts, the mentally ill and for poor people has presented a great challenge to the current CNH Board of Directors, staff and participants. As provincial government services for these groups of people deteriorated as a result of budget cuts, communities like Collingwood found themselves dealing more and more with visible poverty issues. The mass transit system, Skytrain, brought the drug users and dealers; the neighbouring community had managed to push out the prostitutes and johns, while only moving the problem further east into Collingwood; and a huge increase in the population had contributed to an increased crime rate. All of these factors, combined, meant that the CNH Board could not ignore the people whose lives were intertwined with these external events, and these were largely the poor.

Collingwood Neighbourhood House prides itself on the development of sustained relationships. Indeed, relationships have become the cornerstone of CNH's success, but not all relationships have been easy to form. In 2004, the Neighbourhood House developed a plan, in collaboration with a number of local partners, to develop relationships with the homeless that would allow the groups to identify needed supports and assets. They began to provide a shower, breakfast and clean clothes exchange for the growing number of homeless people in the community. The ensuing outreach work to homeless members of the community brought with it various strong reactions from residents. On the one hand, the Neighbourhood House was accused of drawing more homeless people to the neighbourhood, and thereby jeopardizing the safety of residents: on the other hand, there was an immense outpouring of support for the program by people who wanted to help alleviate poverty in their community.

The Homeless Shower and Breakfast Program, now in its second year, provides a hot shower and breakfast. Participants can also get clean clothing and household goods if they are making the transition into housing. Staff and volunteers provide support to participants, help them connect with government agencies, act as advocates, and link people to housing and detoxification and other medical services. This program enjoys strong support from the neighbouring public health unit, which provides nurses, access to doctors and detox programs.

A broad community committee oversees the program, advocates for social housing, and provides training and education opportunities. The committee is made up of representatives from Evergreen (the community health unit), the Collingwood Crime Prevention Office, the Renfrew Community Centre, and the Neighbourhood House. Initially, the committee studied the work done by a similar group on the other side of Vancouver. They were trained to interact with homeless people, learned how to train volunteers, and they learned what elements a successful program should include. In January 2005 they launched the first shower and breakfast, which attracted two participants. By the end of that year, there were ninety people attending.

The benefits to the community have been felt both by participants in this program and by other Neighbourhood House participants who have opened their minds to accepting this vulnerable and often misunderstood group. By the sharing of stories and the focus on relationships, a greater understanding of the "other" has developed. However, there have also been negative aspects of this program. Some people who are less inclined to include homeless people in their community have been outspoken and have voiced strong concerns for personal safety when using the Neighbourhood House.

Collingwood is home to a very active Community Crime Prevention Office, and while it provides a resource and support service for victims of crime, it also joins with community partners to work towards alleviating the perceived causes of crime. The CCPO has a very important role on the Homeless Program Committee. Their task is to build a bridge in understanding between those who believe that all crime is a result of poor and homeless drug addicts, and the goal of accepting these members of the community, treating them with respect, and advocating for government support to reduce the rates of homelessness and poverty. The CCPO took on the role of educating members of the community and also its own volunteers, who were some of the most outspoken critics of the program. Not all of the issues are yet resolved. There will likely always be people who are not supportive of this type of program. But a lot of ground has been gained.

There have been critics from inside CNH programs as well. The breakfast program initially ran twice each week, but was forced to cancel one session recently due to complaints from a small group of very vocal parents. These parents of children attending a preschool program took issue mainly with the appearance of homeless people and the effect that they thought exposure to them was having on their children. While it is true that this population of people often suffer from mental illness, are not dressed in clean clothing, and may be on medication or illegal drugs, the idea of welcoming them into the neighbourhood house was intended to look beyond the superficial and to listen to and value the stories of each individual.

The program has been fraught with other challenges, and those are mainly issues that CNH staff face on a day-to-day basis. The program grew very quickly. News of a decent breakfast, hot shower, clean clothes and the chance to talk to an outreach worker in a secular place spread along the grapevine. CNH staff quickly noticed that after breakfast, people were in no hurry to leave the warm, friendly building. They continued having coffee, smokes, socializing and even sleeping in the lobby long after breakfast. Many stayed until lunch, and this began to occur regularly. The lobby was no longer open for other users, there was additional staff time and attention needed to feed and clean up after people, the outdoor benches were filled with sleeping bodies, and at times there were outbursts and incidents. To some staff and participants, this took the Neighbourhood House in a direction that they didn't think was healthy. People began to comment that CNH was losing participants, that an invisible equilibrium had been disturbed. At the height of the crisis, we were spending dozens of additional hours each week dealing with incidents, meeting with participants, meeting with staff, strategizing with staff, preparing food and coffee, resolving disputes, writing letters, and finding clean clothes for people. It was becoming clear that something needed to change.

At the same time, some of the vocal parents of preschoolers presented a petition to CNH management, demanding the elimination of the program. CNH had no intention of cancelling the program, but they did want to appease the parents, and at the same time rein in the program. The parents were sent a letter outlining changes that were coming, and asking for their patience and understanding while the outreach to this marginalized community continued. The Homeless Committee and CNH staff set out a number of new policies to guide the program back to a more manageable level. The policies dealt with a number of issues, including a maximum number allowed for breakfast, "hanging out" after the programme, and sleeping in and around the building. These were meant to lessen the impact that the program was having on staff and participants. Homeless participants were made aware of the new policies and although they were disappointed, many of them recognized the need to curb behaviours that were negatively affecting others.

Staff training had been ongoing since the beginning of the program. Reception staff and Custodial staff in particular were trained to recognize and respond to drug overdoses, violent and difficult behaviour, waking someone up, and empathic listening. As well, Mental Health, First Aid, and sensitivity training for the homeless was initiated and offered to staff and volunteers in neighbourhood agencies and institutions. Most of these staff responded very well to the new regime. They had become connected to the homeless participants and formed relationships with regulars. They were now being asked to limit those relationships, and to deal with people in a way that was more confrontational. There was a zero tolerance for anyone sleeping in the lobby, and no coffee was available outside of program times. There was a definite adjustment for staff, and training and debriefing were organized along with the new policies. These staff expressed a sense of relief. In spite of their personal feelings for the participants, they recognized that the program was not sustainable in terms of staff time devoted to this one group. But there is always room for personal judgement and discretion at CNH, and even in a zero tolerance environment, staff are trusted to make decisions based on their gut feelings of what is right.

Find yourself in
Collingwood
Neighbourhood House

The strategy to rein in the program had a limited effect. People quickly got the message that hanging around in between program times was not acceptable. Sleeping was harder to deal with, because it can be absolutely impossible to wake someone up and move them on. Staff time dealing with issues decreased slightly, but the ire of the parents did not. Four months after the new directives were put into place, the parents rose up again to challenge the program, and this time they threatened to pull their children from the preschool. This threat would be a serious blow to the Neighbourhood House, which depends on childcare revenues to fund staff positions and other operations. After a series of meetings with staff, parents and the committee, the Wednesday program was postponed until a new location could be found.

The Homeless Committee is working to find another location for the postponed program. In one sense there has been a positive outcome from this, in that it has brought the issue out into the broader community and forced other groups to accept some of the responsibility for helping the homeless and poor. There are now two churches who are interested in taking on the issue, to ensure that the important advocacy and outreach work continues.

Although perhaps too idealistic, many staff and volunteers supported this program and became genuinely engaged with the homeless participants. Relationships continue to evolve and there is a sense of confidence that the program will prevail. The hope is that the homeless and poor in the neighbourhood will eventually be able to find a more inclusive community in Collingwood.

For the time being, the postponement of this program demonstrates the limits of tolerance and inclusivity in this otherwise very open and accepting community. It also illustrates a deep and ongoing commitment to inclusivity and social justice on the part of CNH, as well as demonstrating that such struggles are always unfinished projects, requiring ongoing social learning and conflict resolution.

Chapter 7
Integrating Immigrants Through Community Development

Leonie Sandercock

7.1 Introduction: From Nation to Neighborhood

Policies dealing with immigration and refugees are formulated at national level, but their most significant repercussions are at the local level, where they impact the whole intricate social fabric of urban life, in streets and neighbourhoods, housing estates, shops and schools, parks and places of worship. Immigration policies are motivated primarily by economic concerns, sometimes with an added dash of humanitarianism. But the national economic mindset typically does not take into account the challenges and complexities of strangers entering the urban fabric in significant numbers and the ways in which this can be perceived, rightly or wrongly, as undermining a particular way of life.

Countries facing immigration need to rethink their political and social philosophies to mesh with the 21st century realities of immigration and mongrel cities. Canada is the most advanced example of this bold new experiment in imagining how to organize an increasingly pluralist society.

As Chapter 1 has outlined, multiculturalism in Canada has served as a guideline for government policy since 1971, and also as a framework for national discourse on the construction of Canadian society (Mahtani 2002: 68). Initially conceived as a way of accommodating the separatist impulse of Quebec's French-speaking population and Francophone culture, the policy has had to evolve to take on board, literally, the arrival of increasing numbers of immigrants from "ethnically diverse" (non-Anglo, non-Caucasian) backgrounds. Canadian multiculturalism has encouraged individuals voluntarily to affiliate with the culture and tradition of their choice, and there has been significant spending, through multicultural grants, to support the maintenance of various cultures and languages and to encourage diverse cultural festivals in public places as well as the symbolic gesture of public artworks that recognize and celebrate the multiple peoples who make up the nation. The intention has been to forge

L. Sandercock, G. Attili, *Where Strangers Become Neighbours*, Urban and Landscape Perspectives 4, DOI 10.1007/978-1-4020-9035-6_7
© Springer Science+Business Media 2009

a workable national framework of "unity within diversity", all the while emphasizing the economic benefits of immigration.

Still, there is a significant leap from multicultural rhetoric at the level of national politics and legal frameworks, to what happens in the streets and neighborhoods of Canada's cities. Provincial and local levels of government, in general, have been slower to respond to cultural diversity in terms of examining and changing their policies. There are, however, exceptions, beacons of innovation, and that is the story told in this book and film.

7.2 Learning from the Local

The Collinwood Neighbourhood House was one of the first institutions in Vancouver to develop an intercultural policy, which is part of what makes its story significant. More important, though, are the details of how this was done (Chapters 5 and 6), and the (local and national) circumstances that made it possible (Chapters 1, 2 and 3).

The CNH is now widely recognized for its innovative approach to cultural diversity, its ability to create and maintain "a place for everyone". In March 2007 CNH received the BMW Group Award for Intercultural Learning, the first time that this ten year old prize has been awarded outside of Europe, and recognition of the widening reach of CNH's example.

On the surface, what CNH does is to develop and provide services according to perceived local needs. But there is more to it than that. First, the organization's real purpose (as reflected in its mission statement) is to *build community*, and its belief is that that cannot be achieved by providing culturally specific services. The very idea of a "neighborhood house" implies a place with no subcultural affiliation, no shared interest other than *creating a community based on common residency*. Thus the approach to programming is *intercultural*. Second, the services are not seen as merely services meeting a need. They are also seen as providing meeting places where people come together, and *connect through engaging in activities together*. Third, residents are engaged as researchers in the investigation of their own community, which further helps in establishing contacts and building relationships, as well as empowering locals to become involved in the decision-making and programming at the Neighborhood House. CNH also conducts regular anti-racism education programs, and teaches through its consistent policies and actions that community is built through inclusion rather than through drawing boundaries. This is the daily negotiation of difference in the micro-publics of the city, in everyday activities, that would seem to be the most appropriate way to foster intercultural contact and exchange.

In Collingwood (and other Neighborhood Houses in Vancouver) we have examples to show the world how it is possible to move towards an intercultural society by creating a local institution which is, literally, "a place for everyone" rather than only for the members of one cultural group. These Neighborhood Houses provide services according to perceived local needs. Such services include, of course, language training for immigrants; a range of settlement services; a buddy and host program for youths (very important in addressing youth alienation); and a range of bridging services where the focus is relationship-building between different cultural groups, in order to build an intercultural community. The Neighborhood House approach to providing services is different from traditional service provision agencies in that the services are seen as not only meeting a need, but also as providing meeting places where people can come together and connect through engaging in activities together.

The uniqueness and strength of Neighbourhood Houses stems precisely from the fact that they are *neighborhood-based*. This means that they are easily accessed by people, because they are close to home. They are also well-connected with the whole gamut of institutions that newcomers must deal with, from schools to storekeepers to local law enforcement, which means they can assist newcomers in integrating with local life, and also help out in the inevitable disputes that arise, because they are known and trusted locally.

Another strength of Neighbourhood Houses is that they are *multi-service organizations*, which minimizes the stigmatizing that can come from seeking help from a single-purpose agency. The breadth of language skills available at these Houses in Vancouver is another reason for their success in developing intercultural programs and bringing people together across their cultural differences.

7.2.1 But, What Circumstances Brought This Organization into Being?

The CNH was born in the mid-1980s amidst the emerging philosophies of diversity and multiculturalism at the national level. The City of Vancouver, under new left-of-center leadership was engaged in redefining itself as both a global and a multicultural city in the lead-up to staging Expo in 1986. This City Council was eager to implement culturally sensitive policies. For example, the City of Vancouver created the Hastings Institute to provide leadership in diversity and improve race relations through anti-racist and diversity training programs.

As a new organization, the CNH was not burdened with inherited ways of thinking and doing. It defined itself, from the beginning, as a *learning* organization that would have to constantly reflect on its own programs and ways of operating. It had strong internal advocates for diversity in its early development as an organization and strong leadership of its governing Board. The founding President and the Executive Director had each received training in the practice of diversity through the Hastings Institute, and required that that be an ongoing practice of the organization. Care has always been taken in recruiting new staff, Board members, and volunteers, who are expected to have cross- cultural experience and a demonstrated appreciation of the principles of diversity. Care has also been taken to ensure *ongoing* commitment by requiring that attention to diversity is integrated throughout the entire institution, from its strategic directives to its daily operations. Finally, the funding model is unusual. After initial dependence on the City Council and the United Way, the CNH successfully pursued a wide range of funding sources, so that if any one source is withdrawn, the operation does not collapse.

This intricate web of reasons for the success of the CNH cautions us against generalizing from it as a model to be *imitated* in other cities in other countries. Often, small local initiatives, especially ones that are sparked by strong and inspiring individual leadership, appear replicable if comparably energetic and committed individuals can be found in different places, and some funding provided for them. Clearly the story we have told is far more complicated, involving philosophical, political, and/or financial support from two tiers of government, the engagement of a mobilized civil society, and the development of a complex funding model. Nevertheless, the story is instructive in what it takes to work towards living with diversity, beyond fear, and beyond the American model of "indifference to difference", towards actually building an intercultural community. It is a living example of the principles I will discuss in Chapter 8, most notably, emphasizing the daily and ongoing negotiation of difference through coming together on common projects and in everyday activities of survival and the reproduction of life.

7.3 Conclusion: From Neighborhood Back to Nation, the Web of Change

The neighborhood is important, but it is not enough. It would be remiss to conclude with the local story outlined above, ignoring the many other policy responses that are necessary to address the integration of immigrants. I'll conclude by summarizing these.

The *first* requirement is for commitment by political parties at the municipal level in developing integration initiatives as a central part of their mission. This can only be done cooperatively, involving a breadth of organizations in civil society (Chapter 2).

A *second* requirement is for multi-tiered political and policy support systems, from national through to provincial, city and municipal levels (Chapters 1 and 2).

The *third* requirement for addressing integration at the level of everyday life is to tackle the culture and practices of municipal workers such as the police, teachers, judges, planners, and service providers. Most bureaucracies have needed to undergo sensitivity training on gender issues in order to transform historic patterns of discrimination and domination. Now it is urgent that they address cultural difference and cultivate the qualities necessary to overcome discrimination and marginalization (Chapter 3).

A *fourth* requirement is reform and innovation in the realm of social policy, from the most obvious – language assistance – to the creation of new institutions such as Neighborhood Houses, support for immigrant organizations, official recognition of immigrant rituals and naming rights, and provision of culturally sensitive social services, including culturally appropriate food and recognition rituals at official functions.

A *fifth* requirement is a better understanding of how *urban* policies can and should address cultural difference. This includes issues of design, location, and planning process. For example, if different cultures use public and recreational space differently, then new kinds of public spaces may have to be designed, or old ones re-designed, to accommodate this difference. Buildings like Neighbourhood Houses express their inclusivity in their very design. Space also needs to be made available for the different worshipping practices of immigrant cultures: the building of mosques and temples, for example, has become a source of conflict in many cities. And when cultural conflicts arise over different uses of land and buildings, of private as well as public spaces, planners need to find more communicative, less adversarial ways of resolving these conflicts, through participatory mechanisms which give a voice to all those with a stake in the outcome. This in turn requires new skills for planners and architects in cross-cultural communication.

A *sixth* requirement is the elaboration of new notions of citizenship – *intercultural and urban* – that are more responsive to newcomers' claims of rights to the city and more encouraging of their political participation at the local level. This involves nothing less than openness on the part of host societies to being redefined in the process of migrant integration, and to new notions of a common identity emerging through an always contested notion of the common good and shared destiny of all residents. It also involves an understanding that *citizenship can be actively constructed through the kinds of community development processes embodied in CNH practices* (Chapter 8).

The *seventh* is an understanding of and preparedness to work with the emotions that drive these conflicts over integration: emotions of fear, and attachment to history and memory, as well as the status quo, on the part of host societies; and the (possibly ambivalent) desire for belonging, and fear of exclusion on the part of migrants. Not to acknowledge and deal with these emotions is a recipe for failure in the longer-term project of intercultural co-existence (Chapters 5 and 6).

If the mongrel cities of the 21st century are to be socially sustainable, their citizens, city governments, and city-building professions need to work collaboratively on all of these fronts. We're all immigrants into the future, and we need places like the Collingwood Neighbourhood House to help us make the journey.

Reference

Mahtani M (2002) 'Interrogating the Hyphen-nation: Canadian Multicultural Policy and "Mixed Race" Identities', Social Identities, 8, 1: 67–90

Chapter 8
Towards a Cosmopolitan Urbanism: From Theory to Practice

Leonie Sandercock

Most cities today are demographically multicultural, and more are likely to become so in the foreseeable future. The central question of this chapter is how to come to terms – theoretically, philosophically, and practically – with this empirical urban reality. What can the practice of the Collingwood Neighbourhood House contribute to our theoretical understanding of the possibilities of peaceful co-existence in the mongrel cities of the 21st century? My argument proceeds in four stages. First, I discuss the challenge to our urban sociological imaginations in thinking about how we might live together in all of our differences. Second, I propose the importance of a deeper political and psychological understanding of difference, and its significance in urban politics. Third, I suggest a way of theorizing an intercultural political project for 21st century cities, addressing the shortcomings of 20th century multicultural philosophy. And finally, I link all of these with the actual achievement of the Collingwood Neighbourhood House in the integration of immigrants in Vancouver.

8.1 Introduction

Arriving and departing travelers at Vancouver International Airport are greeted by a huge bronze sculpture of a boatload of strange, mythical creatures. This 7 m long, almost 4 m wide and 4 m high masterpiece, *The Spirit of Haida Gwaii*, is by the late Bill Reid, a member of the Haida Gwaii First Nations from the Pacific Northwest. The canoe has thirteen passengers, spirits or myth creatures from Haida mythology.[1] The bear mother, who is part human, and the bear father sit facing each other at the bow with their two cubs between them. The beaver is paddling menacingly amidships, and behind him is the mysterious intercultural dogfish woman. Shy mouse woman is tucked in the stern. A ferociously playful wolf sinks his fangs into the eagle's wing, and the eagle is attacking the bear's paw. A frog (who symbolizes the ability to cross boundaries between worlds) is partially in, partially out of the canoe.

---

[1] The following description is taken from James Tully's account of the sculpture (Tully 1995: 17–18).

L. Sandercock, G. Attili, *Where Strangers Become Neighbours*, Urban and Landscape Perspectives 4, DOI 10.1007/978-1-4020-9035-6_8
© Springer Science+Business Media 2009

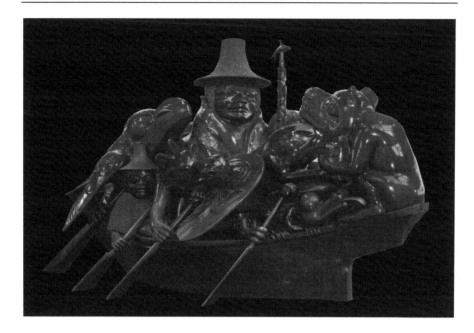

An ancient reluctant conscript paddles stoically. In the centre, holding a speaker's staff in his right hand, stands the chief, whose identity (according to the sculptor) is deliberately uncertain. The legendary raven (master of tricks, transformations, and multiple identities), steers the motley crew. *The Spirit of Haida Gwaii* is a symbol of the "strange multiplicity" of cultural diversity that existed millennia ago and wants to be again (Tully 1995: 18). Amongst other things, this extraordinary work of art speaks of a spirit of mutual recognition and accommodation; a sense of being at home in the multiplicity yet at the same time playfully estranged by it; and the notion of an unending dialogue that is not always harmonious. For the political philosopher James Tully, the wonderfulness of the piece lies in "the ability to see one's own ways as strange and unfamiliar, to stray from and take up a critical attitude toward them and so open cultures to question, reinterpretation, negotiation, transformation, and non-identity (Tully 1995: 206).

The near extermination of the Haida by European imperial expansion is typical of how Aboriginal peoples have fared wherever Europeans settled (Chapter 1). The positioning of the sculpture at Vancouver International Airport, and an identical piece at the Canadian Embassy in Washington, D.C., gives a poignant presence on both coasts of North America to indigenous people who are still struggling today for recognition and restitution.

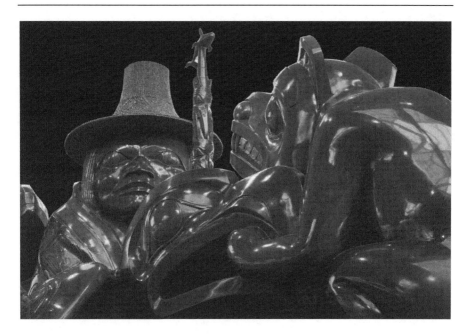

The Spirit of Haida Gwaii stands as a symbol of their survival, resistance, and resurgence, and also perhaps as a more ecumenical symbol for the mutual recognition and affirmation of all cultures that respect other cultures and the earth.

But this sculpture can also be read as a powerful metaphor of contemporary humanity and of the contemporary urban condition, in which people hitherto unused to living side by side are thrust together in what I have called the "mongrel cities" of the 21st century (Sandercock 2003). Most societies today are demographically multicultural, and more are likely to become so in the foreseeable future. The central question of the concluding chapter of this section of the book, then, is how to come to terms with this historical predicament: how can we manage our co-existence in the shared spaces of the multicultural cities of the 21st century? What kind of theoretical challenge is this? In the four-stage argument that follows, I suggest that there is first the challenge to our urban sociological imagination of how we might live together in all of our differences.

In order to act within mongrel cities, we must have a theoretical understanding of "difference" and how it becomes significant in urban politics, in spatial conflicts, in claims over rights to the city.

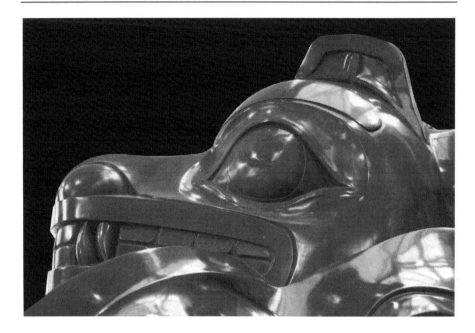

Thus, in the second section, I seek to deepen our psychological and political understanding of the concept of difference and, through this, to explain why a politics of difference is related to basic questions of identity and belonging and therefore cannot be wished away. In the third section, I argue that we need to theorize an intercultural political project for 21st century cities, one that acknowledges and addresses the shortcomings of 20th century multiculturalism and establishes political community rather than ethno-cultural identity as the basis for a sense of belonging in multicultural societies.

And finally, I link all of these with the actual achievement of the Collingwood Neighbourhood House in the integration of immigrants in Vancouver.

8.2 How Might We Live Together? Three Imaginings

8.2.1 Richard Sennett: Togetherness in Difference

In *Flesh and Stone* (1994: 358) Sennett laments that the apparent diversity of Greenwich Village in New York is actually only the diversity of the gaze, rather than a scene of discourse and interaction. He worries that the multiple cultures that inhabit the city are not fused into common purposes, and wonders whether "difference inevitably provokes mutual withdrawal". He assumes (and fears) that if the latter is true, then "a multicultural city cannot have a common civic culture" (Sennett 1994: 358). For Sennett, Greenwich Village poses a particular question of how a diverse civic culture might become something people feel in their bones. He deplores the ethnic separatism of old multi-ethnic New York and longs for evidence of citizens' understanding that they share a common destiny. This becomes a hauntingly reiterated question: nothing less than a moral challenge, the challenge of living together not simply in tolerant indifference to each other, but in active engagement.

For Sennett then, there is a normative imperative in the multicultural city to engage in meaningful intercultural interaction. Why does Sennett assume that sharing a common destiny in the city necessitates more than a willingness to live with difference in the manner of respectful distance? Why should it demand active engagement? He doesn't address these questions, nor does he ask what it would take, sociologically and institutionally, to make such intercultural dialogue and exchange possible, or more likely to happen. But other authors, more recently, have begun to ask, and give tentative answers to, these very questions (Parekh 2000; Amin 2002).

In terms of political philosophy, one might answer that in multicultural societies, composed of many different cultures each of which has different values and practices, and not all of which are entirely comprehensible or acceptable to each other, conflicts are inevitable. In the absence of a *practice* of intercultural dialogue, conflicts are insoluble except by the imposition of one culture's views on another. A society of cultural enclaves and de facto separatism is one in which different cultures do not know how to talk to each other, are not interested in each other's well-being, and assume that they have nothing to learn and nothing to gain from interaction. This becomes a problem for urban governance and for city planning in cities where contact between different cultures is increasingly part of everyday urban life, in spite of the efforts of some groups to avoid "cultural contamination" or ethnic mixture by fleeing to gated communities or so-called ethnic enclaves.

A pragmatic argument then, is that intercultural contact and interaction is a necessary condition for being able to address the inevitable conflicts that will arise in multicultural societies. Another way of looking at the question of why intercultural encounters might be a good thing would start with the acknowledgement that different cultures represent different systems of meaning and versions of the good life.

But each culture realizes only a limited range of human capacities and emotions and grasps only a part of the totality of human existence: it therefore "needs others to understand itself better, expand its intellectual and moral horizon, stretch its imagination and guard it against the obvious temptation to absolutize itself" (Parekh 2000: 336–7). I'd like to think that this latter argument is what Sennett might have had in mind.

8.2.2 James Donald: An Ethical Indifference

In *Imagining the Modern City* (1999), James Donald gives more detailed thought to the question of how we might live together. He is critical of the two most popular contemporary urban imaginings: the traditionalism of the New Urbanism (with its ideal of community firmly rooted in the past), and the cosmopolitanism of Richard Rogers, advisor to former Prime Minister Tony Blair and author of a policy document advocating an urban renaissance, a revitalized and re-enchanted city (Urban Task Force 1999). What's missing from Rogers' vision, according to Donald, is "any real sense of the city not only as a space of community or pleasurable encounters or self-creation, but also as the site of aggression, violence, and paranoia" (Donald 1999: 135).

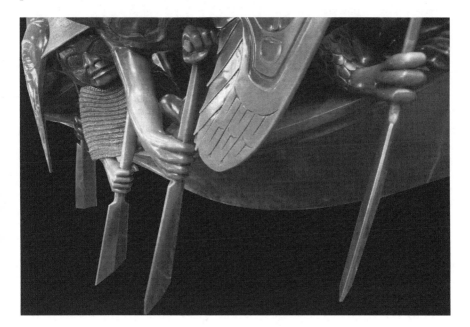

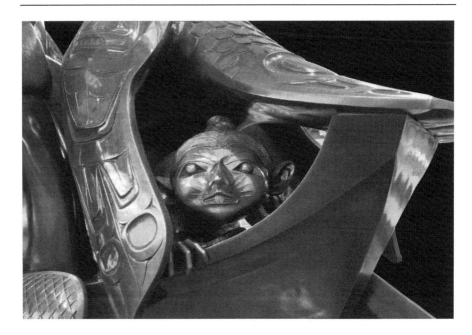

Is it possible, he asks, to imagine change that acknowledges difference without falling into phobic utopianism, communitarian nostalgia, or the disavowal of urban paranoia.

Donald sets up a normative ideal of city life that acknowledges not only the necessary desire for the security of home, but also the inevitability of migration, change and conflict, and thus an "ethical need for an openness to unassimilated otherness" (Donald 1999:145). He argues that it is not possible to domesticate all traces of alterity and difference. "The problem with community is that usually its advocates are referring to some phantom of the past, projected onto some future utopia at the cost of disavowing the unhomely reality of living in the present" (Donald 1999:145). If we start from the reality of living in the present with strangers, then we might ask, what kind of commonality might exist or be brought into being? Donald's answer is "broad social participation in the never completed process of making meanings and creating values … an always emerging, negotiated common culture" (Donald 1999:151). This process requires time and forbearance, not instant fixes. This is community redefined neither as identity nor as place but as a productive process of social interaction, apparently resolving the long-standing problem of the dark side of community, the drawing of boundaries between those who belong and those who don't.

Donald argues that we don't need to share cultural traditions with our neighbors in order to live alongside them, but we do need to be able to talk to them, while also accepting that they are and may remain strangers (as will we).

This is the pragmatic urbanity that can make the violence of living together manageable. Then, urban politics would mean strangers working out how to live together. This is an appropriately political answer to Sennett's question of how multicultural societies might arrive at some workable notion of a common destiny. But when it comes to a thicker description of this "openness to unassimilable difference", the mundane, pragmatic skills of living in the city and sharing urban turf, neither Donald nor Sennett have much to say. Donald suggests

> reading the signs in the street; adapting to different ways of life right on your doorstep; learning tolerance and responsibility – or at least, as Simmel taught us, indifference – towards others and otherness; showing respect, or self-preservation, in not intruding on other people's space; picking up new rules when you migrate to a foreign city" (Donald 1999: 167).

Donald seems to be contradicting himself here in retreating to a position of co-presence and indifference, having earlier advocated something more like an agonistic politics of broad social participation in the *never completed process* of making meanings and an *always emerging* (never congealed), *negotiated common culture.* Surely this participation and negotiation in the interests of peaceful co-existence requires something like daily habits of perhaps quite banal intercultural interaction in order to establish a basis for dialogue, which is difficult, if not impossible, without some pre-existing trust. I will turn to Ash Amin for a discussion of how and where this daily interaction and negotiation of ethnic (and other) differences might be encouraged.

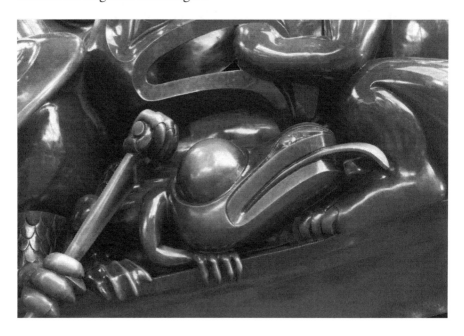

8.2.3 Ash Amin: A Politics of Local Liveability

Ash Amin's report, *Ethnicity and the Multicultural City. Living with Diversity* (2002), was commissioned by the British government's Department of Transport, Local Government and the Regions in the wake of the (so-called) "race riots" in three northern British cities in the summer of 2001. This report is a self-described "think piece" that uses the 2001 riots as a springboard "to discuss what it takes to combat racism, live with difference and encourage mixture in a multicultural and multiethnic society" (Amin 2002:2). Amin's paper is in part a critique of a document produced by the British Home Office (*Building Cohesive Communities*, Home Office 2001). It goes deeper and draws on different sources than the Home Office document. The political economy approach of the Home

Office analysis of the riots never once mentions globalization, or the colonial past (see Chapter 1 of this book). That is Amin's starting point. The dominant ethnic groups present in Bradford, Burnley and Oldham are Pakistani and Bangladeshi, of both recent and longer-term migrations. What this reflects is the twin and interdependent forces of postcolonialism and globalization.

As several scholars have pointed out (Sassen 1996; Rocco 2000), the contemporary phenomena of immigration and ethnicity are constitutive of globalization and are reconfiguring the spaces of and social relations in cities in new ways. Cultures from all over the world are being de- and re-territorialized in global cities, whose neighborhoods accordingly become "globalized localities" (Albrow 1997: 51). The spaces created by the complex and multidimensional processes of globalization have become strategic sites for the formation of transnational identities and communities, as well as for new hybrid identities and complicated experiences and redefinitions of notions of "home". As Sassen has argued:

> What we still narrate in the language of immigration and ethnicity…is actually a series of processes having to do with the globalization of economic activity, of cultural activity, of identity formation. Too often immigration and ethnicity are constituted as otherness. Understanding them as a set of processes whereby global elements are localized, international labor markets are constituted, and cultures from all over the world are de- and re-territorialized, puts them right there at the center along with the internationalization of capital, as a fundamental aspect of globalization (Sassen 1996: 218).

This is the context for Amin's interpretative essay on the civil disturbances, which he sees as having both material and symbolic dimensions. He draws on ethnographic research to deepen understanding of both dimensions, as well as to assist in his argument for a focus on the everyday urban, "the daily negotiation of ethnic difference". Ethnographic research in the UK on areas of significant racial antagonism has identified two types of neighbourhood. The first are old white working class areas in which successive waves of non-white immigration have been accompanied by continuing socio-economic deprivation and cultural and/or physical isolation "between white residents lamenting the loss of a golden ethnically undisturbed past, and non-whites claiming a right of place". The second are "white flight" suburbs and estates that have become the refuge of an upwardly mobile working class and a fearful middle class disturbed by what they see as the replacement of a "homely white nation" by foreign cultural contamination. Here, white supremacist values are activated to terrorize the few immigrants who try to settle there. The riots of 2001 displayed the processes at work in the first type of neighborhood, but also the white fear and antagonism typical of the second type (Amin 2002: 2).

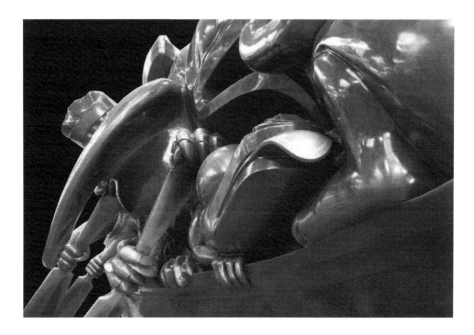

What is important to understand is that the cultural dynamics in these two types of neighbourhood are very different from those in other ethnically mixed cities and neighbourhoods where greater social and physical mobility, a local history of compromises, and a supportive local institutional infrastructure have come to support co-habitation.

For example, in the Tooting neighbourhood of South London, Martin Albrow's research inquired about the strength of "locality" and "community" among a wide range of local inhabitants, from those born there to recent arrivals, and among all the most prominent ethnic groups. His analysis reveals that locality has much less salience for individuals and for social relations than older research paradigms invested in "community" allow. His study reveals a very liquid sense of identity and belonging. His interviewees' stories suggest the possibility that:

> Individuals with very different lifestyles and social networks can live in close proximity without untoward interference with each other. There is an old community for some, for others there is a new site for community which draws its culture from India. For some, Tooting is a setting for peer group leisure activity, for others it provides a place to sleep and access to London. It can be a spectacle for some, for others the anticipation of a better, more multicultural community (Albrow 1997: 51).

In this middle income locality there is nothing like the traditional concept of community based on a shared local culture. Albrow describes a situation of "minimum levels of tolerable co-existence" and civil inattention and avoidance strategies that prevent friction between people living different lifestyles. The locality is criss-crossed by networks of social relations whose scope and extent range from neighbouring houses and a few weeks acquaintance to religious and kin relations spanning generations and continents.

This study gives us an important insight into the changing social relations within globalized localities. Where is community here? It may be nowhere, says Albrow, and this new situation therefore needs a new vocabulary.

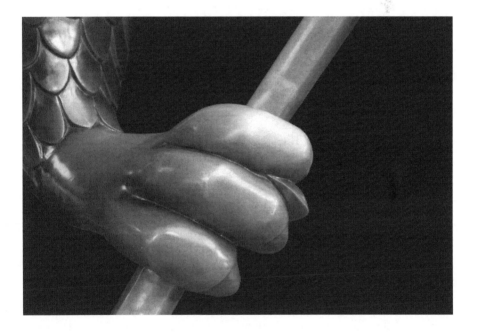

How meaningful is the newly promoted (by the Home Office) notion of community cohesion, when people's affective ties are not necessarily related to the local place where they live? Where is the deconstruction, and reconstruction, of what "community" might mean in the globalized localities of mongrel cities? "Globalization makes co-present enclaves of diverse origins one possible social configuration characterizing a new Europe" (Albrow 1997: 54).

While Albrow's research seems to support the urban imaginings of James Donald, discussed earlier, in terms of the feasibility of an attitude of tolerant indifference and co-presence, the difference between Tooting and the northern mill towns that are the subject of Amin's reflection is significant. In those one-industry towns, when the mills declined, white and non-white workers alike were unemployed. The largest employers soon became the public services, but discrimination kept most of these jobs for whites. Non-whites pooled resources and opened shops, takeaways, minicab businesses. There was intense competition for low-paid and precarious work. Economic uncertainty and related social deprivation has been a constant for over twenty years and "a pathology of social rejection...reinforces family and communalist bonds" (Amin 2002:4). Ethnic resentment has bred on this socio-economic deprivation and sense of desperation. It is in such areas that social cohesion and cultural interchange have failed.

What conclusions does Amin draw from this? How can fear and intolerance be challenged, how might residents begin to negotiate and come to terms with difference in the city? Amin's answer is interesting. The contact spaces of housing estates and public places fall short of nurturing inter-ethnic understanding, he argues, "because they are not spaces of interdependence and habitual engagement" (Amin 2002: 12).

He goes on to suggest that the sites for coming to terms with ethnic (and surely other) differences are the "micro-publics" where dialogue and prosaic negotiations are compulsory, in sites such as the workplace, schools, colleges, youth centers, sports clubs, community centers, neighbourhood houses, and the micro-publics of "banal transgression", (such as colleges of further education) in which people from different cultural backgrounds are thrown together in new settings which disrupt familiar patterns and create the possibility of initiating new attachments. Other sites of banal transgression include community gardens, child-care facilities, community centers, neighbourhood watch schemes, youth projects, and regeneration of derelict spaces. I have provided just such an example (Sandercock 2003: Chapter 7), the Community Fire Station in the Handsworth neighbourhood of Birmingham, where white Britons are working alongside Asian and Afro-Caribbean Britons in a variety of projects for neighborhood regeneration and improvement. The Collingwood Neighbourhood House in Vancouver is an even better example of a successful site of intercultural interaction, as I will argue in the final section of this chapter. Part of what happens in such everyday contacts is the overcoming of feelings of strangeness in the simple process of sharing everyday tasks and comparing ways of doing things. But such initiatives will not automatically become sites of social inclusion. They also need organizational and discursive strategies that are designed to build voice, to foster a sense of common benefit, to develop confidence among disempowered groups, and to arbitrate when disputes arise. The essential point is that "changes in attitude and behavior spring from lived experiences" (Amin 2002: 15).

The practical implication of Amin's work, then, is that the project of living with diversity needs to be worked at "in the city's micro-publics of banal multicultures" (Amin 2002: 13). It is clear from Albrow's work, as well as that of Amin, that in today's globalized localities one cannot assume a shared sense of place and that this is not the best "glue" for understanding and co-existence within multicultural neighbourhoods. Ethnographic research on urban youth cultures referred to by Amin confirms the existence of a strong sense of place among white and non-white ethnic groups, but it is a sense of place based on turf claims and defended in exclusionary ways. The distinctive feature of mixed neighbourhoods is that they are "communities without community, each marked by multiple and hybrid affiliations of varying geographical reach" (Amin 2002: 16).

There are clear limits then to how far "community cohesion" can become the basis of living with difference. Amin suggests a different vocabulary of local accommodation to difference – "a vocabulary of rights of presence, bridging difference, getting along" (Amin 2002: 17). To adopt the language of Henri Lefebvre, this could be expressed as the right to difference, and the right to the city. The achievement of these rights depends on a politics of active local citizenship, an agonistic politics (as sketched by Donald) of broad social participation in the never completed process of making meanings, and an always emerging, negotiated common culture. But it also depends on an *intercultural political culture*, that is, one with effective antiracism policies, with strong legal, institutional and informal sanctions against racial and cultural hatred, a public culture that no longer treats immigrants as "guests", and a truly inclusive political system at all levels of governance. This is the subject of the third section of this chapter. In the second section I take up the issue of difference and identity in relation to national belonging and question the adequacy of framing the issues of an intercultural society through the language of race and minority ethnicity. A significant dimension of the civil disturbances in Britain in 2001 was this aspect of identity and belonging, and this spills over into the next section.

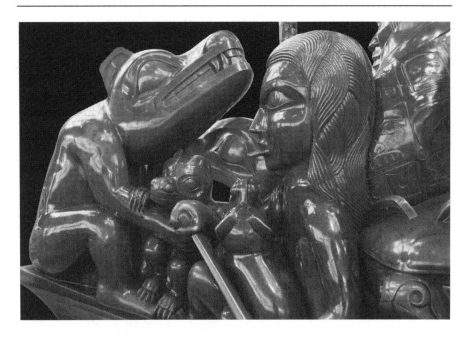

8.3 Thinking Through Identity/Difference

We have norms of acceptability and those who come into our home – for that is what it is – should accept those norms (David Blunkett, quoted in Alibhai-Brown 2001).

> ...seven years ago I finally decided this place was my place, and that was because I had a daughter whose father was of these islands. This did not make me any less black, Asian or Muslim – those identities are in my blood, thick and forever. But it made me kick more vigorously at those stern, steely gates that keep people of color outside the heart of the nation then blame them for fighting each other in the multicultural wastelands into which the establishment has pushed them. A number of us broke through. The going was (and still is) incredibly hard but we are in now and, bit by bit, the very essence of Britishness is being transformed (Alibhai-Brown 2001).

The above remarks of David Blunkett were made in December of 2001, after Britain's summer of "race riots". It was a time of questioning of the previous half-century of immigration, the race relations problems that had emerged, and the policy response of multiculturalism. At the heart of this questioning was a perturbation over what it meant/means to be British (an agonizing which has only heightened since the terrorist bombings in

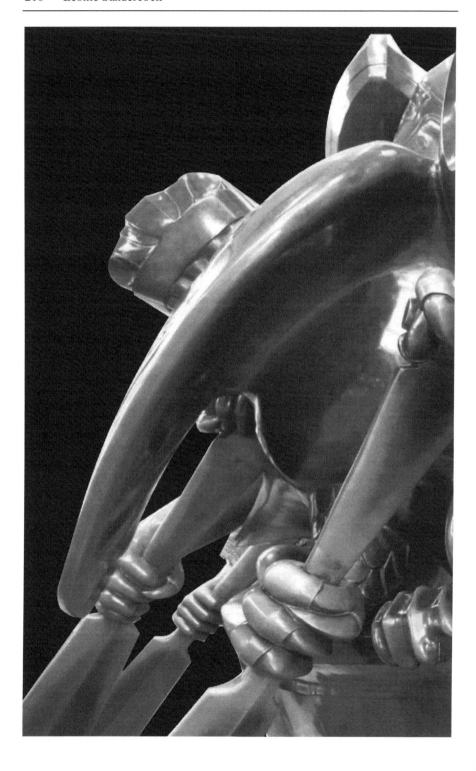

London in the summer of 2005). Notions of identity were being unsettled. The response of Blunkett, the Home Secretary in the Blair government, was a rather crude reassertion of us-and-them thinking. His words epitomize a long-standing but much-contested view that immigrants are guests in the home of the host nation and must behave the way their hosts want them to behave: adopt the norms of "Britishness", or get out. Implicit in this view is that there is only one correct way to be British and that it is the responsibility of newcomers to learn how to fit in with that way. Yasmin Alibhai-Brown, herself an immigrant of three decades standing, contests this pure and static notion of national identity, counterposing it with a notion of a more inclusive, dynamic and evolving identity which can accommodate the new hybrid realities of a changing culture. She urges "a national conversation about our collective identity" (Alibhai-Brown 2000:10)

At stake here, and across European (or any of the large number of globalizing) cities today, are contested notions of identity and understandings of difference, and conflicting ways of belonging and feeling at home in the world. The Home Secretary expresses the view that there is a historic Britishness that must be protected from impurity. (Sections of the Austrian, Danish, French, Italian and Dutch populations have expressed similar antagonisms in recent years). In this view, what it means to be British, to be "at home" in Britain, is being threatened by immigrants who bring a different cultural baggage with them. Interestingly, the (fragile) notion of identity at the heart of this view is one that is both afraid of and yet dependent on difference. How does this apparent psychological paradox work?

When a person's self-identity is insecure or fragile, doubts about that identity (and how it relates to national identity may be part of the insecurity), are posed and resolved by the constitution of an Other against which that identity may define itself, and assert its superiority. In order to feel "at home" in the nation and in the wider world, this fragile sense of identity seeks to subdue or erase from consciousness (or worse) that which is strange, those who are "not like us". Attempts to protect the purity and certainty of a hegemonic identity – Britishness, Danishness, and so on - by defining certain differences as independent sites of evil, or disloyalty, or disorder, have a long history.[2] There are diverse political tactics through which doubts about self-identity are posed and resolved, but the general

---

[2] For much of my interpretation in this section I am indebted to the work of William Connolly (1991, 1995) and Julia Kristeva (1991).

strategy is the establishing of a *system of identity and difference* which is given legal sanctions, which defines who belongs and who does not. Over long periods of time, these systems of identity and difference become congealed as cultural norms and beliefs, entrenching themselves as the hegemonic status quo. Evil infiltrates the public domain, Connolly (1991) argues, when attempts are made to secure the surety of self- and national identity – and the powers and privileges that accompany it – with spatial and social and economic policies that demand conformity with a previously scripted identity, while defining the outsider as an outsider, (a polluter of pure identities), in perpetuity.

There is a fascinating paradox in the relationship between identity and difference. The quest for a pure and unchanging *identity* (an undiluted Britishness, or Brummie-ness, or Danishness...) is at once framed by and yet seeks to eliminate difference; it seeks the conformity, disappearance, or invisibility of the Other. That is the paradox of identity. But what of *difference* and *its* political strategies? Surely difference, too, is constituted by its Other – as woman is in patriarchal societies, or to be gay and lesbian in heterosexual societies, or to be Black in white societies – and so is constituted by the hegemonic identity which it resists and seeks to change. Difference, defined as that which is outside, in opposition to the congealed norms of any society, is constituted by/against hegemonic identity. Identity and difference then are an intertwined and always historically specific system of dialectical relations, fundamental to which is inclusion (belonging) and its opposite, exclusion (not belonging). Here then is a double paradox. Some notion of identity is, arguably, indispensable to life itself (Connolly 1991), and some sense of culturally-based identity would seem to be inescapable, in that all human beings are culturally embedded (Parekh 2000: 336).[3] But while the politics of pure identity seeks to eliminate the Other, the politics of difference seeks recognition and inclusion.

A more robust sense of identity must be able to embrace cultural autonomy and, at the same time, work to strengthen intercultural solidarity. If one dimension of such a cultural pluralism is a concern with reconciling old and new identities by accepting the inevitability of "hybridity", or "mongrelization", then another is the commitment to actively contest what

---

[3] "Culturally embedded" in the sense that we grow up and live within a culturally structured world, organise our lives and social relations within its system of meaning and significance, and place some value on our cultural identity (Parekh 200: 336)

is to be valued across diverse cultures. Thus Alibhai-Brown feels "under no obligation to bring my daughter and son up to drink themselves to death in a pub for a laugh", nor does she want to see young Asian and Muslim women imprisoned in "high-pressure ghettoes…in the name of *culture*", a culture that forces obedience to patriarchal authority and arranged marriages (Alibhai-Brown 2001). Negotiating new identities, then, becomes central to daily social and spatial practices, as newcomers assert their rights to the city, to make a home for themselves, to occupy and transform space.[4]

What now seems insidious in terms of debates about belonging in relation to the nation is the way in which the identities of minorities have been essentialised on the grounds of culture and ethnicity. The ethnicization and racialization of the identities of non-white or non-Anglo people in western liberal democracies, even the most officially multicultural among them (Canada and Australia), has had the effect of bracketing them as minorities, as people whose claims can only ever be minor within a national culture and frame of national belonging defined by others and their majority histories, usually read as histories of white belonging and white supremacy (Amin 2002: 21; Hage 1998). But the claims of the Asian youths in Britain's northern mill towns, just as those of Black Britons or "Lebanese Australians" or "Chinese Canadians", are claims for more than minority recognition and minority rights. Theirs is a claim for the mainstream, (or perhaps it is a claim for "the end of mainstream" (Dang 2002)), for a metaphorical shift from the margins to the centre, both in terms of the right to visibility and the right to reshape that mainstream. It is nothing less than a claim to full citizenship and a public naming of what has hitherto prevented that full citizenship – the assumption that to be British, Canadian, Danish, Dutch, and so on, is to be white, and part of white culture. As long as that assumption remains intact, the status of minority ethnic groups in all the western democracies will remain of a different order to that of whites, always under question, always at the mercy of the "tolerance" of the dominant culture, a tolerance built on an unequal power relationship (Hage 1998).

The crucial implication of this discussion is that in order to enable all citizens, regardless of "race" or ethnicity or any other cultural criteria, to become equal members of the nation and contribute to an *evolving*

---

[4] Or as previously dominated groups such as gays and lesbians, women, people with disabilities, decide to engage in a politics of identity/difference, a politics of place-claiming and place-making (Kenney 2001).

national identity, "the ethnic moorings of national belonging need to be exposed and replaced by criteria that have nothing to do with whiteness" (Amin 2002: 22). Or as Gilroy (2000: 328) puts it, "the racial ontology of sovereign territory" needs to be recognized and contested. This requires an imagination of the nation as something other than a racial or ethnic territorial space, perhaps an imagination that conceives the nation as a space of traveling cultures and peoples with varying degrees and geographies of attachment. Such a move must insist that race and ethnicity are taken out of the definition of national identity and national belonging "and replaced by ideals of citizenship, democracy and political community" (Amin 2002: 23). This brings me to the necessity of rethinking 20th century notions of multiculturalism (based on ethno-cultural recognition), and that is the subject of the third section of this chapter.

8.4 Reconsidering Multiculturalism

As a *fact*, multiculturalism describes the increasing cultural diversity of societies in late modernity. Empirically, many societies and many cities could be described today as multicultural. But very few countries have embraced and institutionalised an *ideology* of multiculturalism. Australia and Canada have done so since the late 1960s, as have Singapore and

Malaysia, although the latter pair of countries have a different interpretation of multiculturalism than do the former pair. During the same period, the USA has lived through its "multicultural wars", still uneasy with the whole notion, preferring the traditional "melting pot" metaphor and its associated politics of assimilation. France has been most adamant that there is no place for any kind of political recognition of difference in their republic. The Dutch and the Danish, once the most open to multicultural policy claims, have each begun to pull up the drawbridges since 2002. Each country has a different definition of multiculturalism, different sets of public policies to deal with/respond to cultural difference, and correspondingly different definitions of citizenship.

As an *ideology*, then, multiculturalism has a multiplicity of meanings. What is common in the sociological content of the term in the West – but never spoken of – is that it was formulated as a framework, a set of policies, for the national accommodation of non-white immigration. It was a liberal response that skirted the reality of the already racialized constitution of these societies and masked the existence of institutionalised racism.[5] The histories of multicultural philosophies are in fact much more complex and contested than this, and genealogical justice cannot be done without a much more contextualised discussion of each country, which is not my purpose here. So instead, drawing on the distinguished British cultural studies scholar Stuart Hall, I will simply summarise the *range* of meanings that have been given to multiculturalism as ideology, and some of the dangers embedded in it.

Hall (2000) theorizes the multicultural question as both a global and local terrain of political contestation with crucial implications for the West. It is contested by the conservative Right, in defense of the purity and cultural integrity of the nation. It is contested by liberals, who claim that the "cult of ethnicity", the notion of "group rights", and the pursuit of "difference" threaten the universalism and neutrality of the liberal state. Multiculturalism is also contested by "modernizers of various political persuasions". For them, the triumph of the (alleged) universalism of western civilization over the particularisms of ethnic, religious, and racial belonging established in the Enlightenment marked an entirely worthy transition from tradition to modernity that is, and should be, irreversible. Some postmodern versions of *cosmopolitanism* oppose multiculturalism as imposing a too narrow, or closed, sense of identity. Some radicals argue

---

[5]   See Hage (1998), on Australia; Hesse (2000) and Hall (2000), on the UK; Bannerji (1995, 2000), on Canada.

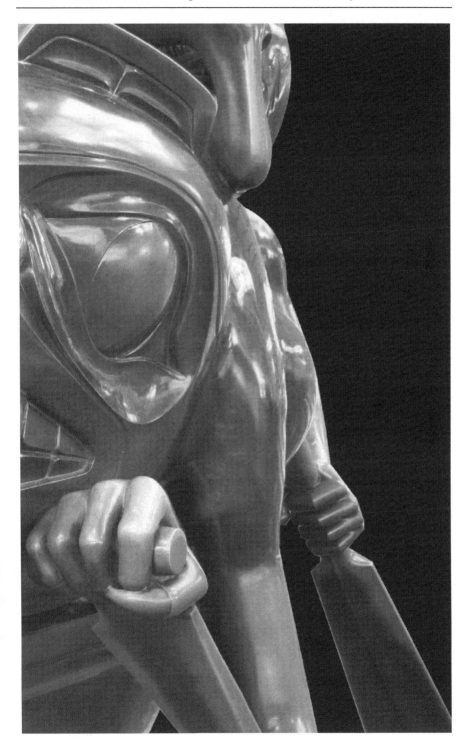

that multiculturalism divides along ethnic lines what should be a united front of race and class against injustice and exploitation. Others point to commercialised, boutique, or consumerist multiculturalism as celebrating difference without making a difference (Hall 2000: 211).

Clearly, multiculturalism is not a single doctrine and does not represent an already achieved state of affairs. It describes a variety of political strategies and processes that are everywhere incomplete. Just as there are different multicultural societies, so there are different multiculturalisms.

Conservative multiculturalism insists on the assimilation of difference into the traditions and customs of the majority. Liberal multiculturalism seeks to integrate the different cultural groups as fast as possible into the "mainstream" provided by a universal individual citizenship... Pluralist multiculturalism formally enfranchises the differences between groups along cultural lines and accords different group rights to different communities within a more...communitarian political order. Commercial multiculturalism assumes that if the diversity of individuals from different communities is recognized in the marketplace, then the problems of cultural difference will be dissolved through private consumption, without any need for a redistribution of power and resources. Corporate multiculturalism (public or private) seeks to "manage" minority cultural differences in the interests of the center. Critical or "revolutionary"

multiculturalism foregrounds power, privilege, the hierarchy of oppressions and the movements of resistance... And so on (Hall 2000: 210).

Can a concept that has so many valences and such diverse and contradictory enemies possibly have any further use value? Alternatively, is its contested status precisely its value, an indication that a radical pluralist ethos is alive and well?

Given that we live in an age of migration (Castles and Miller 1998), we are inevitably implicated in the politics of multiculturalism. This in turn demands a rethinking of traditional notions of citizenship as well as a lot of new thinking about the social integration of immigrants. Given this 21st century urban reality, we need to find a way to publicly manifest the significance of cultural diversity, and to debate the value of various identitics/differences; that is, to ask which differences exist, but should not, and which do not exist, but should.[6] Far from banishing the concept to political purgatory, we need to give it as rich a substance as possible, a substance that expands political possibilities and identities rather than purifying or closing them down. This leads me to re-theorise multi-culturalism, *which I prefer to re-name as interculturalism,* as a poli-tical and philosophical basis for thinking about how to deal with the challenge of difference in the mongrel cities of the 21st century.

My intercultural theory is composed of the following premises:

> The cultural embeddedness of humans is inescapable. We grow up in a culturally structured world, are deeply shaped by it, and necessarily view the world from within a specific culture. We are also capable of critically evaluating our own culture's beliefs and practices, and of understanding and appreciating as well as criticizing those of other cultures. But some form of cultural identity and belonging seems unavoidable.
>
> "Culture" cannot be understood as static, eternally given, essentialist. It is always evolving, dynamic and hybrid of necessity. All cultures, even allegedly conservative or traditional ones, contain multiple differences within themselves that are continually being re-negotiated.

---

[6] See Chantal Mouffe's discussion of this dilemma in her case for an agonistic democratic politics in *The Democratic Paradox* (2000).

Cultural diversity is a positive thing, and intercultural dialogue is a necessary element of culturally diverse societies. No culture is perfect or can be perfected, but all cultures have something to learn from and contribute to others. Cultures grow through the everyday practices of social interaction.

The political contestation of interculturalism is inevitable, as diverse publics debate the merits of multiple identity/difference claims for rights.

At the core of interculturalism as a daily political practice are two rights: the right to difference and the right to the city. The right to difference means recognizing the legitimacy and specific needs of minority or subaltern cultures. The right to the city is the right to presence, to occupy public space, and to participate as an equal in public affairs.

The "right to difference" at the heart of interculturalism must be perpetually contested against other rights (for example, human rights) and redefined according to new formulations and considerations.

The notion of the perpetual contestation of interculturalism implies an agonistic democratic politics that demands active citizenship and daily negotiations of difference in all of the banal sites of intercultural interaction.

A sense of belonging in an intercultural society cannot be based on race, religion, or ethnicity but needs to be based on a shared commitment to political community. Such a commitment requires an empowered citizenry.

Reducing fear and intolerance can only be achieved by addressing the material as well as cultural dimensions of 'recognition'. This means addressing the prevailing inequalities of political and economic power as well as developing new stories about and symbols of national and local identity and belonging.

There are (at least) two public goods embedded in a version of interculturalism based on these understandings. One is the critical freedom to question in thought, and challenge in practice, one's inherited cultural ways. The other is the recognition of the widely-shared aspiration to belong to a culture and a place, and so to be at home in the world (Tully 1995). This sense of belonging would be lost if one's culture were

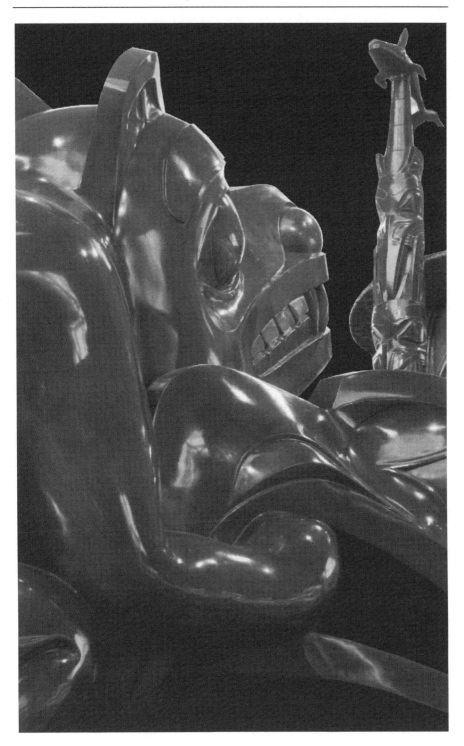

excluded, or if it was imposed on everyone. But there can also be a sense of belonging that comes from being associated with other cultures, gaining in strength and compassion from accommodation among and interrelations with others, and it is important to recognize and nurture those spaces of accommodation and intermingling.

This understanding of interculturalism accepts the indispensability of group identity to human life (and therefore to politics), precisely because it is inseparable from belonging. But this acceptance needs to be complicated by an insistence, a vigorous struggle against the idea that one's own group identity has a claim to intrinsic truth. If we can acknowledge a drive within ourselves, and within all of our particular cultures, to naturalise the identities given to us, we can simultaneously be vigilant about the danger implicit in this drive, which is the almost irresistible desire to impose one's identity, one's way of life, one's very definition of normality and of goodness, on others. Thus we arrive at a lived conception of identity/difference that recognizes itself as *historically contingent and inherently relational*; and a cultivation of a care for difference through strategies of critical detachment from the identities that constitute us (Connolly 1991; Tully 1995). In this intercultural imagination, the twin goods of belonging and of freedom can be made to support rather than oppose each other.

From an intercultural perspective, the good society does not commit itself to a particular vision of the good life and then ask how much diversity it can tolerate within the limits set by this vision. To do so would be to foreclose future societal development. Rather, an intercultural perspective advocates accepting the reality and desirability of cultural diversity and then structuring political life accordingly. At the very least, this political life must be dialogically and agonistically constituted. But the dialogue requires certain *institutional preconditions*, such as freedom of speech, participatory public spaces, empowered citizens, agreed procedures and basic ethical norms, and the active policing of discriminatory practices. It also calls for

> such essential political virtues as mutual respect and concern, tolerance, self-restraint, willingness to enter into unfamiliar worlds of thought, love of diversity, a mind open to new ideas and a heart open to others' needs, and the ability to persuade and live with unresolved differences (Parekh 2000: 340).

A notion of the common good is vital to any political community. From an intercultural perspective, this common good must be generated not by transcending or ignoring cultural and other differences (the liberal position), but through their interplay in a dialogical, agonistic political life. Finally, a sense of belonging, which is important in any society, cannot in multicultural societies be based on ethnicity or on shared cultural, ethnic or other characteristics. An intercultural society is too diverse for that. A sense of belonging must ultimately be political, based on a shared commitment to a political community (Parekh 2000: 341; Amin 2002: 23).

Since commitment, or belonging, must be reciprocal, citizens will not feel these things unless their political community is also committed to them and makes them feel that they belong. And here is the challenge. An intercultural political community

> cannot expect its members to develop a sense of belonging to it unless it equally values and cherishes them in all their diversity, and reflects this in its structure, policies, conduct of public affairs, self-understanding and self-definition (Parekh 2000:342).

It would be safe to say that no existing (self-described) multicultural society can yet claim to have achieved this state of affairs, for reasons that have already been elaborated: political and economic inequalities accompanied by an unresolved postcolonial condition that we may as well name as racism. But in recent years these issues have been identified, increasingly documented, and are becoming the focus of political activity in many countries.

8.5 Conclusions: The Marriage of Theory and Practice

This chapter has outlined three main elements of a cosmopolitan urbanism, or intercultural political philosophy. What has emerged from the descriptions and analysis of the Collingwood Neighbourhood House in previous chapters is that this local institution is a catalyst for and a working example of living together and bridging vast cultural differences. With many different ethnocultural groups living in this one territorially defined neighbourhood, it is neither the existence of a common culture (ethnically defined) nor a shared sense of attachment to place that makes this neighbourhood a community. Rather, what has happened in the period of twenty years of rapid demographic change from a predominantly Anglo-European to a much more ethnically mixed population is exactly what James Donald theorized, "a broad social participation in the never completed process of making meanings and creating values, an always emerging, negotiated common culture".

But that "common culture" is not ethno-culturally grounded, nor is it the result of one dominant culture imposing its lifeways on all the rest. Rather, it is a negotiated sharing of values, established through broad social participation. This is community redefined neither as identity nor as place, but as a productive process of social interaction. The CNH is indeed a physical place: many folks even refer to it as a blessed place (as the DVD shows), one that has helped to create a sense of belonging. But, perhaps paradoxically, that belonging is only partially to do with the actual physical place, and more profoundly to do with the lived experience of building relationships. As James Donald proposed in his normative ideal, we don't need to share cultural traditions with our neighbours in order to live alongside them, but we do need to be able to talk to them. CNH has created that space for intercultural dialogue, for exchange across cultural difference, which is the precondition for relationship building.

The secret of this remarkable achievement is in the CNH mission, which embodies Ash Amin's normative ideal of a politics of local liveability, nurtured through daily habits of "quite banal intercultural interaction in order to establish a basis for dialogue". At CNH, these daily habits of banal interaction occur around childcare, around the learning of English as a second language, around preparing and/or sharing meals together, and sharing a multitude of other training and learning and recreational opportunities. In these "micro-public spaces", these sites of everyday encounter and prosaic negotiation of difference, people from different cultural backgrounds come together, initially in quite practical ways, but in these moments of coming together there is always the possibility of dialogue, of initiating new attachments. And that is what happens at and through CNH. Part of what happens through such everyday contact is the gradual overcoming of feelings of strangeness in the simple process of sharing everyday tasks and/or challenges and comparing ways of doing things.

But such initiatives do not automatically become sites of social inclusion. They need organizational and discursive strategies that are designed to build voice, to foster a sense of common benefit, to develop confidence among disempowered groups, and to arbitrate when disputes arise. And that is precisely, and systematically, what the CNH Board and leadership have done through two decades of social and demographic change. They have consciously diversified as a Board, and in the selection of staff and nurturing of volunteers. They have consciously chosen not to provide any programs or services on an ethno-culturally specific basis. They have systematically conducted outreach to marginalized groups such as First Nations and youth. They have systematically organized anti-racism and diversity training for staff and volunteers, and empowered youth to run their own anti-bullying, anti-racism and drug counseling programs. And they have proactively developed programs for homeless people. All of which reflects the values of social justice and social inclusion embedded in the mission of CNH.

CNH's vocabulary of accommodation to difference is a vocabulary of "rights of presence, bridging difference, getting along", just as proposed in Amin's normative ideal. And an important part of this pragmatic vocabulary is the recognition of conflict as inevitable, and a commitment (described in detail in Chapter 6 by Paula Carr and Val Cavers) to work through such conflict, acknowledging whatever fears and anxieties have been triggered, and devoting time to listening, talking through and arriving at new accommodations that work for residents. But these local, neighbourhood-based organizational and discursive strategies cannot endure, let alone thrive, in the absence of a broader intercultural political culture: that is, one with effective anti-racism policies, with strong legal, institutional and informal sanctions against racial and cultural hatred and a public culture that no longer treats immigrants as "guests". We saw in Chapter 3 why such a local experiment, in Frankfurt, failed in the 1990s in the absence of this broader political culture. We also saw, in all of Part 1, how Canada as a nation and Vancouver as a city have striven, albeit imperfectly, to create such a political culture over the past three decades.

One very important aspect of Canada's evolving political culture at federal government level, especially in the past decade, through the Department of Canadian Heritage, has been the effort to create a sense of national identity and national belonging that is grounded in ideals of active citizenship, democracy and political community, rather than in notions of "Canadianness" grounded in race or ethnicity (the latter being the case in most European countries). This very important shift is also a shift in the meaning of multiculturalism, from its earlier incarnation emphasizing recognition and support of all immigrant cultures and the celebration of ethno-cultural differences, to an intercultural position emphasising the building of bridges between cultures. And this has been reflected in actual funding shifts, away from the support of ethno-culturally specific organizations or facilities (such as a Chinese Cultural Centre or a Vietnamese Seniors Centre) to organizations with explicit intercultural mandates, like CNH. In the process, the essential political virtues of a cosmopolitan urbanism (or an intercultural society) are being nurtured: the virtues of mutual respect and concern, tolerance, self-restraint, love of diversity, minds open to new ideas and hearts open to the needs of others. In embodying these virtues, nurturing them, and pursuing them through relationship building in everyday life, the Collingwood Neighbourhood House is a microcosm of all that Canada aspires to be (but is not, yet). It is a marriage of the theory and practice of cosmopolitan urbanism.

References

Albrow M (1997) Travelling beyond local cultures: Socioscapes in a global city. In: Eade J (ed) Living the global city. Globalization as a local process. Routledge, London

Alibhai-Brown Y (2000) Diversity versus Multiculturalism, The Daily Telegraph, 23 May

Alibhai-Brown Y (2001) Mr. Blunkett has insulted all of us, The Independent, 10 December.

Amin A (2002) Ethnicity and the multicultural city. Living with Diversity. Report for the Department of Transport, Local Government and the Regions. University of Durham, Durham

Bannerji H (1995) Thinking through. Women's Press, Toronto

Bannerji H (2000). The Dark side of the nation: Essays on multiculturalism, nationalism and gender. Canadian Scholars' Press Inc., Toronto

Castles S and M Miller (1998) The Age of Migration, 2nd ed. The Guilford Press: New York

Connolly W (1991) Identity\difference. Cornell University Press, Ithaca

Connolly W (1995) The ethos of pluralization. University of Minnesota Press, Minneapolis

Dang S (2002) Creating cosmopolis: The end of mainstream Unpublished Masters Thesis, School of Community and Regional Planning, University of British Columbia

Donald J (1999) Imagining the modern city. The Athlone Press, London

Gilroy P (2000) Between camps. Penguin, London

Hage G (1998) White nation: Fantasies of white supremacy in a multicultural society. Pluto Press, Sydney

Hall S (2000) Conclusion: The multi-cultural question. In: Hesse B (ed) Un/settled multiculturalisms. Zed Books, London

Hesse B (2000) Introduction: Un/settled multiculturalisms. In: Hesse B (ed) Un/settled multiculturalisms. Zed Books, London

Home Office (2001) Building cohesive communities: A report of the ministerial group on public order and community cohesion. Home Office/Her Majesty's Government, London

Kenney M (2001) Mapping gay L.A. The intersection of place and politics. Temple University Press, Philadelphia

Kristeva J (1991) Strangers to ourselves Columbia University Press, New York. Translated by Leon S. Roudiez

Mouffe C (2000) The democratic paradox. Verso, London

Parekh B (2000) Rethinking multiculturalism. Macmillan, London

Rocco R (2000) Associational rights-claims, civil society and place. In: Isin E (ed) Democracy, Citizenship and the global city. Routledge, London

Sandercock L (2003) Cosmopolis 2: Mongrel cities of the 21st century. Continuum, London

Sassen S (1996) Whose city is it? Globalization and the formation of new claims, Public Culture, 8:pp 205–223

Sennett R (1994) Flesh and stone. The body and the city in Western Civilization. Norton, New York

Tully J (1995) Strange multiplicity. Constitutionalism in an age of diversity. Cambridge University Press, Cambridge

Urban Task Force (1999) Towards an urban renaissance. E & FN Spon, London

Young I (1990) Justice and the politics of difference. Princeton University Press, Princeton, NJ

Part III
Film as Action Research

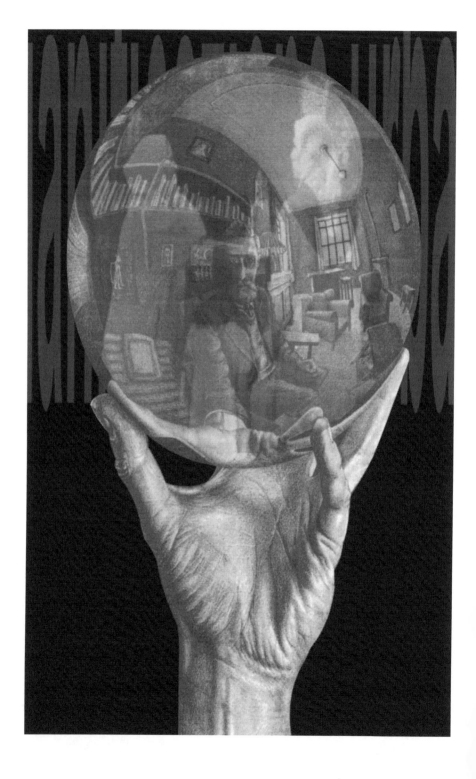

Chapter 9
"Where Strangers Become Neighbours":
The Story of a Research, the Research of a Story

Giovanni Attili

9.1 Storytelling and Planning

The documentary "Where strangers become neighbours" is part of a research project called "From the Campfire to the Computer: the powers and limitations of story and storytelling in planning research and practice" which was funded by Canada's Social Sciences and Humanities Research Council (SSHRC), a federal agency that promotes and supports university-based research and training in the social sciences and humanities.

The main goal of this research was to explore the potentialities of storytelling in the planning field. Nowadays a significant number of scholars are investigating the important relationship between story and planning, critically scrutinizing the so-called "story turn" in planning theory (Forester 1989; Mandelbaum 1991; Eckstein and Throgmorton 2003; Sandercock 2003). They highlight how planning is performed through stories, how rhetoric and poetics become crucial in interactive processes, how the communicative dimension is central to planning practices, how a story can awaken energies and imaginations, becoming a catalyst for an involving urban conversation.

According to this reflective framework, we decided to turn theory into practice by giving voice to a narrative which was worth telling: the inspiring story of the Collingwood Neighbourhood House. A tangled web of stimulating narratives was there, written over the course of twenty years of hopes, conflicts, and activities of this local institution. It is a multifaceted story that could have been told in many ways, with diverse accents and tones, applying different colours or interpretative filters, selecting disparate events and voices. What follows is the narration of the genesis of our documentary: the construction of the story we chose to represent, the authorial perspective, the research process we engaged in and finally, the making of the film itself. It is the only way to put ourselves into the narration, revealing the presence of the observer in the observed field,

L. Sandercock, G. Attili, *Where Strangers Become Neighbours*, Urban and Landscape Perspectives 4, DOI 10.1007/978-1-4020-9035-6_9

claiming subjectivity and partiality. Before going into the story itself, we wish to narrate ourselves in this chapter, disclosing the invisible threads that may hide either fear or desire.

But what is the thread we followed in making this documentary? The CNH is many things at the same time: a gathering place, a service provider, an incubator of sociality, a community-building catalyst. In this complex panorama, we decided to focus our attention on the role that this institution developed over the years, dedicated to the social integration of immigrants into the neighbourhood. By exploring a place where "strangers can become neighbours," we tried to understand how the diversity mission of the CNH was achieved by creating a place for everyone, supporting the newcomers, addressing their needs, and creating a new sense of belonging. This focus shaped all our work from the beginning, a process in which teaching and research were deeply interconnected.

9.2 A Class Where It All Started

Everything started during the course "Digital Ethnographies and Urban Planning"[1] which was taught at the School of Community and Regional Planning of the University of British Columbia in Vancouver in 2005. In that context, fourteen students began learning how to approach the study of the city through an ethnographic perspective. From the start, they were challenged to abandon a strictly quantitative understanding of space and the sterile cartographic approach that is traditional to the planning field. At the same time, they were asked to transgress the rationalist operation which reduces urban complexities to morphologies, models, systems, compositions, and numbers. One of the learning objectives of the course was to understand that the city is much more than an isotropic, metrical space. Grasped as a whole, the city cannot be reduced to a bi-dimensional surface crossed by lines, marked by geometries, and filled with homogeneous colors. It cannot be fully understood by adopting only an arrogant over-flying technique which photographs the physical shape of the city through zenithal views projected on scaled, papery surfaces. The urban space cannot be considered only in its physical-material dimension and frozen into abstract cartographies.

---

[1] This course was taught by Giovanni Attili and Leonie Sandercock in the Winter term.

Starting from these premises, the course tried to focus on a different concept of space crossed and signified by a kaleidoscope of different subjectivities, conflicts, signification practices, and relational webs. It is a space where expectations, feelings, reminiscences, bodies, and voices are stratified in living urbanities. This spatial vision is able to abandon the silenced shapes of an objectified city, exploring the invisible which loves hiding and elusively pulsates in the interstices of maps and of the morphological design of the city.

In doing this, the course did not deny the relevance of the physical dimension of the city. Rather, it evoked the simultaneous need of an expressive and analytical path in which symbolic levels, physical dimensions, and social practices are complexly interwoven. It evoked an alternative vision of spatiality as illustrated in the heterotopologies of Foucault, the trialectics and thirdings of Lefebvre, the marginality and radical openness of bell hooks, and the hybridities of Homi Bhabha, all of which challenge conventional modes of spatial thinking: the demolition of all the flatlands that traditionally permeate our disciplinary field.

In order to capture this complexity, students were stimulated to embrace a qualitative research path through which values, stories, desires and fears could find a place: a thick description of a life space capable of narrating what's beyond the morphological structure of the city. This methodological leap was particularly relevant when students were asked to tell the story of the CNH. It was evident that this local institution could not have been narrated by simply designing its location on a cartographic map or describing its morphological context, nor by using only numbers or statistics. The CNH appeared from the beginning as a complex system of layered and interconnected stories that needed to be understood through more sensitive analytical tools.

In order to achieve this goal, the course tried to outline a methodological framework for guiding the in-depth interviews that the students would engage in. Important reflections were particularly developed around the concept of "living speech": an open and dynamic encounter between people in a dialogue whose outline cannot be perceived a priori, because it is generated from moment to moment among the participants. Ultimately, this is what qualitative interviews are about: to generate an unpredictable interactive process in which the roles of the interviewers and of the interviewees are constantly being challenged through a communicative process that tries not to be controlling and aims at avoiding imposed languages. The result is a germinative, empowering dialogue characterized by spontaneity and creativity.

In the course, students performed different role games to experience directly diverse types of communicative interactions. They were asked to reflect on the formulation of their questions, on the power structure of the relationships, on the expected outcomes of the interviews, on the ethical issues which accompany this kind of research, and on the new epistemological assumptions that shape this ethnographic form of social inquiry.

9.3 The First Themes

Divided into small groups, students used this theoretical background to narrate pieces of the Collingwood Neighbourhood House story. They had to immerse themselves in the pulsating life of this dynamic neighbourhood, interact with a diversity of people, listen to different stories, and focus on a number of themes that we had pre-selected. We selected seven themes which reflected the life of this institution:

The Arts Pow Wow was a CNH initiative aimed at nourishing different cultural projects through a perspective of community-building. In this initiative, art played the important role of a social connector: a tool through which cultural and linguistic barriers could be transgressed, improve cultural capabilities of individuals and their community, and allow residents to express themselves. The Arts Pow Wow program had four main themes: Aboriginal development, neighbourhood development, community development, and communication networks. In keeping with the mission of the Neighbourhood House, the idea was to foster cultural pride and self-worth among all residents; to increase human connections through stories, visual arts, festivals, and public celebrations; to increase cross-cultural learning; and to beautify and personalize the neighbourhood through public art production and cultural programs and performances. In the Pow Wow, the role of artists as facilitators of community connections would be emphasized.

The Slocan Park story is the narrative of the transformation of a park, a formerly run-down area where drug users and youth gangs hung out, that was redesigned by local residents, led by environmental artist January Wolodarsky, working together to reclaim the park for the neighbourhood. Local artists worked with more than 6000 local residents, young and old, newcomers and oldtimers, collaborating on murals, mosaics, music, lantern making, aboriginal carving, gardening, puppetry, and physical recreation. Through the park regeneration process, neighbours worked side by side, had fun together, using old rituals as well as creating new ones in the process.

"Leaving, arriving, belonging" is a theme selected to emphasize the difficult paths followed by many people coming to a new country. Specifically, it was addressed by interviewing three immigrant women who powerfully narrated their personal stories of painful separation from their homelands. Arriving in Vancouver, their tears turned into a sense of loss and bewilderment. In this context, the CNH played an important role by offering help that in time would create a new sense of belonging during the arduous process of integration into the new society. An open, intercultural community thus came into being. As a result, these three women found in the CNH their new home as Satinder's words suggest: "I feel like this is my place, this is my second family and this is where I belong."

Multiweek is the story of an annual celebration that takes place in the Collingwood Neighbourhood House. For one week every February, the many cultures that co-exist in this neighborhood come together and share traditions and customs. It is a way of learning from other cultures, of understanding each other, of living the differences in a welcoming place.

The Leadership Institute story focuses attention on the role of a program that would help people to acquire leadership skills in the community. This is a central part of the mission of the Neighbourhood House: the attempt to build a community not just by delivering services but by empowering people to achieve collective goals on their own. The Leadership Institute prepares men and women, newcomers as well older residents, and youth to become effective leaders, ready to take on important roles in the community.

The *Buddy Program* is an after-school program offered by the Collingwood Neighbourhood House. It is directed to youth and its goal is to help young immigrants adjust to their new culture and home. It is a very successful program which in 2005 involved more than 100 participants. The *Host Buddy Program* runs in parallel with the Buddy Program, which trains older teens in youth work, imparting skills that will enable them to assist younger immigrants in settling into their new country. This program also allows teens to later volunteer for other CNH programs.

The History of the CNH was one of the main themes chosen to outline the different stages in the development of this institution. The CNH pilot project in 1985 was housed in a small storefront on Joyce Street. Demand for its programs quickly outgrew this space and expanded into a second storefront on Joyce. Soon that, too, was bursting at the seams, and a bigger space was found on Kingsway. As programs and services continued to expand in the early 1990s, the Board began negotiations with the City for a permanent facility. In 1995 there were 200 volunteers, 65 staff, and 12.000 users of programs each year, with an annual budget of $1.9 million. By 2005, the number of volunteers had almost doubled to 375 and staff numbers had risen to 95, but these folks were now serving 106.000 clients each year. In other words, there was a 900 percent increase in the users of CNH programs, yet its budget had only grown by 50 percent.

9.4 Digital Experimentations in the Cosmopolis Laboratory

In order to narrate these seven themes, students spent a lot of time interviewing people, learning from their stories, and experiencing the beauty (as well as the hard work) of a deep dialogical exchange. They used a video-camera to collect the voices of the interviewees, adding a further level of difficulty in the interaction process. The presence of the video-camera is not neutral: it shapes the conversation, induces anxiety or excitement, and may or may not cool the exchange through a distancing effect. Consequently, the use of the video-camera was an object of a delicate reflection during the class.

Students had to learn not only how to use it in a technical sense but they were also solicited to think critically about the impact of this tool on the interview process itself. The outcomes of students' work were a series of digital narratives based on in-depth interviews. From this perspective, the course gave them the technical skills that would allow them to create their own movies and digitally narrate their ethnographic research.Using specific editing and graphic software, students gave expression to the small pieces of the story of the Collingwood Neighbourhood House. They produced impressive art works that played with the potentialities of digital languages and creatively decided upon the formats of their own stories, for example, whether they would be hypermedia narratives or linear stories. As a result, students were able to create their own graphics, to choose the music they wanted, and to edit the interviews in a variety of imaginative ways.

Moreover, they were asked to put themselves into these digital narratives. They had to create a self-reflective section in which they could narrate their presence in the research, including the role they played in the interviews, the selection of the questions they asked, the reasoning behind their editing work, their sense-making path, how they dealt with ethically sensitive issues, and their choices of creative digital work in the awareness that medium and message are deeply connected.

The entire process was truly demanding for each student, but the effort turned out to be rewarding once we decided to obtain direct feedback from CNH staff. We organized the screening of the students' work in a crowded hall of the neighbourhood house. And the response was amazing. People appreciated the work they had done, themes selected, and how the stories were narrated. This session revealed that we were on the right path.

This course and the related student work were developed in a fully equipped laboratory, the "Cosmopolis Lab." The Lab had been established with a Canada Foundation for Innovation grant that provided funds to renovate a physical space and pay for the necessary equipment. The Lab is named after the title of a book by Leonie Sandercock, Towards Cosmopolis: Planning for Multicultural Cities (and the award winning sequel, Cosmopolis 2: Mongrel Cities of the 21st Century).[2] According to its manifesto, the main research themes of the Cosmopolis Laboratory are (and continue to be) the challenges to planners and planning systems of the multicultural, multiethnic cities of the 21st century; how to create cities and neighborhoods where there is genuine connection with and respect and

---

[2] This book received the Paul Davidoff award from the American Collegiate Schools of Planning in 2005. The Davidoff Award is made every two years to the best book published in North America addressing the ideals of equity and social justice advocated by the late Paul Davidoff.

space for all the different inhabitants of the city and the possibility of working together on matters on common destiny; how to live together in all of our differences, and how to live sustainably on the planet; how to develop an inclusive planning process; and how to pay attention to the city of spirit, of memory, and of desire, as well as to the functional/rational city.

The CNH research was the first project of the Cosmopolis Lab, a project in which teaching and research were to be significantly interwoven. On one hand, the Lab was where the "Digital Ethnographies and Urban Planning" course took place. But it was also the space where each student could learn about ethnographic and qualitative research approaches, where they could practice, experiment and play with editing software, cameras, microphones and computers. In short, it was a learning space that allowed a deeply interactive didactic approach.

Didactic tools were used throughout the course and were strictly congruent with the main topics described above. Talking about the role of images in planning meant to use images as didactic tools. Talking about the relevance of stories meant to narrate stories and reflect on their role. Talking about qualitative interviews meant to simulate interactive processes through role plays. The whole course was thus sustained by the consciousness that to teach something it is necessary to embody what you teach. And if you are teaching a new language you cannot do anything but use this language itself.

The Cosmopolis Lab was the workshop where experiments were conducted such as video projections, collective graphic works, digital storytelling, and multimedia productions – a multiplication of the didactic tools and of the possibilities of interaction.

9.5 The Construction of the Story

Once the work of the students was completed, Leonie Sandercock and I started to work on a new phase of the research project, expanding the horizon of the interviewees and reflecting on the construction of the story we wanted to tell: the story of a neighbourhood that, just twenty years earlier had locked its doors, was afraid of change, and told immigrants "to go back to where they came from," but that is now a totally changed place, a welcoming place for everyone. We realized that we needed more voices to add to this story. Many gaps had to be filled. Many more pieces of information had to be discovered. So we started again, going around the neighbourhood, interviewing more people during the following three months. This was a period of intensive work which allowed us to weave our web of relations in Collingwood and more particularly to consolidate our relationship with CNH. We used a snowball sampling approach to identify potential interlocutors where first contacts led to others in an ever widening web of relations. A key role was played by people who worked at the neighbourhood house, and this helped us in making our first contacts for the interviews.

使命

願應高羚活社區居民在社交、教育、經濟、
健康、文化及康樂方面之需要，
而提供所需的領導、服務及活動，
並提高本區居民和社區整體的生活質素。

價值觀及信念

1. 人與人之間的合作及互相尊重。
2. 個人自力更新，人們和高羚活社區整體的自強自主。
3. 社會公義及人人享有平等待遇。
4. 向社區負責，配合社區時刻在改變的需要。
5. 人人全面參與高羚活社區的社交、文化及經濟生活。
6. 承認及獎勵高羚活鄰舍中心員工及義工的工作及成
就，並不斷給予他們支持、訓練和繼續進修的機會。
7. 居民在解決難題及決策方面的參與。
8. 服務人員之間，以至機構內部和社區內部的融洽、合
作及協同。
9. 高羚活社區多樣化及多元文化的特色。

CNH捐贈基金

綠屋溫哥華基金會的兩名成員、高羚活朱清福利設施捐
贈基金及高羚活鄰舍中心協會捐贈基金，分別在一九九
四年九月和一九九三年十一月成立，目的是贊助高羚活
鄰舍中心的營運經費。每年來自捐贈基金的收益都撥作
協會的財政來源。

CNH承辦的計劃和服務以及很多設備的添購均由固定的
捐贈基金質助。而把贈基金個別撥捐者界入、參加活動
人士以及區內眾多居民的支持。很多人都不知道可以在
遺囑或遺產件捐贈給予自己關懷的非牟利團體。慷慨捐
助有需要人士或推動一項自己追求的理想或目標。捐贈
成的可享有稅務優惠。

如希望更進一步了解如何支持高羚活鄰舍中心捐贈基
金，請致電604-435-0323聯絡鄰舍中心。

RC 7704

COLLINGWOOD NEIGHBOURHOOD HOUSE

高羚活鄰舍中心
活動及服務指南
2004-2005

Collingwood
Neighbourhood House

鄰舍中心大樓
5288 Joyce Street
Vancouver, B.C. V5R 6C9
電話：604-435-0323
傳真：604-451-1191

辦公時間：
星期一至星期五　上午八時至晚上九時
星期六　上午九時至晚上八時
星期日　上午十時至晚上八時

Website: www.cnh.bc.ca

What really impressed us was the power of the life stories we had the privilege to listen to, revealing the richness of human experience where frailty and compassion intersect. Caught by the intensity of passionate voices, we were sometimes moved to tears. But we had to pay attention, trying to be in and out at the same moment, avoiding identification dynamics, role ambiguity, and the well-known phenomenon of transference. We were only too aware that a deeper personal involvement would not allow us to consciously and critically read the relationship between interviewer and interviewee. The risk was to lose an analytical view of the process and of the main characters, including ourselves. So we had to be walking a tightrope, following a pendulum-like movement from inside to outside, from empathic compassion to distanced observation.

After each interview we spent a lot of time talking about what we had experienced, trying to find what was interesting about the story we wanted to narrate. This reflective part of the process became crucial during the editing phase of the film. We had a lot of filmed interviews that had to be transformed into a documentary of reasonable length. So cuts were necessary. But which parts of the interview were essential to our telling of the CNH story?

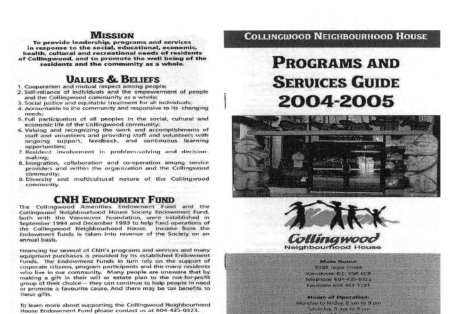

Sometimes we found that the interviews, though extremely passionate and emotional, didn't find a place in the final, edited work. This surprised us. It was evident that we were struggling between what we had experienced and what we judged was relevant for the film as it evolved. Sometimes we had to make some hard decisions. Such was the case of Cecilia, a Chilean woman who narrated the precious story of her adolescence, the disappearance of her father during the Pinochet dictatorship, the interruption of her studies, and the oppressive military regime in her country of birth. Her story was intense, but we couldn't incorporate the entire interview into the 45 min film we were producing. We simply had to select those pieces that were directly connected with the CNH story.

Some editing cuts were also necessary to protect interviewees whose personal stories, we felt, should not be publicised. In a larger sense, we were always wondering how this film might, in turn, affect the lives of the

people we had interviewed. This was our beacon and a thought which was constantly in our mind during the editing process. And there was another preoccupation: whether or not to include in the film every single person who had given us their precious time to be interviewed. In one specific case, we decided that we had to exclude an interview, for reasons of fluidity and the comprehension of the story. During the first projection of the film at the CNH, that person left the room in disappointment or anger. But it is what, as professionals, we believed we had to do.

The editing phase was also characterised by several crucial moments with key people working at the neighbourhood house. Rough versions of the documentary were shown to them in order to get their feedback. In this process we discovered that we had neglected some important parts of the story which they wanted us to tell. For example, initially we hadn't put much emphasis on the presence of a First Nations community in the neighbourhood and on the struggles between native and non-native communities in Collingwood. Some other things had not been explained properly, or the music wasn't functioning in the way we had hoped. So we had to go back to the editing room and change some pieces of our work in progress in answer to the criticisms we had received.

To amalgamate different sections of the documentary and to round out the narrative by adding essential information, we had to add some voice-over. We also added a few statistics about CNH which we believed were essential to our story. Other parts of the narrative had to be shortened in order to give space to some voices that had at first been excluded from our narrative. In all, editing the documentary was a great learning trip for us, a complex spiral process in which going back to where we had started meant moving forward.

As we worked on the film, it became more and more evident to us that we were building an advocacy documentary, something which could help the CNH in its financial crisis and which could be used to demonstrate the achievements of this institution.

Through this documentary we were clearly performing a political act as well, assuming the responsibility of narrating an inspiring story, showing how a local place-based institution managed to overcome the fear of strangers through community development processes.

Every single choice we made during the editing process was connected with these emerging objectives that affected not only the construction of the story itself but the way it was told visually. From this perspective, what we produced was a multi-stratified visual layout, a complex web of images and information that were interconnected and displayed on the same screen. The documentary was thus not merely talking heads, but an intricate tangle of visions potentially able to allow the spectator to dive into the story's depth. What we pursued was the possibility of creating aesthetic connections intended as different ways of learning through visual, narrative and musical languages.

This phase of the work had an important deadline: the 20th birthday celebration of the Collingwood Neighbourhood House. On that occasion, their gym was transformed into a big movie theatre holding more than 300 people. There was a general sense of excitement in the air. It was the first official projection of our documentary and the audience's reactions were incredible. Many people were in tears after the screening. Most of the people we had interviewed ended up seeing their own story in the film along with the net of connections that tied them to CNH. It was an incredible and meaningful moment for each of them. Others told us that the film was able to tell the bigger picture of a complex story of which they knew only the small segments in which they had themselves been

REALIZING

A

COMMUNITY

VISION

3185
Kingsway
Vancouver
B.C.
V5R 5K2
435-0323

personally involved. The consciousness of being part of a bigger story was for them an important step in the construction of a renewed sense of belonging. The film's projection contributed to this process. For many, it was a ritual passage that enabled them to make sense of the twenty years of history of this institution, arousing their awareness of what had been achieved and renewing their energies.

The audience at this first formal screening was heterogeneous. Some of the city planners who had played a role in the early stages of CNH were there and found the documentary helpful in depicting what had happened in that neighbourhood twenty years earlier when they had worked hard to deal with the planning aspects of its establishment. Others were representatives from several of Vancouver's neighbourhood houses who requested copies of the documentary to show to their own organisations. And many, of course, came from the Collingwood neighbourhood itself. As a whole, the audience was impressed because the film showed them not only the story of the CNH but a more universal story of loss, struggle, fear, and renewed belonging. "Where Strangers Become Neighbours" was thus more than a story of one neighbourhood house and its history; it was a story that spoke a more universal language accessible to everyone.

9.6 Disseminating the CNH Story

During the research process we learned how positive change processes can happen in a community thanks to the role played by a local institution which succeeded in developing a sense of citizenship and belonging anchored in shared values and a shared identity. Building on this, we decided to share what we had learned with others and to take the documentary on the road.

The projection of the documentary at the Collingwood Neighbourhood House was the beginning of this new phase. For one year now we have been travelling around the world, showing our documentary to different audiences, in diverse academic and professional settings[3] as well as at

---

[3] Among these: *City of Vancouver, Department of Planning, Central Area division* (Vancouver, British Columbia); *City of Vancouver, Department of Planning, Social Planning Division* (Vancouver, British Columbia); *Immigration and Canada's Place in a Changing World,* national conference (Metropolis, Vancouver, British Columbia); *Narrative Matters,* international conference (Arcadia University, Nova Scotia); *Eyes on the City,* international conference

several international film festivals[4] where the documentary was awarded with an honourable mention (International Federation of Housing & Planning, International Film & Video Competition, Geneva, Sept. 2006) and a special mention (Berkeley Video and Film Festival, Oct. 2006).

(International Visual Sociology Association, Urbino, Italy); *Paths & Crossroads: Moving People, Changing Places,* international conference (Metropolis, Lisbon, Portugal); *Borders and Cores. What is Planning in the New Era?* Conference (American Collegiate Schools of Planning, Fort Worth, Texas); *Sustainable Urbanization: Turning Ideas into Action,* World Planning Congress (Canadian Institute of Planners and the Planning Institute of BC, Vancouver, British Columbia); *Urban Futures, Continuities and Discontinuities,* World-Congress (International Federation for Housing and Planning, Rome, Italy); and *Global Studio Workshop* (Vancouver, British Columbia). In addition, we decided to use the film as a catalyst for discussion in different architecture and planning schools (School of Community and Regional Planning, Vancouver, British Columbia; Engineering Faculty of La Sapienza University, Rome, Italy; Architecture faculty of "Roma III", Rome, Italy; Planning Faculty of IUAV, Venice, Italy; Architecture Faculty, Alghero, Italy; and the Architecture Faculty of Politecnico, Milan, Italy).

[4] New York International Independent Film and Video Festival (2006), Los Angeles International Independent Film Festival (2006), Toni Corti Indipendent Video Festival (2006), Berkley Film Festival (2006).

Social issues, immigration policies, planning themes, media and communication topics became objects of intense discussion in the different places where we showed the film. This variety of issues is due to the complexity of the story that we narrated as well as to the wide range of communicative impulses which characterize this film, a multiplicity of narratives and languages which are simultaneously interwoven on the screen, going beyond the traditional documentary format.

The film's abundant and exuberant mixture of signs allows people to select and keep the information they find most relevant to their own interests and personal stories. As a result, very different sense-making processes happened, revealing the power of a communicative tool that is able to tell a story while recalling further and diverse narrations.

The success of this way of disseminating knowledge, of raising questions and of discussing sensitive social issues is related to the use of a narrative and ordinary speech. This kind of speech is based on a more accessible and common language which is able to target a wider audience. In fact, stories are an accessible, comprehensible and familiar way of communicating, while technical and expert forms of communication usually reduce the possibility of interaction to only a small number of people who share the same professional or academic language.

These reflections accompanied us in the construction of an educational package including a community development manual to complement the film. Both film and manual were taken to a series of workshops held in strategic locations throughout Canada. This final stage of our adventure was funded by a RIIM Metropolis[5] grant which allowed Leonie Sandercock and Paula Carr, executive director of CNH, to use the Metropolis Research Network and take advantage of its Centres of Excellence in four Canadian cities: Edmonton, Halifax, Moncton and Toronto.

By documenting the twenty year achievement of the Collingwood Neighbourhood House in Vancouver, the workshops' goal was to illuminate some of the factors that shape public attitudes about immigration and can lead to a sense of welcome and inclusion. These workshops were the occasion to ask what lessons can be learned from an institution such as CNH, that has developed positive practices related to the diversity of its work force, its volunteers, and its clients. They were an

---

[5] RIIM: Research on Immigration and Integration in the Metropolis.

occasion to reflect on how citizenship can be actively constructed through community development, so long as this is underpinned by an intercultural philosophy of the kind that continues to inform the work of CNH.

Workshop attendees were given a copy of the manual "How Strangers Become Neighbours: Constructing Citizenship Through Community Development", which tells how the CNH developed its unique approach of relationship-building; what kinds of programs and services it offers; where it gets its funding; how it trains staff and volunteers; how its outreach programs work; how the resident-run Board operates; how they develop community leadership; why its approach is intercultural rather than multicultural; and above all, the values that have shaped this very special place.

By showing the documentary and using the manual, each workshop was shaped according to the topics and themes identified by the participants and relating to the lessons of the CNH experience. Many people attended the workshops from federal, provincial and local governments, as well as from various immigrant and refugee serving organisations, from the arts sector, and from universities. The response was again extremely positive. In a follow-up evaluation, a remarkably high percentage (90%) of attendees rated the workshops in the top category. In addition, an interesting dynamic emerged in the course of these workshops as people working in the same field and in the same city discovered each other for the first time, thus establishing new networks concerned with the social integration of immigrants. We hope that this dissemination and germinative process will continue even through the present publication by inspiring people who are struggling with one of the greatest challenges of our times, which is to live peacefully in the mongrel cities of the world.

References

Eckstein B and J. Throgmorton eds. (2003) Story and Sustainability. MIT Press, Cambridge Massachusetts

Forester J (1989) Planning in the Face of Power. University of California Press, Berkeley

Mandelbaum S (1991) 'Telling Stories', Journal of Planning Education and Research, 10, 1:209–14

Sandercock L (2003) Cosmopolis 2: Mongrel Cities in the 21st Century. Continuum, London

Chapter 10
Qualitative Inquiries and Film Languages in the Planning Field: A Manifesto

Giovanni Attili

The story of the Collingwood Neighbourhood House was shaped and expressed through the language of film. This language is not new in urban planning. During the last century, several planners have promoted their projects and visions through this medium.[1] The goal of these early experiments was to address a wider audience by using the more accessible, inclusive language of moving images supplemented by narration. They were deeply rhetorical, even populist films that proceeded from the conviction that the visual language of motion pictures was more persuasive than merely technical writing and would help build a popular consensus for specific proposals. Over the years, a new sensibility in the use of film in planning has emerged based on a post-modern, self-reflective epistemology. This helped reshape the spectrum of narrative expression and opened the path to participatory planning research and practices having transformative potential. What follows is an inquiry into the new potentialities of digital storytelling.

---

[1] Neues Bauen in Frankfurt am Main, Germany 1928 (subjects by Ernst May), Die Stadt von morgen, 1930 (subject by Maximilian V. Golbeck), La giornata nella casa popolare, Italy 1933 (directed by Piero Bottoni), Pour mieux comprendre Paris, France 1935 (directed by Marcel Poëte), The City, USA 1939 (narrative by Lewis Mumford), Trilogia della X Triennale di Milano, Italy 1954 (subjects by Giancarlo De Carlo, Carlo Doglio and Ludovico Quaroni), Comunità millenarie . Paesi della Lunigiana and Lucca città comunale, Italy 1954 and 1955 (subjects by Edoardo Detti), Città e terre del'Umbria, Italy 1961 (directed by Giovanni Astengo).

L. Sandercock, G. Attili, *Where Strangers Become Neighbours*, Urban and Landscape Perspectives 4, DOI 10.1007/978-1-4020-9035-6_10
© Springer Science+Business Media 2009

10.1 Starting from a Qualitative Analysis

The language of film can give expression to a dense qualitative analysis of social phenomena in a territorial context. It can be used to give thick and complex accounts of the city focused on stories, interviews, and narration. Qualitative analysis succeeds in expressing what lies beyond the surface of maps, physical objects, classifications and aggregate quantitative data. It intentionally focuses on individual lives in urban settings made up of changing densities, memories, perceptions and aesthetics. It is an attentive, extremely focused analysis of urban space, where existence, intersections, languages and interstitial freedoms delineate controversial and palpitating urban landscapes.

The goal of this kind of analysis is to probe deeply into inhabitants' lived practices, conflicts, and modalities of space appropriation which will reveal principles, rationalities and potential writings that interrogate the ordered text of the planned city. Intercepting these multiform practices means to be able to listen to the city's murmurs, to catch stories, and to read signs and spatial poetics, all of which are generative of new meanings. Using film is to research what normally remains invisible in planning (though not in life) and ends by questioning the way planners typically explore, analyze, and represent urban space.

Bypassing the ideology of the Archimedean observer who stands outside the observed, the qualitative approach privileges collaborative contexts to produce a collective invention of interconnected stories. In this perspective, there is no longer a single eye that encompasses "everything" in its vision, but a multiplicity of stories told by the inhabitants of specific neighborhoods who no longer can be thought of as isolated monads (as for example in survey research), and whose stories must be understood as an inter-connected web.

Through in-depth interviews and the confrontation of diverse visions of the world, this approach becomes a powerful tool for a deeper comprehension of what animates the many souls, conflicts and resources of the city. The result is an ethnographic narrative that is built on the intersection of multiple narratives captured by the ethnographer. It is a story that doesn't pretend to represent "the truth;" rather, it is explicitly subjective, even partial. The key word to comprehend the fulcrum of ethnographic analysis is "to evoke," that is, to create a plausible world – one of many such worlds – taken from everyday life. Assuming this perspective, ethnography rids itself of the obsession of a mimesis rooted in objects, facts, empirical generalizations, and ultimately in a single truth. Rather, it becomes an inter-connected patchwork of evocative images imbued with ambiguity and indeterminacy. Their full comprehension escapes the researcher's intentionality, as the film creates a dynamic field that is open to diverse interpretations and possibilities. This level of interpretative openness transforms a digital ethnography into a potential catalyst for participatory planning. In other words, digital ethnographies represent a new way of provoking dialogue in decision-making contexts. It is a way of starting a public conversation.

10.2 Digital Poetics and Multi-Sensory Aesthetics

Ethnographic analysis can be expressed through a linguistic medium that is not necessarily restricted to the written word. It can avail itself of different communicative codes (verbal, film, graphics, photography, etc.). More specifically, it can feed on the potentialities of new technologies (ICT) which, according to Gargani, is "a new system of restraints and limits, but also with unpredictable and unprecedented possibilities that can lead to new paths of thought, action and behavior" (Gargani 1999: 16, author's translation).

New media have the intrinsic ability of deploying different expressive languages. They are complex scores of multi-sensory idioms that can be creatively re-assembled to express and communicate a specific content. They represent an extremely versatile and dynamic tool through which it is possible to build complex "images" composed of forests of signs and communicative metaphors that are mutually involved and interpenetrating. ICTs allow the creative bricolage of diversified media that produces something more than a summation of its parts.

Photography, music, spoken words, written texts, graphics, digital animation and videos play together in generating a wider resonance. Their combined use multiplies aesthetic connections and allows for the transition from rhetoric to poetics, a leap that allows us to move from referential and argumentative languages to germinative and constructive ones. This multiplication of aesthetic languages represents a significant reservoir which has the possibility to expand the horizons of logical and scientific argument.

In principle, digital languages can reinforce the expressiveness of storytelling, connecting a qualitative study of the city to the potentialities of a deeply communicative language. Digital qualitative inquiries give rise to narratives through an aesthetics that is inherent in all social interactions. They can tell inspiring stories capable of triggering planning interventions by revealing new possibilities and sense worlds. This is the case of the Collingwood Neighbourhood House digital narrative, the filmic ethnography of an organization that is able to inspire, provoke questions, and play with different scenarios. All these characteristics are extremely important in awakening new imaginaries and creating spaces for renewed and more involving forms of interaction in social planning. To create real communication and interactive spaces, it isn't sufficient merely "to say something;" it's also necessary to transfer energies and awaken new aspirations, knowledge and dormant creativity.

The aim of digital stories is to extend the right to participate in the work of the imagination by focusing on new desires, imaginaries and potential urban transformations; and by creating resonance in the viewer's heart, thus generating emotional responses and launching innovative metaphors that can activate imaginative processes. These characteristics represent a significant potential for social planning. Digital stories can awaken astonishment, surprise, and actions in people who are receptive to aesthetics and perceptive drifts. They can be used as real and innovative catalysts for urban change and as incubators of collective action.

10.3 Interactive Astonishment

Not unlike artistic gestures, digital ethnographies often succeed in arousing astonishment, producing a state of interrogation that is suspended between light and shadow, between known things and invisible horizons. Or, as Gargani writes,

> the amazement in front of the unknown becomes the thought which enlarges the investigated field. From this perspective, astonishment leads to the infinite. It is the beginning of knowledge and of philosophical thought. It is intended as an emotion which follows something that cannot be totally and integrally absorbed (Gargani 1999: 22, author's translation).

Paradoxically, the pretension to an exhaustive and all-inclusive knowledge overwhelms what is being investigated and prevents its deeper comprehension. This is the epistemological limit that characterizes any disciplinary specialization when it attempts to control its specific object-in-view. A disciplined, formalized translation of reality ends up removing its many ambiguities, its depth of meanings, its inherent alienation through abstraction. Astonishment awakens only when we abandon rational, comprehensive controls and start exploring the world in questioning terms, putting objectivity between brackets.

Digital ethnographies embody a possible knowledge path that comprises imagination, poetical gestures, and aesthetic experience. The astonishment theme, fundamental to a different cognitive approach, is particularly relevant here, because it is a presupposition for action. Only if we are astonished can we reinvent the frameworks of meaning through which people organize their own experience of the world. Poetic and evocative digital ethnographies offer a space for suggestions and drifting imaginaries. These aesthetic and perceptive drifts are creative impulses that can create a space of new possibilities. By opening this space, digital ethnographies create a field in which new actions become possible. Just as in the Veda, Vishnu creates a space for the warlike action of Indra through his spectacular dance, so digital ethnographies, by becoming an occasion for social interaction, prefigure potential actions (Dumezil 1969, cited in de Certeau 1990: 185).

Digital ethnographies act somewhat like deforming mirrors that alter events or relations which in the ordinary flow of life are not recognizable. These mirrors are not unidirectional. They don't passively photograph reality. Rather, "they act as reflecting consciences and the reflected images are their product. These images are modeled in vocabulary and rules, in meta-linguistic grammars through which unprecedented performances can occur" (Turner 1993: 76). In other words, digital ethnographers re/present reality in a mood of supposition, desire, hypothesis, and possibility. They can be interpreted as potential change agents helping to bring about occasions for social interaction that, in turn, call forth emotional and aesthetic-perceptive responses. But this is only possible because digital ethnographies bypass the technical, specialized languages of planning that are typically uninvolving in an emotional sense.

All these potentialities rely on how digital ethnographies are constructed, on the authorial judgment which shapes them, and on the social and political views of the ethnographer. From this perspective, a digital ethnography cannot be deterministically interpreted as a change agent, though it embodies important and unprecedented potentialities in challenging traditional scientific languages and can open up new possibilities of involving interactions.

10.4 Performatory Situations

Outside their lives and interests, outside their skill areas, and separated from one another, individuals have nothing to say. The difficulty is to catch them – both in an emotional and topological sense – and to group them together, involving them in an adventure through which they could enjoy imagining, exploring, building together sensitive environments (Levy 1997: 131, author's translation). Digital ethnographies aim to reach this goal. They can be used as fulcrums of strongly interactive events. Such events are performatory situations that may be able to rouse diverse subjectivities, remembrances, fantasies, and creativities. The central idea is the "concrete construction of momentary ambiances of life and their transformation into a superior passional quality" (Debord 1957) to be molecularly disseminated throughout the city in a series of Situationist experiments. In these events, the digital narrative becomes a magnet for interaction that recalls "a multiplication of the narrations that try to explain it, to exalt it, to find the moral from it, to forgive it, to abhor it, to repudiate it, to use it in order to characterize a collective experience and as a model for the future" (Turner 1993: 93).

The projection of the CNH film in different urban contexts embodied this potential. It was experienced as an intense moment of interaction where propositions, creative listening, metaphors and symbolic acts interconnected. This example leads us to think of the city as a net of interactive moments, a new theater that can host cultural operations resolutely built through the collective organization of interactive environments. The astonishment and the interactive potential connected with the use of digital ethnographies allow new city building processes to emerge. They are interactive occasions that can help to define future scenarios and to nourish endogenous and creative capabilities to produce changes in urban life.

From this point of view, digital ethnographies can be seen as *relational and communicative tools* that "help to build social bonds through learning and knowledge exchange; communicative tools that are able to listen to, to combine and to give expression to diversity" (Levy 1997: 133, author's translation). They invite people to suggest modifications, initiate new narrations through a dynamic knowledge management to be explored "not only conversationally but even through sensitive modalities according to significant paths and associations" (Levy 1997: 210, author's translation). If we reject Reason because it cannot produce the totality of potential actions nor create a genuine communicative space that ultimately induces people to act, it is not sufficient to "tell." Rather, it is necessary to transfer energies from ethnographer to audience, so that sentiments and emotions will vibrate, awaken latent aspirations, knowledge and energies, and so rediscover the powerful role of artistic and poetic languages in life. It is therefore necessary to focus on the cognitive and communicative performance that will give aesthetic pleasure, not as an accessory of the message but as a central moment of every communicative process (Gargani 1999).

10.5 Propulsive Planning

Refined, poetical filmic formats allow qualitative inquiries to be communicated on different levels, thus becoming generators of a renewed form of aesthetic learning. They are the foundations of a different concept of planning than the current understandings of the profession. In this new sense, planning becomes a way of creating gatherings of people where reflections, inspirations and ideas can emerge from deep interaction catalyzed by meaningful communicative tools. This new form of planning is no longer the top-down, argumentative, categorical and controlling style of communication. Instead, it is a process that is rooted in the power of narrative exchange and the constructions of endogenous territorial practices.

The assumption of such a perspective would mean abandoning the idea of an intentional, comprehensive, state-controlled, and panoptical planning in favor of the construction of *strong* interactive processes and of the "images", dispositions and situations that could potentially catalyze them. It would mean to think about a *propulsive* planning capable of stimulating occasions for exploring meanings, valorizing socially hidden potentialities, empowering communities, multiplying different learning situations in small-scale contexts. I am arguing here for a less normative planning that is more inclined to make needs, actions and politics emerge from territorially based communities.

The implications of this perspective are particularly important for a cultural turn in territorial politics (and planning) which is oriented to multiplication of occasions for social interaction. This approach is difficult; it will require more rather than less intervention.

It will also require a deep comprehension of the power differences that shape political and social networks. It will call for planners who have a deep comprehension of social phenomena, a less normative attitude than they commonly bring to their work, abandoning the standardization of behaviors traditionally considered to be the best solution for exercising social control (Tosi 2000: 1218). The unforeseeable outcomes of social interactions (produced locally and contextually) may become the fulcrum of a different kind of planning. If we assume this perspective, the planners' control anxiety breaks down. Given the crisis of political representation and of state-controlled planning in most countries, it is urgent to creatively imagine other paths such as the multiplication of occasions for collective learning that can produce innovative change. The use of film language seems to answer this kind of exigency. Film has the potential to catalyze people's interaction, create evocative and powerful stories-images of the city, and involve residents in discussing the interconnected dimensionalities of the spaces in which they live. The language of film is intended as a way to prefigure possible change. It can do this by creating "sonorous buildings, cities of voices and songs, instantaneous, luminous, and moving like flames" (Levy 1997: 134, author's translation).

References

de Certeau M (1990), L'invenzione del quotidiano. Edizioni Lavoro, Roma

Debord G (1957) Report on the construction of Situations and on the International Situationist Tendency's Conditions of Organization and Action. http://www.cddc.vt.edu/sionline/si/report.html

Gargani AG (1999) Il filtro creativo. Editori Laterza, Bari

Levy P (1997) L'intelligenza collettiva. Feltinelli, Milano

Tosi A (2000) L'inserimento urbano degli immigrati. In: Migrazioni Scenari per il XXI secolo. Dossier di Ricerca vol II. Agenzia Romana per la preparazione del Giubileo, Roma

Turner V (1993) Antropologia della performance. Il Mulino, Bologna

Appendix

Film's Credits

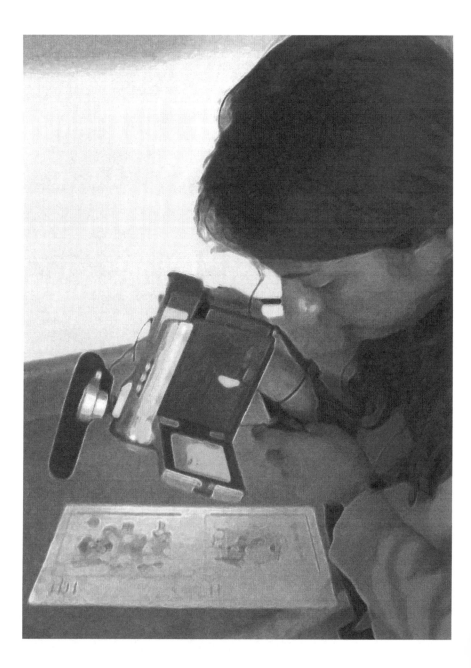

Where Strangers Become Neighbours:
The Story of the Collingwood Neighbourhood House
and the Integration of Immigrants in Vancouver

A documentary film by
Giovanni Attili and Leonie Sandercock

Directed and edited
by Giovanni Attili

Produced and written
by Leonie Sandercock

Music
by Gianluca Misiti

Research
by Leonie Sandercock and Giovanni Attili

with **research assistance** from the following Masters students
at the School of Community & Regional Planning,
University of British Columbia:

A. Khanderia, K. Hassan, H. Willard
Carmen, Cecilia and Ami's stories

B. Suderman, D. Welch
CNH History

A Brzozowski, E. Finnigan
Carmen, Cecilia and Ami's stories

K.Wong, J. Solorzano
Buddy Program

S. Beresky, J. Starke
Collingwood History

M.Riesmeyer, I. Marcuse, D. Parker
Leadership Institute

L. Moffat
Slocan Park and Technical assistance

S. Brock
Lab Equipment

Special thanks to:

PAULA CARR
Executive director of the
CNH and director of
Community Development

VAL CAVERS
Former Coordinator of
Settlement Service

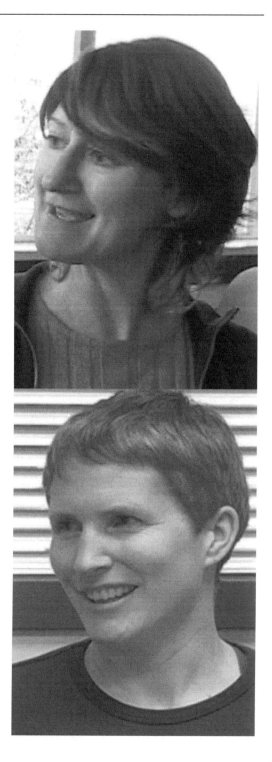

and thanks to all those who gave their time to be interviewed

AMY WU

resident
volunteer
former staff member

CARMEN CORREAL

resident
volunteer
current staff member
Recreation Co-ordinator

CARMEN ROSEN

resident
artist
Community Organiser
member of Arts Pow Wow

CECELIA TAGLE

resident
volunteer
current Board member

CHRIS TAULU

resident
chair of Joyce Street Area Planning
Committee
Executive Director of Community
Policing Centre

COMFORT ERO

resident
current Board member
storyteller

DON VAN DYKE

resident
member of Joyce Street Area Planning
Committee
Steering Committee for CNH
past Board member

EMANUELA SHEENA

resident
volunteer
staff
artist,
community organizer
member of Arts Pow Wow

JEANNE PIERRE MAKOSSO

artist

JANUARY WOLODARSKY

resident
environmental artist
community organizer
member of Arts Pow Wow

JULIE CHENG

resident
community organizer
coordinator of Arts Pow Wow

KARTHI SIVALINGAM

resident
volunteer
current Board member

KERRY JANG

resident
current President of CNH Board

LAWRENCE YUEN

resident
volunteer
computer lab assistant

NATHAN EDELSON

senior planner City of Vancouver
member of City of Vancouver planning, team on Joyce Street Area Planning Committee

SANJEEV KARWAL

resident
volunteer
staff member Youth Co-ordinator

SATINDER SINGH

resident
volunteer
staff member
Family Life Education Co-ordinator

SUSAN GORDON

member of the Vancouver
Parks Board Staff

TERESA DALBY

volunteer
resident
programme participant

TERRY TAYLER

Resident
member of Joyce Street Area Planning
Committee
member of Steering Committee for
CNH first President of CNH Board

VILIEN CHEN

resident
volunteer
ESL instructor

VISHY SIVALINGAM

resident
local businessman

   This film was made possible by a grant from the Social Sciences and Humanities Research Council of Canada and by a Canada Foundation for innovation grant which built and equipped the Vancouver Cosmopolis Laboratory in the School of Community & Regional Planning at the University of British Columbia

Film's Screening History and Awards

Special Mention, International Federation of Housing and Planning International Film Festival, Geneva, Sept. 2006

Honorable Mention, Documentary section, Berkeley Video and Film Festival, Oct. 2006.

Official Selection New York International Independent Film and Video Festival, 2006

Official Selection Los Angeles International Independent Film Festival, 2006

Official Selection Toni Corti Independent Video Festival, 2006

Film's Synopsis

Migration has always been an important feature of human history, but never more so than the past two decades. But what happens when increasing numbers of strangers move into a neighbourhood, bringing with them different histories and cultures, religions and social practices, and often, urgent needs for housing, language training, schools and jobs? How do newcomers, as well as members of the "host" society, develop an everyday capacity to live alongside those perceived as different, strange?

Our story explores this contemporary global social issue by looking at one neighbourhood – Collingwood – in the City of Vancouver. 38% of metropolitan Vancouver, and 51% of the City's residents are foreign born. Collingwood, a predominantly Anglo-European community until the 1980s, has been transformed since then by the arrival of large numbers of East, South, and South East Asians, Africans, and Latin Americans. A neighborhood that, just 20 years ago was locking its doors, afraid of change, and telling immigrants to go back where they came from, is now a welcoming place for everyone.

How did this happen? How do strangers become neighbours?

This is the story of the transformation of one neighbourhood, over a twenty year period, from fear and hostility towards immigrants to a remarkably integrated and welcoming community. It is the story of how an integrated community was created, through the work of the Collingwood Neighbourhood House (CNH). The story is told primarily through the voices, and lives, of immigrant women (from Nigeria, Chile, Colombia, Taiwan, and India), who describe their feelings of isolation and invisibility on arriving in Canada and not being able to speak the language. "You feel invisible. You are nobody." These women first came to the CNH to use its language or childcare programs, and then became involved as volunteers, received training, and went on to find jobs in the city. Now their teenage children, who were once in the childcare programs, are volunteers at CNH in the Youth Buddy Program, for example, or youth counseling other youth about drugs, bullying, and so on.

The film begins with a portrait of this low income neighbourhood twenty years ago, a neighbourhood fearful of and antagonistic towards the newcomers. We then tell the story of the birth of the CNH in 1985, with its mission of diversity, of creating a place for everyone, and we follow the development of the CNH and of the community through a series of innovative social and community development programs such as the Arts Pow Wow (a community cultural development program in which thousands of local residents participated), MultiWeek, and the Community Leadership Institute.

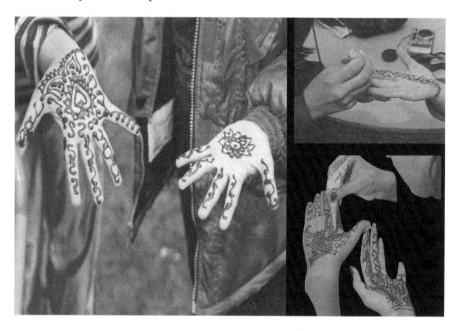

This is now a very respectful community, but it wasn't always like that. A longtime Collingwood resident tells the story of the effort to build a Native housing coop in the neighbourhood, and the initial resistance to that, the stereotypes about "Indians" and reservations, that had to be dispelled before the community could see that the Native population brought real assets to this neighbourhood, as well as needs. Various residents, newcomers as well as oldtimers, discuss the various forms of racism that have existed, and how the CNH works to combat this.

One of the most remarkable stories involves the reclamation of a local park that had been taken over by gang members and drug dealers. Through the local leadership of an environmental artist and a native elder, thousands of residents worked together to come up with a plan for making the park more attractive and hospitable to people from all cultures. Chinese seniors from a tai chi group worked side by side with African drummers and Native carvers to create, with their own sweat and artistic abilities, a place that everyone is proud of. During this lengthy participatory process, people worked together, had fun together, celebrated together, and got to know each other. Strangers became neighbours. Our immigrant women interviewees describe the CNH as a "blessed place" a place where everyone feels "at home" and learns about other cultures. We explore what is so special about this place, how "the Collingwood spirit" emerged, and what struggles it still faces.

Name Index

Subject Index

Druck:
Customized Business Services GmbH
im Auftrag der KNV-Gruppe
Ferdinand-Jühlke-Str. 7
99095 Erfurt